Envisioning Critical Race Praxis in K–12 Leadership Through Counter-Storytelling

A volume in
Educational Leadership for Social Justice
Jeffrey S. Brooks, *Series Editor*

Envisioning Critical Race Praxis in K–12 Leadership Through Counter-Storytelling

edited by

Tyson E. J. Marsh
University of New Mexico

Natasha N. Croom
Iowa State University

INFORMATION AGE PUBLISHING, INC.
Charlotte, NC • www.infoagepub.com

Library of Congress Cataloging-in-Publication Data

A CIP record for this book is available from the Library of Congress
http://www.loc.gov

ISBN: 978-1-68123-408-3 (Paperback)
       978-1-68123-409-0 (Hardcover)
       978-1-68123-410-6 (ebook)

CONTENTS

PART I
STUDENT VOICE

PART II
LEADERSHIP

PART III
TEACHING AND LEADING

SERIES EDITOR'S PREFACE

Jeffrey S. Brooks
Monash University

I am pleased to serve as series editor for this book series, Educational Leadership for Social Justice, with Information Age Publishing. The idea for this series grew out of the work of a committed group of leadership for scholars associated with the American Educational Research Association's (AERA) Leadership for Social Justice Special Interest Group (LSJ SIG). This group existed for many years before being officially affiliated with AERA and has benefitted greatly from the ongoing leadership, support, and counsel of many leaders, but particularly Dr. Catherine Marshall (University of North Carolina-Chapel Hill). It is also important to acknowledge the contributions of the LSJ SIG's first chair, Dr. Ernestine Enomoto (University of Hawaii at Manoa), whose wisdom, stewardship, and guidance helped ease a transition into AERA's more formal organizational structures. This organizational change was at times difficult to reconcile with scholars who largely identified as nontraditional thinkers and who push toward innovation rather than accept the status quo. As the second chair of the LSJ SIG, I appreciate all of Ernestine's hard work and friendship. Moreover, I also thank Drs. Gaetane Jean-Marie, Whitney Sherman Newcomb, and Judy Alston, the third, fourth, and fifth chairs of the LSJ SIG for their visionary leadership, steadfast commitment to high standards and collaborative scholarship, and friendship.

Envisioning a Critical Race Praxis in K–12 Leadership Through Counter-Storytelling, pages vii–ix
Copyright © 2016 by Information Age Publishing
All rights of reproduction in any form reserved.

I am particularly indebted to my colleagues on the LSJ SIG's first Publications Committee, which I chaired from 2005–2007: Dr. Denise Armstrong, Brock University; Dr. Ira Bogotch, Florida Atlantic University; Dr. Sandra Harris, Lamar University; Dr. Whitney Sherman Newcomb, Virginia Commonwealth University; and Dr. George Theoharis, Syracuse University. This committee was a joy to work with, and I am pleased we have found many more ways to collaborate—now as my fellow series editors of this book series—as we seek to provide publication opportunities for scholarship in the area of leadership for social justice.

This book, *Envisioning Critical Race Praxis in K–12 Leadership through Counter-Storytelling*, co-edited by Dr. Tyson Marsh of the University of New Mexico, and Dr. Natasha Croom of Iowa State University, is the twentieth in the series. The book explores many understudied concepts and advances a variety of perspectives through which we can understand various issues related to race and racism in K–12 settings.

Again, welcome to this twentieth book in this Information Age Publishing series, Educational Leadership for Social Justice. You can learn more about the series at our web site: http://www.infoagepub.com/series/Educational-Leadership-for-Social-Justice. I invite you to contribute your own work on equity and influence to the series. We look forward to you joining the conversation.

Dr. Jeffrey S. Brooks
Monash University

OTHER BOOKS IN THE EDUCATIONAL LEADERSHIP FOR SOCIAL JUSTICE BOOK SERIES

Jo Bennett (2012). *Profiles of care: At the intersection of social justice, leadership, & the ethic of care.*

Elizabeth Murakami-Ramalho & Anita Pankake (2012). *Educational leaders encouraging the intellectual and professional capacity of others: A social justice agenda.*

Jeffrey S. Brooks & Noelle Witherspoon Arnold, Editors (2013). *Antiracist school leadership: Toward equity in education for America's students.*

Jeffrey S. Brooks & Noelle Witherspoon Arnold, Editors (2013). *Confronting racism in higher education: Problems and possibilities for fighting ignorance, bigotry and isolation.*

Mary Green (2014). *Caring leadership in turbulent times: Tackling neoliberal education reform.*

Carol Mullen (2014). *Shifting to fit: The politics of black and white identity in school leadership.*

Anthony H. Normore & Jeffrey S. Brooks, Editors (2014). *Educational leadership for ethics and social justice: Views from the social sciences.*

Whitney N. Sherman & Katherine Mansfield, Editors (2014). *Women interrupting, disrupting, and revolutionizing educational policy and practice.*

Carlos McCray & Floyd Beachum (2014). *School leadership in a diverse society: Helping schools to prepare all students for success.*

M.C. Kate Esposito & Anthony H. Normore, Editors (2015). *Inclusive practices for special populations in urban settings: The need for social justice leadership.*

Jeffrey S. Brooks & Melanie C. Brooks, Editors (2015). *Urban educational leadership for social justice: International perspectives.*

Natasha Croom & Tyson Marsh (2015). *Envisioning a Critical Race Praxis in K–12 Leadership through Counter-Storytelling.*

NOTE

1. Winner of the American Educational Studies Association 2011 Critics Choice Award.

ENVISIONING CRITICAL RACE PRAXIS IN K–12 LEADERSHIP THROUGH COUNTER-STORYTELLING

"So What Do We Do Now?"

Tyson E.J. Marsh and Natasha N. Croom

As faculty members in our respective colleges of education at Iowa State University and the University of New Mexico, we teach a range of courses preparing the next generation of teachers and educational leaders for K–12 and higher education, with an emphasis on social justice and equity. Charged with the task of connecting theory to practice, as faculty of color, we strive to work with our students in helping them develop a mastery of the language of numerous critical theoretical frameworks that can assist them in looking at the world in different ways, through the lens of power and knowledge production in relation to race, class, gender, sexuality, ability, and religion. As our students will one day be responsible for the educational trajectory of hundreds and in some cases thousands of youth and young adults, we take

Envisioning Critical Race Praxis in K–12 Leadership Through Counter-Storytelling, pages xi–xxv
Copyright © 2016 by Information Age Publishing
xi

this work seriously and recognize the urgency with which our students must work to interrogate and dismantle inequitable social and educational structures including but not limited to white supremacy, class-based oppression, sexism, heterosexism, ableism, and religious persecution, through translating critical theoretical approaches into tangible, socially just praxis.

Together, we have often reflected on how we can do this work better, as it is not uncommon for us to face resistance within and throughout the context of educational institutions, policies, and practices that we contend are set up to reproduce what hooks (2000) has referred to as imperialist, White supremacist, capitalist patriarchy. While we strive to ultimately transform these institutions, as junior faculty we recognize that the classroom is where this work must begin. As such, we contemplate how we can improve our work with practicing and future teachers and educational leaders to ensure that they can name and resist the multiple manifestations of oppression within and throughout educational institutions towards the end of creating more socially just possibilities in a world rife with injustice. Engaging in this work, one of the most common phrases we hear from students in response to classroom readings, discussions, and interactions with life and the everyday world typically comes in the form of the question: "So what do we do now?" Through the critical insights and counterstories of our colleagues that have contributed to this edited volume, this book represents a collective and critical response to this important question.

As scholars, we acknowledge the need, value, and urgency of drawing on multiple critical theoretical frameworks and languages to make sense of the manner in which power and knowledge production contribute to imperialist, White supremacist, capitalist patriarchy (hooks, 2000). However, for the purpose of responding to the question at hand, we have come to see the value of centering critical race theory in creating a venue for broadly incorporating multiple critical theoretical approaches to addressing the above question. In addition, we have come to recognize the value of counterstorytelling and the concept of critical race praxis as a starting point from which we can begin to establish tangible approaches to educational leadership for social and racial justice. In what follows, we offer a brief but concise background of critical race theory, particularly as it relates to the field of education. We move on to discuss the powerful implications of creating critical spaces for counterstorytelling to occur and how that can assist scholars, practitioners, and community activists in envisioning critical race praxis. Concluding this introduction, we offer a concise summary of chapters.

CRITICAL RACE THEORY: A BRIEF LOOK AT SOME OF THE MAJOR CONCEPTS

As the nation approaches the end of the second term of our first non-White president, it is ever more pronounced that despite promises of hope, the audacious claims of imperialist, White supremacist, capitalist patriarchs (hooks, 2000) citing the Obama presidency as indicative of "the end of racism" and a "post-racial" America, we recognize that Derrick Bell's (1987) claim documenting the elusiveness of racial justice, made over 25 years ago, rings true to this day. From U.S. border politics to racial violence in New York, Baltimore, and Ferguson, Missourri, as well as the persistence of government policies geared toward the assimilation and elimination of indigenous peoples, it is easy to look at the purported progress of our nation and feel as if we have progressed little, if at all, since the 1960s (Simpson, 1998). Though geneticists, legal scholars, and social scientists have established that race is a biological, legal, and social construct, the persistence of racism is very real (Bonilla-Silva, 2003; Lawrence, 1987; Patterson, 1997; Selden, 1999; Tapper, 1999). However, differing conceptualizations of what constitutes racism is a topic of social debate and much scholarly research. As expressed by Bonilla-Silva (2003), "For most whites racism is prejudice, for most people of color racism is systemic or institutionalized" (p. 8). Upon considering the notion of systemic and institutionalized racism, it is critical that we pose the question: What end does systemic and institutionalized racism serve? Omi and Winant (1994) contend that, like other forms of racism, systemic and institutionalized racism serve the end of maintaining racial categories to ensure the reproduction of the existing racial hierarchy. To be raced in American society is to find one's place in that hierarchy. Within this hierarchy, to be White is to be placed at the top of that hierarchy, bestowed with the material benefits of White privilege (Harris, 1995; McIntosh, 1988). To be non-White is to be systemically denied the most basic rights and benefits while always being reminded of your "other-ness" (Bell, 2004; Du Bois, 1903; Haney-Lopez, 1994, 1996; West, 1993). The social construction of race is deeply engrained in our psyche, as well as our institutions (Omi & Winant, 1994).

As public schools have been charged with the task of serving an increasingly diverse student body, racial disparities persist as communities of color continue to be denied access to an equitable education (Bell, 2004; Fischer, Hout, Sanchez-Jankowski, Lucas, Swidler & Voss, 1996; Hilfiker, 2002; Kozol, 1991; Ladson-Billings, 1998; Lopez, 2003; Love, 2004; Mickelson, 2003). With regard to schooling for communities of color, this inequality includes, but is not limited to, access to basic instructional materials, qualified teachers, facilities, disproportionate representation in the school-to-prison pipeline, and underrepresentation in college access (Earthman, 2002; Fine, 2002; Heitzeg, 2009; Lee, Ready, & Welner, 2002; López, 2010; Losen, Hewitt, & Kim, 2010; Noguera, 2002). As demonstrated by Oakes, Rogers, Silver, and Goode (2004), this "opportunity gap has profound consequences for students' educational and life chances" (p. ii). In addition to structural inequalities, students of color must also learn to cope within a system ultimately created to reinforce

White power and privilege. Ladson-Billings (1998) posits that the curriculum as well as modes of instruction and assessment serves to reproduce and maintain White supremacy and what she has referred to as the "White supremacist master script" (p. 18). The resulting power structure, kept intact by racism, serves to disproportionately impede and limit the educational opportunities and access to power for communities and students of color (Banks, 1993; Knaus, 2006; Wright, Weekes, & McLaughlin, 2000). Critical race theory is concerned with illuminating, naming, and addressing the material outcomes and realities of systemic and institutionalized racism. The central argument of critical race theorists is that racism is inherent in American law, policy, and institutions (Delgado & Stefancic, 2001).

Birthed from critical legal studies in the 1970s, critical race theory is a movement created by activists and scholars engaged in the struggle to challenge and transform the relationship between race, racism, and power in the post-Civil Rights era (Bell, 1980, 1987, 1992, 1998, 2004; Delgado & Stefancic, 2001). Although critical race theorists center on racial discourse, they acknowledge and address its intersection with class, gender, and sexuality (Arriola, 2000; Caldwell, 2000; Delgado & Stefancic, 2001; Harris, 1990; Hutchinson, 2000; Valdes, 2000). In addition, critical race theorists employ an interdisciplinary framework, drawing from discourse in fields such as history, sociology, women studies, and ethnic studies (Delgado & Stefancic, 2001; Ladson-Billings & Tate, 1995; Solórzano, 1998; Solórzano & Yosso, 2002; Tate, 1997).

In relation to education, Ladson-Billings and Tate (1995) formally introduced critical race theory to the field of education,

> Argu[ing] for a critical race theoretical perspective in education analogous to that of critical race theory in legal scholarship by developing three propositions: (1) race continues to be significant in the United States; (2) U.S. society is based on property rights rather than human rights; and (3) the intersection of race and property creates an analytical tool for understanding inequity. (p. 47)

Building on this work, Tate (1997) delineated five defining elements as a starting point for critical race theory in relation to educational research. To summarize, critical race theory in education: (1) recognizes that racism is endemic in U.S. society, deeply engrained legally, culturally, and even psychologically; (2) crosses epistemological boundaries; (3) reinterprets civil rights law in light of its limitations, illustrating that laws and policies to remedy racial inequality are often undermined before they can be fully implemented; (4) portrays dominant legal and social claims of neutrality, objectivity, colorblindness, and meritocracy as camouflages for the self-interest of the powerful entities of society; and (5) challenges ahistoricism and insists on a contextual/historical examination of the law and a recognition of the experiential knowledge of people of color in analyzing law and society (pp. 234–235). Furthering this work, Solórzano (1998) identified five themes specific to critical race theory in education, including: (1) the centrality and intersectionality of race and racism, (2) the challenge to dominant ideology, (3) the centrality of experiential knowledge, (4) the interdisciplinary perspective, and (5) the commitment to social justice (pp. 122–123). Though the defining features of critical race theory in education are contested and always evolving, for the purpose of this book, we present the following themes, thoughtfully crafted by Natasha:

- Racism as Endemic: Race is a product of social thought and interactions rather than simply a set of objective fixed characteristics. Founders of critical race theory posit that racism is normal, ordinary, and ingrained in American society, making it difficult, at times, to recognize due to its embeddedness in social structures, laws, and practices that shape our social worlds. (Bell, 1992; Delgado & Stefancic, 2012; Ladson-Billings, 2000)
- Interest Convergence: Critical race scholars argue that there is little incentive to eradicate racism; therefore, the interests of people of color will only be met if those interests converge with elite-White people, and often only when there is a greater benefit to the dominant group. Further, in order to reveal the self-interests of benefiting dominant groups and the historic and contemporary ingrained systems of power and privilege, dominant ideologies of liberalism, race-neutrality, objectivity, colorblindness, and meritocracy must be unmasked and challenged. (Calmore, 1992; Crenshaw, 1991; Harper & Patton, 2007; Solórzano, 1997; Sweeney, 2006)
- Intersectionality: Critical race feminist scholars pushed forward the notion that each person has many intersecting social identities that are experienced and perceived in a variety of ways depending on the convergences of power, privilege, and oppression associated with each identity. Thus, Black working-class women may experience the social world in dramatically different ways than White working-class women or Black middle-class women and men. Additionally, while we could assume that there are marginalized and subordinated groups, there is no monolithic or essentialist experience. All Black middle-class women do not automatically have the same experiences simply because they identify with or are perceived to be a part of any particular identity groups.
- Experiential Knowledge: This tenet supposes that the voices of communities of color who experience racism are valuable, valid, and crucial to uncovering, addressing, and eliminating the persistence of racial inequity and inequality. Moreover, this knowledge is often provided through narrative and counterstorytelling and used to

challenge majoritarian interpretations of ideologies, policies, and practices, which lack more contextually and historically accurate analyses of race and racism as they are enacted upon people of color in the U.S. (Delgado-Bernal, 2002; Harper, Patton, & Wooden, 2009; Ladson-Billings, 2000; Solórzano & Yosso, 2001)

- Social Justice: Critical race theory scholars agree that the broader goal of this work is to end racial oppression as a part of a larger agenda to end all forms of oppression (Tate, 1997, p. 234). If the larger goal is to be met, an interdisciplinary approach must be taken to address social oppression (Bell, 1987; Solórzano & Delgado Bernal, 2001). Lastly, praxis, or an "iterative process by which the knowledge gained from theory, research, personal experiences, and practices inform one another" (Ford & Airhihenbuwa, 2010, p. S31), is necessary to bring the empowerment of people.

With these overarching themes in mind, we now turn to a brief discussion of counterstorytelling and praxis to highlight the impetus of this book.

Counter-Storytelling and Praxis

Educators cannot require anyone to listen.... But educators can share tools to express ourselves without fear, knowing we may be penalized, but that voice is too important to silence. Structurally, that is what critical race theory's application to education requires: to no longer penalize students for speaking their realities, and to instead shift reality by demanding that all voices be included, particularly voices that are silenced by the structures of racism. (Knaus, 2009, p. 152)

Critical race theory in education demands that the experiential knowledge of people of color be centered in examining how race and racism have functioned as a centerpiece in our nations educational institutions (Tate, 1997). In opposition to racism's one-sided stories, counterstories and narratives can play a critical role in outlining the experiences of people of color in education, while drawing on their voices (Ladson-Billings, 1998, Ladson-Billings & Tate, 1995; Love, 2004; Solórzano & Yosso, 2002). Counterstories offer insight and ownership to people of color in highlighting their lived realities and experiences with racism within inequitable educational and social structures that reify and reproduce white privilege. As a result of this power structure, it is important to consider when and where people of color might feel safe in freely expressing themselves and their experience with racism, particularly in acknowledging the potential repercussions of such expression. Given the power dynamic between students, teachers, and administrators in which adults are allocated the authority and responsibility of guiding discussions and managing discipline, it can be assumed that some students, particularly students of color, might feel hesitant to fully express their reality as that reality may be in opposition to the purportedly race-neutral curriculum and the discourses of schooling that implicitly and explicitly privileges Whiteness (Knaus, 2006). In acknowledging this reality, the expression and reception of counterstories can be coupled with counterspaces co-created with students of color that support and validate their experiences (Solórzano, Ceja & Yosso, 2000; Yosso, 2005). While the expression of students' counterstories can and may take place within the physical context of the school, they may require a space and time that is set aside for their specific and free expression within and outside of the formal context of schooling (Desai & Marsh, 2005; Fisher, 2005; Mahiri & Sablo, 1996).

In discussing racial discourse, it is imperative that we critically examine Whiteness and the privileges that accompany it (Delgado & Stefancic, 1997; Harris, 1995). As put forth by Wildman and Davis (1997), "Whites do not look at the world through a filter of racial awareness, even though whites are, of course, members of a race. The power to ignore race, when white is the race, is a privilege, a societal advantage" (pp. 317–318). Critical race theory emphasizes revisionist histories that allow us to understand the role that history has played in the continual shaping of racial inequities (Delgado & Stefancic, 2001). The concept of counterstorytelling serves to offer an oppositional narrative that exposes White racism and its resulting privileges. As Solórzano et al. (2000) and Ladson-Billings (1998) have argued, the counterstories told by people of color who experience racism are often not given the same credence as those who possess White privilege. However, counterstories can emerge in "counter-spaces" where people of color are allowed the safety to "foster their own learning and to nurture a supportive environment where their experiences are validated and viewed as important knowledge" (Solórzano et al., 2000, p. 70).

In considering the aforementioned factors, in relation to education, critical race theory serves a critical purpose in calling the racial hierarchy of education and schooling into question. While the core concepts of critical race theory have been and continue to be contested, revisited, and reiterated to offer a more succinct understanding of how students and communities of color have experienced racism, the concepts of voice, experiential knowledge, and counterstorytelling remain central to its theoretical and practical underpinnings (Delgado, 1989). While traditional approaches to counterstorytelling include but are not limited to autobiographical, biographical, and composite narrative, for the purpose of soliciting contributors for this work, we placed emphasis on the value of counterstorytelling, as opposed to method. As expressed by Solórzano and Yosso (2002), "Within the histories and lives of people of color, there are numerous unheard counter-stories. Storytelling and counter-storytelling these experiences can help strengthen the traditions of social, political, and cultural survival and resistance" (p. 32). For this edited volume, it is our intention to draw on counterstorytelling for the purpose of strengthening these traditions, in relation to critical race leadership praxis.

> *Philosophers have only interpreted the world, in various ways;*
> *the point, however, is to change it.*
> —Marx, 1845/1977, p. 158

One of the primary objectives of critical race theory in education is work towards social justice and the elimination of racial injustice. While theory offers critical insight into the construction of race and the existing hierarchical power structure resulting from systemic and institutionalized racism, critical thought and insight are not enough. As indicated in the quote above, we must engage in praxis to disrupt, dismantle, and overthrow racism, as well as other forms of domination including class-based oppression, sexism, heterosexism, ableism, religious persecution, and other forms of oppression, as they are connected and interlocking systems (Collins, 1986). Drawing on Marx and Gramsci, Paulo Freire (2005) outlined critical pedagogical praxis in his landmark book *Pedagogy of the Oppressed*. For the purpose of this book, our conceptualization of praxis is rooted in the work of Freire (2005) and his understanding of praxis as "reflection and action upon the world in order to transform it" (p. 51). Connecting Freire's concept of praxis to critical race theory, Yamamoto (1997) describes critical race praxis as "critical pragmatic socio-legal analysis with political lawyering and community organizing for justice practice by and for racialized communities. Its central idea is racial justice as antisubordination practice" (p. 875). Building on the work of Yamamoto in relation to educational leadership, Stovall (2004) offers suggestions for engaging in critical race praxis leadership, arguing that critical race praxis for school leaders "involves forging relationships with parents, students, community organizations, student-teachers, and first-year and veteran teachers" (p. 11). The intent of this edited volume is to extend Stovall's (2004) initial conceptualization of critical race leadership praxis while also, in the spirit of praxis, provide practicing educational leaders, and leaders-in-training, with tangible examples in response to the question "So what do we do now?" It should be noted that this book is not meant to be prescriptive, as every educational context is unique, informed by unique local histories and voices. However, we encourage readers to acknowledge and critically reflect on the manner and process in which contributors engage in the struggle for social justice and critical race praxis in their respective context.

THE CHAPTERS

Part I—Student Voice

In Chapter 1, "'We Talk but We Don't Say Shit': Education and the Silencing of Voice," Christopher B. Knaus documents the ways in which schooling and educational reform serve to silence youth, students, and college professors. Informed by critical race theory, and through self-reflection, counterstorytelling, and interviews, Knaus, along with his co-researcher, Dwele—an African American high school student, remind us that there is much to learn, should we choose to listen. Together, they offer a powerful argument for the fostering and centering of youth voices in challenging academic imperialism, and the White, male, heterosexual, middle-class norms and values embedded in educational research, policy, and practice.

Chapter 2 reiterates that we must do more to listen to the voices of the young people we aim to serve in K–12 education. In "Reclaiming the Innocence of Latino Males: A Message from Middle School Latino Boys to their Teachers," author Eligio Martinez and then-middle school students David Fernandez, Isaac Perez, and Guadalupe Montes critique top-down approaches to research and reform that are intended to address educational inequities for Latinos. As an alternative, they propose that if we are to fully understand and address the educational obstacles that Latinos face, we must co-create spaces and opportunities for them to express their views regarding what works and how we can improve their educational experience. Focusing on middle school, a critical stage in youth development, Martinez, Fernandez, Perez, and Montes present a composite narrative that models what middle school teachers can gain from listening to the voices of their Latino students, particularly with regard to classroom engagement, and challenging of deficit perspectives.

Concluding the first section of the book, in "Fitting 'Out': How American Indian Students Make Sense of School Success," Stephanie Zywicki draws on critical race theory and tribal critical race theory to present and challenge the master narrative of student success at her former middle school. Drawing on the voices of American Indian middle school students at Leaf Lake Middle School, a nontribal school, she presents a counterstory documenting how these students internalize the master narrative and dominant discourse of what it means to be a successful student. Connecting the discourse of school success at Leaf Lake Middle School to historical efforts to assimilate American Indian students to White culture, she pushes school leaders to disrupt policies and practices that reproduce the damaging effects of dominant ideology while advocating that they foster a school environment that is supportive of American Indian student values.

Part II—Leadership

In Chapter 4, "The Burden of Admission: Profile of an African American Female Leader," Rachelle Rogers-Ard shares a powerful composite narrative articulating her struggle as a Black female leader navigating and inherently racist and sexist urban education system. Intricately weaving together her experience throughout and within the unique educational context in which she has served, Rogers-Ard reflects on her personal identity in relation to her navigation of historical stereotypes, racism, sexism, gender roles, and class oppression. Positioned at the intersection of race, gender, and class, she reflects how the voices of African American female leaders are often silenced. However, through the process of reflection, and in rearticulating her commitment to action, Rogers-Ard models that which is both essential and central to critical race leadership praxis.

Chapter 5 makes the case for a nuanced approach in the push for the recruitment, training, and retention of leaders of color. In "Educational Leadership: A Critical, Racial, and Theoretical Examination of the 'We-Need-More-Leaders-of-Color' Discourse," Nicholas D. Hartlep and Aza A. Baylor problematize the symbolic representation of education leaders of color. Drawing on concepts at the core of critical race theory, including whiteness as property (Harris, 1995), and White interest convergence, they present parallels in the way that the model minority myth and the Black Bourgeoisie stereotype can contribute to the underrepresentation of Asian Americans and Black women in educational leadership. Sharing their personal counter-stories, the authors challenge these stereotypes, while advocating for the establishment of leadership pipelines focused on the development, recruitment, and retention of leaders of color that are fluent in the cultural wealth (Yosso, 2005), and sociopolitical needs of the communities they are meant to serve.

Rounding out the second section of this book, Antonette Aragon exposes the majoritarian discourse behind Desert School District's attempt to close five schools disproportionately serving students of color in Chapter 6, "Ignored by the Board: Disrupting School Closure and Illuminating White Racism through Counterstorytelling." Combining her work as a parent, community leader, activist, and teacher educator, Aragon places herself in dialogue with a former district leader towards the end of successfully resisting the closure of Mariposa Dual Language Elementary School, where the former leadership pushed teachers to address systemic inequities including poverty and racism, as well as deficit perspectives of language and culture. Presenting her counterstory as a series of email exchanges with Dr. Martínez, the former principal of Mariposa, Aragon discusses key elements of critical race theory, Latina/o critical race theory, and culturally responsive education to document her community's struggle and ultimate success in resisting school closure.

Part III—Teaching and Leading

In Chapter 7, "Transformative Leadership and Creating Conditions to Empower Students Marginalized by Low Academic Expectations," Daniel D. Liou and René Antrop-González present personal vignettes to articulate how low teacher expectations can impede the success of students of color. Drawing on their work as practitioners and combined experience preparing teachers and leaders, they demonstrate the importance of critical theories of race in leadership preparation programs to inform critical race praxis. Liou and Antrop-González offer tangible insight into the how leaders can put critical race frameworks into practice in relation to low teacher expectations within the current context of educational reform.

Chapter 8, "Preparing Teachers to Work in Disenfranchised Communities: Deconstructing Latina/o Historical Trauma and Internalized Racism," models how critical theories of race are valuable in assisting scholars and education practitioners in exposing the historical and present day forces that continue to shape Latina/o schooling. In this chapter, Marcos Pizarro discusses the process of MAESTR@S, a community collective, in understanding and developing approaches to support Latina/o youth in their struggle for an education. Describing MAESTR@S's translation of critical perspectives on deficit thinking, historical trauma, school failure, and internalized racism into applied critical practice, Pizarro documents process of theory building for the purpose of deconstructing racial injustice. He concludes the chapter in advocating that school leaders work to co-create counterspaces in schools for this work to take place.

This book concludes with Chapter 9, "Racial Justice Leadership in Disenfranchised Latina/o Communities: A Model for Walking Social Justice in Schools." Co-authored by Marcos Pizarro, with Jaime, Rosalva Gaytan, Martha Naranjo, Carlos Navarrette, and the MAESTR@S Collective, this chapter serves as a reminder that critical race praxis is an ongoing, evolving process, always informed by multiple voices and stories. In this chapter, the authors model how leaders, teachers, and community can engage in social and racial justice in a sustained fashion. Building on the previous chapter, Chapter 9 situates research and practice, thought and action, or praxis, as a continual and communal conversation, with the aim of naming and addressing the needs of raza youth and their teachers, so that they may heal. As aptly expressed by the authors, "It is our definition of what school leadership needs to be."

REFERENCES

Arriola, E. R. (2000). Gendered inequality. In R. Delgado & J. Stefancic (Eds.), *Critical race theory: The cutting edge* (pp. 322–324). Philadelphia, PA: Temple University Press.

Banks, J. (1993). Multicultural education: Historical development, dimensions, and practice. *Review of Research in Education, 19*, 3–49.

Bell, D. (1980). *Brown v. Board of Education* and the interest-convergence dilemma. *Harvard Law Review, 93*(3), 518–533.

Bell, D. (1987). *And we are not saved: The elusive quest for racial justice.* New York, NY: Basic Books.

Bell, D. (1992). *Faces at the bottom of the well: The permanence of racism.* New York, NY: Basic Books.

Bell, D. (1998). *Afrolantica legacies.* Chicago, IL: Third World Press.

Bell, D. (2004). *Silent covenants: Brown v. Board of Education and the unfulfilled hopes for racial reform.* New York, NY: Oxford University Press.

Bonilla-Silva, E. (2003). *Racism without racists: Color-blind racism and the persistence of racial inequality in the United States.* Lanham, MD: Rowman & Littlefield.

Caldwell, P. M. (2000). A hair piece: Perspectives on the intersection of race and gender. In R. Delgado & J. Stefancic (Eds.), *Critical race theory: The cutting edge* (pp. 267–277). Philadelphia, PA: Temple University Press.

Calmore, J. (1992). Critical race theory, Archie Shepp, and fire music: Securing an authentic intellectual life in a multicultural world. *Southern California Law Review, 65*, 2129–2231.

Collins, P. H. (1986). Learning from the outsider within: The sociological significance of black feminist thought. *Social problems, 33*(6), S14–S32.

Crenshaw, K. (1991). Mapping the margins: Intersectionality, identity politics, and violence against women of color. *Stanford Law Review, 43*(6), 1241–1299.

Delgado, R. (1989). Storytelling for oppositionists and others: A plea for narrative. *Michigan Law Review, 87*(8), 2411–2441.

Delgado-Bernal, D. (2002). Critical race theory, Latino critical theory, and critical raced-gendered epistemologies: Recognizing students of color as holders and creators of knowledge. *Qualitative Inquiry, 8*(1), 105–126.

Delgado, R., & Stefancic, J. (1997). *Critical White studies: Looking behind the mirror.* Philadelphia, PA: Temple University Press.

Delgado, R., & Stefancic, J. (2001). *Critical race theory: An introduction.* New York, NY: New York University Press.

Delgado, R., & Stefancic, J. (2012). *Critical race theory: An introduction* (2nd ed.). New York, NY: New York University.

Desai, S., & Marsh, T. E. (2005). Weaving multiple dialects in the classroom discourse: Poetry and spoken word as a critical teaching tool. *Taboo: The Journal of Education and Culture, 9*(2), 71–90.

Du Bois, W. E. B. (1903). *The souls of black folk.* New York, NY: Norton & Company.

Earthman, G. I. (2002). *School facility conditions and student academic achievement.* Los Angeles, CA: UCLA's Institute for Democracy, Education, & Access (IDEA).

Fine, M. (2002). *Civic lessons.* Los Angeles, CA: UCLA's Institute for Democracy, Education, & Access (IDEA).

Fisher, M. T. (2005). From the coffee house to the school house: The promise and potential of spoken word poetry in school contexts. *English Education, 37*(2), 115–131

Fischer, C. S., Hout, M., Sanchez-Jankowski, M. S., Lucas, S. R., Swidler, A., & Voss, K. (1996). *Inequality by design: Cracking the bell curve myth.* Princeton, NJ: Princeton University Press.

Ford, C. L., & Airhihenbuwa, C. O. (2010). Critical race theory, race equity, and public health: Toward antiracism praxis. *American Journal of Public Health, 100*(S1), S30–S35.

Freire, P. (2005). *Pedagogy of the oppressed.* New York, NY: Continuum.

Haney-Lopez, I. F. (1994). The social construction of race: Some observations on illusions, fabrication, and choice. *Harvard Civil Rights Civil Liberties Law Review, 29*(1), 1–62.

Haney-Lopez, I. F. (1996). *White by law: The legal construction of race.* New York, NY: New York University Press.

Harper, S. R., & Patton, L. D. (Eds.). (2007). *Responding to the realities of race on campus.* New Directions for Student Services. San Francisco, CA: Jossey-Bass.

Harper, S. R., Patton, L. D., & Wooden, O. S. (2009). Access and equity for African American students in higher education: A critical race historical analysis of policy efforts. *The Journal of Higher Education, 80*(4), 389–414.

Harris, A. P. (1990). Race and essentialism in feminist legal theory. *Stanford Law Review, 42,* 581–616.

Harris, C. I. (1995). Whiteness as property. In K. Crenshaw, N. Gotanda, G. Peller, & K. Thomas (Eds.), *Critical race theory: The key writings that formed the movement* (pp. 276–291). New York, NY: The New Press.

Heitzeg, N. A. (2009). Education or incarceration: Zero tolerance policies and the school to prison pipeline. *Forum on Public Policy Online, 9*(2), 1–21.

Hilfiker, D. (2002). *Urban injustice: How ghettos happen.* New York, NY: Seven Stories Press.

hooks, b. (2000). *Feminist theory: From margin to the center.* London, UK: Pluto Press

Hutchinson, D. L. (2000). Out yet unseen. A racial critique of gay and lesbian legal theory and political discourse. In R. Delgado & J. Stefancic (Eds.), *Critical race theory: The cutting edge* (pp. 325–333). Philadelphia, PA: Temple University Press.

Knaus, C. B. (2006). *Race, racism and multiraciality in American education.* Washington, D.C.: Academica Press.

Knaus, C. B. (2009). Shut up and listen: Applied critical race theory in the classroom. *Race Ethnicity and Education, 12*(2), 133–154.

Kozol, J. (1991). *Savage inequalities: Children in America's schools.* New York, NY: Crown Publishers.

Ladson-Billings, G. (1998). Just what is critical race theory and what's it doing in a *nice* field like education? *Qualitative Studies in Education, 11*(1), 7–24.

Ladson-Billings, G. (2000). Racialized discourses and ethnic epistemologies. *Handbook of Qualitative Research, 2,* 257–277.

Ladson-Billings, G., & Tate, W. F. (1995). Toward a critical race theory of education. *Teachers College Press, 97*(1), 47–68.

Lawrence, C. R. (1987). The ID, the ego, and equal protection: Reckoning with unconscious racism. *Stanford Law Review, 39*, 317–388.

Lee, V. E., Ready, D. D., & Welner, K. (2002). *Educational equity and school structure: school size, school overcrowding, and alternative organizational structures.* Los Angeles, CA: UCLA's Institute for Democracy, Education, & Access (IDEA).

Lopez, G. R. (2003). The (racially neutral) politics of education: A critical race theory perspective. *Education Administration Quarterly, 39*(1), 68–94.

López, N. (2010). Schools under surveillance: Cultures of control in public education. *Contemporary Sociology: A Journal of Reviews, 39*(6), 729–730.

Losen, D. J., Hewitt, D. T., & Kim, C. Y. (2010). *The school-to-prison pipeline: Structuring legal reform.* New York, NY: NYU Press.

Love, B. J. (2004). *Brown* plus 50 counter-storytelling: A critical race theory analysis of the "majoritarian achievement gap" story. *Equity & Excellence in Education, 37*, 227–246.

Mahiri, J., & Sablo, S. (1996). Writing for their lives: The non-school literacy of California's urban African American youth. *The Journal of Negro Education, 65*(2), 164–180.

Marx, K. (1977). Theses on Feuerbach. In D. McLellan (Ed.), *Karl Marx: Selected writings* (p. 13). New York, NY: Oxford University Press. (Original work published in 1845)

McIntosh, P. (1988). White privilege and male privilege: A personal account of coming to see correspondences through work in women's studies. In R. Delgado & J. Stefancic (Eds.), *Critical white studies: Looking behind the mirror* (pp. 291–299). Philadelphia, PA: Temple University Press.

Mickelson, R. A. (2003). When are racial disparities in education the result of racial discrimination? A social science perspective. *Teachers College Record, 195*(6), 1052–1086.

Noguera, P. A. (2002). *Racial isolation, poverty and the limits of local control as a means for holding public schools accountable.* Los Angeles, CA: UCLA's Institute for Democracy, Education, and Access (IDEA).

Oakes, J., Rogers, J., Silver, D., & Goode, J. (2004). *Separate and unequal 50 years after Brown: California's racial "opportunity gap."* Los Angeles, CA: UCLA's Institute for Democracy, Education, and Access (IDEA).

Omi, M., & Winant, H. (1994). *Racial formation in the United States: From the 1960's to the 1990's.* New York, NY: Routledge.

Patterson, T. C. (1997). *Inventing western civilization.* New York, NY: Monthly Review Press.

Selden, S. (1999). *Inheriting shame: The story of eugenics and racism in education.* New York, NY: Teachers College Press.

Simpson, A. Y. (1998). *The tie that binds: Identity and political attitudes in the post-civil rights generation.* New York, NY: NYU Press.

Solórzano, D. G. (1997). Images and words that wound: Critical race theory, racial stereotyping, and teacher education. *Teacher Education Quarterly, 24*(3), 5–19.

Solórzano, D. G. (1998). Critical race theory, race and gender microaggressions, and the experience of Chicana and Chicano scholars. *Qualitative Studies in Education, 11*(1), 121–136.

Solórzano, D. G., & Bernal, D. D. (2001). Examining transformational resistance through a critical race and LatCrit theory framework: Chicana and Chicano students in an urban context. *Urban Education, 36*(3), 308–342.

Solórzano, D., Ceja, M., & Yosso, T (2000). Critical race theory, racial microaggressions, and campus racial climate: The experiences of African American college students. *Journal of Negro Education, 69*(1/2), 60–73.

Solórzano, D. G., & Yosso, T. J. (2001). Marinating social justice hopes within academic realities: A Freirean approach to critical race/LatCrit pedagogy. *University of Denver Law Review, 78*(4), 593–621.

Solórzano, D. G., & Yosso, T. J. (2002). Critical race methodology: Counter-storytelling as an analytical framework for education research. *Qualitative Inquiry, 8*(1), 23–44.

Sweeney, K. A. (2006). The blame game: Racialized responses to hurricane Katrina. *DuBois Review, 3*(1), 161–174.

Stovall, D. (2004). School leader as negotiator: Critical race theory, praxis, and the creation of productive space. *Multicultural Education, 12*(2), 8–12.

Tapper, M. (1999). *In the blood: Sickle cell anemia and the politics of race.* Philadelphia, PA: University of Pennsylvania Press.

Tate, W. F. (1997). Critical race theory and education: History, theory, and implications. *Review of Research in Education, 22*, 195–247.

Valdes, F. (2000). Sex and race in queer legal culture: Ruminations on identities and interconnectivities. In R. Delgado & J. Stefancic (Eds.), *Critical race theory: The cutting edge* (pp. 334–339). Philadelphia, PA: Temple University Press.

West, C. (1993). *Race matters.* New York, NY: Vintage Books.

Wildman, S. M. & Davis, A. D. (1997). Making systems of privilege visible. In R. Delgado & J. Stefancic (Eds.), *Critical White studies: Looking behind the mirror* (pp. 314–319). Philadelphia, PA: Temple University Press.

Wright, C., Weekes, D., & McLaughlin, A. (2000). *'Race', class and gender in exclusion from school.* New York, NY: Falmer Press.

Yamamoto, E. K. (1997). Critical race praxis: Race theory and political lawyering practice in post-civil rights America. *Michigan Law Review, 95*(4), 821–900.

Yosso, T. J. (2005). Whose culture has capital? A critical race theory discussion of community cultural wealth. *Race, Ethnicity and Education, 8*(1), 69–91.

PART I

STUDENT VOICE

CHAPTER 1

"WE TALK BUT WE DON'T SAY SHIT"

Education and the Silencing of Voice

Christopher B. Knaus
University of Washington, Tacoma

You deprive your enemies of most of their ammunition when you tell the truth.
Derrick Bell (2002, p. 119)

The tears of joy were overflowing as my mother, stepfather, and I lingered in nervous anticipation. Soon the telltale cries pierced our impatient silence; my older sister had just given birth to Liam, the first child of my siblings' generation, and my mother now had a new name: "Oma." As we crowded around the bed, Liam's tiny body wrapped in a starchy hospital blanket burrito, we held hands, eyes glazed over from the incredibly beautiful—and taxing—experience of birth. And then what happens to babies all over the world began to take shape: Liam erupted into tears, his already sharp, shrill voice screaming. And he wouldn't stop. Immediately, instinctively, my older sister Glory wrapped her motherly arms around his frail new skin. She began shushing him, trying to soften his newfound baby voice, reassuring him that everything was okay. And I remember reflecting on how the first words directed at his newborn ears were about being quiet as

Envisioning Critical Race Praxis in K–12 Leadership Through Counter-Storytelling, pages 3–23
Copyright © 2016 by Information Age Publishing

3

a way of being okay. As he was being shushed, I thought about how babies are often quieted just seconds after they enter this world. As he grew, the shushing continued, "time outs" became regular, and through his toddler years, we collectively told him (and every other toddler) to be quiet when cries became too much for our adult ears.

"Shhhh!" We tell children all the time, "Don't cry." But what other words do they have to communicate? How else do they begin to explore the concept of voice? How else do they begin to talk, if not first through cries? And as I watched Liam grow, I was reminded that as he began to learn language, as he began to form vowel sounds, play with consonants, connect sounds to create words, we were telling him, his family and his teachers, which was the "right way" to communicate, and which ways were wrong. Indeed, he, like all other public school children, would soon figure out that creativity with words resulted in red ink scribbled on his papers. The students who did exactly as they were told were given cute smiley apple stickers and asked to share their answers in front of the class. The students who spoke with accents (or had parents who spoke with accents), those who took longer to learn how to manipulate their mouths into the right shapes as they pushed air into the "correct" annunciations—they were not the favorite students. Their work was not talked about on back-to-school night, and years later, if they maintained their cultural distance from the way they were being taught to speak, with the way to write, they began failing classes, blamed for bringing down a classroom's accumulated standardized test scores. The cumulative failing of such tests impacted their teachers; soon their teachers pushed, cajoled, and begged them to learn to speak, to write in the formulaic ways with which their professional worth was measured, with afterschool tutoring, interventions, and when those did not work, referrals that led to suspensions.

While certainly not all children are pushed out of school in this way, many are. With urban high school dropout rates for students of color hovering in the 50% range (Stillwell, 2010), one thing educators can be sure about: School is dramatically failing students. The silencing of voice is the primary tool through which schools push children away from learning, away from education, and ultimately away from mainstream society. The ways parents have been taught to soothe our own babies (through shushing) aligns directly to the purpose of education in the United States: Regardless of intention, our efforts silence children through teaching one right way to speak, when to speak, and what (if anything) to say.

The purpose of this chapter is to clarify, through interviews and brief narratives, precisely how schooling silences students, teachers, and college professors. This silencing is exacerbated by race, culture, language, and gender, and through commitment to centering racism. This chapter demonstrates critical race theory's (CRT) notion of counterstorytelling by capturing the ways in which schooling sculpts the right way of speaking and teaching, while sharply limiting critical, creative, and cultural expression. This silencing expands for students and adult educators who veer from norms of Whiteness, maleness, heterosexuality, and middle-class values by directly challenging the status quo. This chapter concludes by positioning applied CRT as a framework to guide systems transformation, through a direct centering of the voices and experiences of those most excluded by educational design.

PARTICIPATORY METHODS

This chapter combines several research methods into a storytelling dialogue between myself, a White male academic; an African American male teacher; an African American male high school student (and co-researcher); and two African American male high school juniors. Dwele[1] (the co-researcher) conducted interviews and observations of Mr. Billings in his classroom at an urban high school, at a café, and as he co-taught with other teachers. I conducted three group interviews with two African American male high school juniors (Juquon and Marcelito) at another urban school; these students coined the term "diatribe" to refer to the research method of them talking to each other and the interviewer. In addition to these two qualitative data-gathering methods, I clarify my own experiences conducting voice-centered research methods. I use multiple methods to argue that research can, and should, directly inform counterstorytelling processes through meaningful discussions that inform both the researcher and the "researched." This chapter aims to model conducting research with participants in ways that exchange ideas, as each draft of the paper, data notes, and the articles I use to provide citations led to additional conversations with study participants. The point in this chapter was to use transparent research methods to invite four African American men into conversation about the role of schooling in limiting voice.

Voice and Silencing

Language is a loosely agreed upon combination of letters and sounds, and despite the immensely vast range of words and possible ways to arrange them into sentences, schools in the U.S. teach language, in this case English, as if there is one right way to spell, one right way to talk, one right way to say something (Macedo & Bartolomé, 1999). That, in essence, is the five-paragraph essay, the scripted multiple-choice exam that requires readers to choose the one main point of a paragraph, the one perspective determined by a standard (Delpit, 2012). I am not against learning the beautiful art of language. The way urban schools teach English as a language, however, denies the arbitrary and situational nature of language rules and often ignores the power dynamics inherent within a language structure (Freire, 1973; Macedo & Bartolomé, 1999).

Yet we still teach children to talk and write as if these rigid rules of grammar, punctuation, and spelling are valid. Underlying the contradictory nature of the way we teach English as a society, through schools, required tests, and false notions of a "proper" way to speak and write, rests a notion of White supremacy. Activist poet and scholar Jordan (2002) argued, "white standards of English persist, supreme and unquestioned, in these United States" (p. 158). Jordan further clarified: "Despite our multi-lingual population," she continued, "and despite the deepening Black and white cleavage within that conglomerate, white standards control our official and popular judgments of verbal proficiency and correct, or incorrect, language skills, including speech" (p. 158). In short, the United States uses schooling to teach students how to talk and write in English in a monolithic, racist way.

Voice, the individual, creative, cultural manifestations of who we are, often communicated through words, is not what we teach in schools. Yet diverse, cultural voice is what makes a democratic society (Barber, 1994; hooks, 1994). Without citizens who express themselves, who share how they see the world and advocate for the world they wish to live in, there can be no democracy, no place for communication of difference, distance, disagreements, or dissidence (Barber, 1994; Macedo, 1994; Wa Thiong'o, 1986). Voice is the language of who we are, how we communicate, share stories, share experience, and relate to each other (Silvera, 1989; Smith, 1999). Voice is the strum of a guitar, the pound of a drum, the language of what Brock (2005) called "the third space of indigenous knowledge" where voice is the literal sound of our accents, perspectives, pain, and positionality (p. xvi). The way we talk when we are not told how, the things we want desperately to scream aloud, but know deep inside that we should not—for such screams are, in short, unacceptable, out of bounds, non-academic, and non-intellectual—this is voice.

Importance of Expression

Jordan (1995) argues for poetry in the same way I conceive of voice: "Poetry means taking control of the language of your life" (p. 3). Brock (2005) argues that "language is personal and needs to bring forth the personal stories it is trying to relate to the reader" (p. 3). *Poetry for the People*, Jordan's movement for voice at the University of California, Berkeley, had a ground rule that stated: "the art of telling the truth is a necessary and a healthy way to create powerful, and positive, connections among people" (Muller et al., 1995, p. 16). Truth-telling in our most intimate languages is not only necessary and healthy; voice is how we sustain life. Consider how isolation from other prisoners (solitary confinement) is often considered the worst, most gregarious form of torture (Gawande, 2009). Without human interaction, without listening to others, at even the most basic of levels, we edge toward insanity. Yet, despite being framed as a punitive approach, "time outs" remain a common form of punishment for children, where children are encouraged to reflect (alone) on actions adults have perceived as negative (Everett, Hupp, & Olmi, 2010). Further, consider the incredibly universal notion of music; everywhere around the world, people create and listen to music, voice-filled reminders of our need to listen, and sometimes to dance (Fritz et al., 2009).

SILENCING CULTURAL RESPONSIVENESS

Mr. Billings, a 58-year-old African American teacher from Oakland, California, tells me he has a lot to say about "how we talk and how we ain't 'posed to talk." When he says "we," Mr. Billings means "Black folk." I ask him if White people are all supposed to talk in the same way, too, and he laughs: "The White people who don't talk White, well, probly just a handful of y'all, but I'd bet they don't know what to do with you all." The conversation shifted to his voice:

> It don't really matter how I talk, cause these White people ain't gonna hear me. But I realized long time ago, in my first years of teaching, if they was gonna let me in the classroom, I hadta learn to speak they language. They ain't ever gonna hear me, but they always listening for when I don't speak what they think is right.

Mr. Billings has taught in 12 different schools for over 30 years. He has taught physical education, math, English, social studies, and special education to middle and high school students, though he typically teaches "all them youngsters they just don't know how to handle." Mr. Billings reminds me of my own high school teacher, Mr. Calhoun, who taught Black studies to a relatively privileged suburban context in Davis, California over 20 years ago. Mr. Calhoun, the only African American teacher during my high school years, was forced to teach all of the students the other teachers did not want to teach. Those of us kicked out of other teachers' classrooms always ended up in his, though bad as we were, I learned years later in Oakland, Richmond, Sacramento, and New Orleans, we were relatively tame. Like Mr. Calhoun before him, Mr. Billings is old school, wears clothes from the 70s, and references Parliament, Funkadelic, and James Brown as often as he'll quote Malcolm X, Dr. Martin Luther King, or James Baldwin.

I was introduced to Mr. Billings through Dwele, an African American high school junior who told me I needed to meet his "favorite teacher-man." After Dwele introduced us, I spent five days over the course of two months with Mr. Billings. He was not a particularly good teacher, at least in terms of classroom management, student achievement, and teaching the curriculum the school expects him to teach (and he laughed and laughed when he read my notes about how disengaged students are in his class, shaking his head and dismissing me with a telling comment: "Y'all looking at the wrong things"). I ask Dwele to help me observe Mr. Billings, pay him as a research assistant, and he follows Mr. Billings around school (since he's a student, he can hide in plain sight, observe things I cannot), as we both try to understand what Mr. Billings thinks "the right things" are.

My time with Mr. Billings is not like my time with the dozens of educators I observe each month. I observe new teachers, student teachers, long-time teachers, mentor teachers, and school leaders, but Mr. Billings is perhaps the only educator who almost convinces me that teaching is irrelevant. "My students, the Black children I work for, they need to learn how to survive," he chastises me one day between classes. "You know this, but you still expect me to teach in ways that make them conform. Well I ain't gonna do that to them."

After a handful of meetings with Dwele and Mr. Billings, Dwele and I conclude: Mr. Billings must drive other teachers and the school administration crazy. He does not teach (or even reference) the required curriculum. He follows very few school rules. He does, however, have seniority within the district, knows most of the African American parents, and is an incredible wealth of local knowledge. His personal community is comprised of former Black Panthers and other community activists. He is extremely well read, which Dwele and I learn when we visit him at his house: The walls are hidden behind overflowing bookshelves of thousands of books on African history. And Mr. Billings tells first-person stories about local history, always with a lesson for young people to live more aware of their surroundings, of what history happened in their neighborhood.

The problem, Dwele points out, is that his contemporaries don't have the patience to listen to him. They do, however, respect Mr. Billings in a way they do not other teachers. Mr. Billings lives in their community. They see him walk to school. They see him walk home. They see him at the local liquor store. They see him at the soul food restaurant two blocks from the school. They have known him, *or someone like him,* their entire life. And he is the only adult teacher in their high school who reminds students of their families, their community. After conveying all of this, Dwele comes to a conclusion: "Mr. Billings' role is not as a teacher. He represents us. He makes us think about our families, our cousins. He's always telling us to live right. He's always in our minds, even if we don't listen to him now." After I tell Dwele about Mr. Calhoun, Dwele agrees, then pushes back: "See, and you still thinkin' about Mr. Calhoun. But the difference is Mr. Billings could be my father, my uncle, my grandfather. And that is why we—my Black brothers and sisters—need him in our school."

"The real problem," Mr. Billings clarifies, "is that these muthafuckas don't want me here because of who I am to these children." He continues, "These White teachers scared of me. They know I represent these students. I live here. I am these students. . . . It's why they act right in my classroom or when I am around." After spending time with Mr. Billings, I begin to see how he is targeted by other teachers, who are mostly young, elite, educated, and not from the local community. He is culturally responsive, reflecting the local cultural context of poverty, racism, and violence in the neighborhood; his "peer" teachers are the opposite, reflecting a privileged suburban world in which he and these students do not live. Mr. Billings explains:

> School, the way we do it now—not back in the day when we had a collective community—it's designed to make all these children the same. We ain't got no passion. We fail children who think for theyselves. We teach stupid curricula—I mean the dumbest of things that make no sense. We don't teach them about local history or how many Black people have resisted this, I'd call it colonial, colonizational school. We numb down our students without realizing that being numb might mean they just gonna accept their lot. I don't accept that. I didn't allow my own children to just be passive and I ain't gonna allow these students that choice neither. So I'm punished, excluded, man you should see how they react if I sit next to them. They freakin' scared of me, man. And they don't even realize how many of our children have wanted to jump them, scrub them out, and somedays, I'm the only reason these children don't.

Mr. Billings argued that school, as we teach it now, is designed to punish educators who are told to "just follow the same stream of thought, even though we all know that just gets our students to drop out of school." Yet Mr. Billings became a teacher because he wanted to help students be part of a larger struggle:

> I became a teacher because I wanted to give something back to the youth in this community. And I knew what that meant—long nights, knowing students who are killed, abused, working with drug-addicted parents, the works. But what I didn't expect was to have these White and Black principals continually disparaging everything that matters to me—and to these students. I swear, the more I show that I care about my students, the more my principal gets intimidated. And it don't matter what principal, they all just want me in my classroom, not agitating parents. But you know damn well parents already agitated by them!

While Mr. Billings is repeatedly chastised by what he called a "revolving door of principals," he argued that he maintained his support of a number of teachers, particularly the "Latino and Black ones, cause they the ones who might be able to reach our children, and they the ones treated bad by the White teachers and principals." I observed him visiting the classrooms of two first-year teachers of color during his preparation period, where he joined them in the front of the class, helping to calm students down and demonstrate how to engage students by developing a classroom presence. Meanwhile, the two new teachers talked about how the mentor-teacher that was assigned to them (and paid to support them), had never showed up to their classrooms. Dwele was surprised Mr. Billings cared about other teachers and asked Mr. Billings to clarify. He said,

> I mentor these other teachers, mostly the first- and second-year teachers, or teachers new to our school. Just show 'em where stuff is, how to order paper, supplies, and I ask them if they want to come with me to do home visits so they become comfortable doing them on they own. I ain't never been invited to do this formally. We have some quote-unquote coach—this little young thing from [the suburbs]. She and the principal are friends, like they go to happy hour together, so they just do they thing, unaware of who these children respect, who they listen to, and who they know loves them. So I gotta help show these other teachers that they's other ways of teachin' our kids.

Dwele was able to observe a number of conversations with White teachers and the White principal, and in one of his journals, he wrote: "She seems to not want him to show passion. That way he'll be like her, and not a threat." Dwele reported several interactions that reflected what he saw as "fear that his energy was contagious," and argued that in many ways, "the teachers and students, like, are pushed away because of what they don't teach. But at least he like students." Dwele talked about how Mr. Billings was "not like them other teachers 'cause maybe he isn't teaching us the book stuff, but he's teaching us life stuff. And because they can't teach the life stuff, I think they see him as a threat." I asked Mr. Billings to talk about how he was evaluated and supported as a teacher, particularly by educators he said "don't understand" him, and he laughed back:

> They came in the other day, just snap open the door, poke their heads in, two little White heads, smile their little nice-day smiles, and then close the door. Next thing I know, I'm sitting in the principal's office, and these nice White ladies have this 12-page form filled out about what they saw. But they didn't even step foot in my classroom, watched for like two minutes.

With both Mr. Billings' and Dwele's permission, I shared a draft of this section with the school principal, Ms. Willingham, a 42-year-old White woman from the suburbs, whose lack of knowledge about the local community is reinforced by the hour-long commute to and from school each day. After essentially chastising me for spending my time with "a crankshot," she argued that she knew what I "was trying to do," but thought I should instead focus on "the good teachers who actually teach these students how to get to college" (personal communication, Willingham, 2013). When I clarified that just 5% of students from this high school go to college, and that they might perhaps need some of the teaching that Mr. Billings was providing, she argued that what I was writing was ridiculous and should never be published. Instead, she argued, "we need strategies to get these kids in line, to get them in their seats, learning how to be quiet, not talk back, and follow directions." Mr. Billings, she made clear to me, was and should be an anomaly, and good teachers would teach these children how to "navigate and earn a decent income and operate in a democracy."

Dwele laughed angrily when he read my inclusion of the principal's perspective and replied, "She don't realize that cheap Brown and Black labor are her democracy. Without us being poor, she wouldn't have anyone to save." Dwele recognized that Mr. Billings could be a better teacher and argued "if we had more Black teachers, probably I can see how we'd need to push him to teach better." But Dwele also argued that Mr. Billings was the "only person who has a cultural reference to us." Without Mr. Billings, the only other educators the students related to, Dwele argued, was the Latino custodian and African American secretary. The importance of having an educator who is like the students was repeatedly highlighted by Mr. Billings and Dwele. Dwele argued that he saw "Black students talkin' an' stuff, jus' kinda hangin' out with Mr. Billings and they—I mean we, really—don't do that with the White teachers." Mr. Billings further clarified that "this hangin' out stuff is when I finds out which students are plannin' on leavin' school, so I can go follow up with 'em." Yet this similarity with students is precisely why most teachers and administrators did not support Mr. Billings. Indeed, Mr. Billings had been repeatedly told throughout his many years of teaching that he was "too damn close to those kids."

Mr. Billings, with his commitment to recognizing the cultural context of his students, had never actually been supported in developing as an educator. Rather than considering how to help him integrate the cultural foundation of his approach into a curriculum that aligned to the standards, his 16 previous principals at 12 different schools treated him as a pariah, even as students flocked to him as a resource, as well as caring teacher and mentor. In essence, Mr. Billings was silenced and barely tolerated rather than seen as a valuable resource who teaches new teachers how to engage urban students. His resistance to denying the cultural context of his students was (and is) continually met with disdain, silencing, and dismissiveness by educators who do not understand his larger commitment to seeing students as children growing up in difficult community contexts.

Through Dwele's insight and our shared observations, I came to recognize how Mr. Billings has been silenced throughout his career as one of the very few African American male teachers in every urban school he taught at. The negative treatment he calls his "professional reality" reminds Dwele that he, too, will face such treatment as he ages. But it is Mr. Billings' silencing, what Dwele refers to as the way "White adults be invisibilizing him" that teaches Dwele about himself and his own family members. Dwele concluded, "Mr. Billings makes me want to speak up, to walk proud, and even if I don't want to walk just like him, I still see that I need to so I don't end up walking like those White teachers." In recognizing the impact Mr. Billings had (and has) on his own efforts to maintain his cultural context, Dwele was identifying what Yosso (2005) calls community cultural wealth and learning to see his cultural context as a concrete set of strengths that enable him to navigate through the Whiteness of K–12 education.

SILENCING STUDENT PERSPECTIVES

After working with Dwele and Mr. Billings, I reached out to Juquon and Marcelito, two African American male high school juniors at a nearby urban high school, to learn about the impact of White-framed schooling on their voices. In particular, Marcelito and Juquon provided insight into how African American students are taught to think of "smart" as those who follow directions and those who distance themselves from urban and poor communities. Juquon argued that how students think of academic "smartness" is often equated with those who think the least. Marcelito clarified by stating, "Them that talk the least just sittin' there all quiet-like, smiling, they get rewarded for not being Black-Black, 'cause they quiet like we think of them 'yes-mister-White' kids."

I first met Juquon and Marcelito after a teacher acquaintance suggested they'd be great to talk to about voice because they write and rap together. The first time we met they were slow to open up, and they just kept asking me questions about why a White man would study racism in schools. The second time we met a week later, they read my notes and laughed at my details, and began opening up (and ended on the below 45 minute diatribe). The third time we met, they talked about how proud they were about what I had captured from what I was calling their dialogue. They told me to call their discussion a "diatribe, 'cause," as Marcelito clarified, "we a tribe and tribe is how we gonna stay not-White."

If measured by their grade point averages, Marcelito and Juquon are not very good students: Marcelito reports a 2.1 GPA, while Juquon argues that "if you use the good math, then the 1.97 rounds up to a 2.0, baby!" When measured by their attendance rates, teacher perceptions and peer students, however, both Marcelito and Juquon are referred to as "outstanding," "model students," "who I go to when I need some support," and "really just good, stable young men." The school they attend reports an overall 50% dropout rate, while Juquon argues that "about a third of my friends from elementary school still with us at school." Juquon's older cousin works as a teacher at a nearby junior high school, while Marcelito's mother (actually his grandmother) taught for 30 years before she recently retired. However, Marcelito is clear to frame Juquon and himself as "anti-teachin' men." We ain't goin' nowhere near school once we done here, the way these fools be treating our peoples."

I ask for clarification, and the two of them spend 45 minutes finishing each other's sentences, arguing how the Black adults they know are treated offensively by educators at the schools they attend. Marcelito makes me promise to not say "*his* school" in how I write about the school they attend because he argues that "this ain't my school. Ain't been designed for me and ain't been about me. It about the teachers who be workin' here, not any of us students." Juquon jumps in, not missing a beat: "but you know daaaaaamn well that teachers love claimin' us. They be like: 'yeah, *my* students this, and *my* students that.'" I ask why that bothers them, and they dive into their heated diatribe:

> **J:** Bruh, you know they be lovin' to act responsible for any damn thing we do. Like I took a poo and they'd claim that shit was their shit.
>
> **M:** You know! They act like we can't talk without them, like without their help we won't become White . . .
>
> **J:** Cause they really want to be the ones to teach us to assmilate. They teach us how to talk man, like we don't know White people talk like that. Like we don't have to listen to them teach classes and like we ain't never seen White people.
>
> **M:** That's what kills me though, for realz. The whole notion that without them, like without them being White, we'd be starving . . .
>
> **J:** . . . Or dead . . .
>
> **M:** It's like they teach so that they can make us how they want us to. What's that God quote—make us in their image or something.
>
> **J:** Right!
>
> **M:** Like we're a little toy of theirs, so they can show us off. Look at my little Black boy! See how well . . .
>
> **J:** Behaved and articulate and . . .
>
> **M:** Quiet.

J: That's the real thing they want.

M: What is? Articulate?

J: No man, quiet. They want us, no they need us, quiet. If we have to talk, then maybe articulate and polite. But they really just want to not have to deal with us. And that means the less we talk n' shit, the less they have to.

M: 'Member that class we just had—with what's-her-face...

J: Miss Twisp or some shit

M: Yup, 'member how she gave points for the quietest tables, like we were in fourth fuckin' grade!

J: Sometimes I think we just learnin' to be voice cops, like we gonna stop ourselves from speaking 'cause we graduated. Ain't that what graduated means—like we talk but we don't say shit.

M: We talk but we don't say shit.

J & M: (in unison) We talk but we don't say shit.

After reviewing their diatribe, Juquon argued that they knew how to "say shit," but that what they considered "relevant shit" was precisely what their White teachers argued should not be part of school. Marcelito wanted to be sure that I wrote that he understood that Black folk "be knowing tings that White folk don't even know is knowledge." He argued that he learned to be skeptical of White people who "try to teach us without ever getting to know us." Juquon clarified that "not all White people are dumb—it's just that most of y'all just don't really try to think that hard. Instead y'all just believe what you've been told about us, and to deal with that, y'all teachers just try to get us to stop being." Marcelito concluded the conversation by connecting to standardized testing:

> Sometimes I think that's what those tests you were asking us about measure. They measure how quiet we can become, how silent we could be. Maybe that's what the achievement gap means, just the difference between how quiet Whites are and how loud Black folk are.

Not to let Marcelito have the final word, Juquon added: "And I think we gotta maintain loudness, that's what got us outta fuckin' shackles, man."

ACADEMIC IMPERIALISM

While the personal research approaches I use allow me access to raw, unadulterated language, as demonstrated by Juquon, Marcelito, Dwele, and Mr. Billings, I have been repeatedly told (and taught) by academics that such voices are not valid research. I was taught that quantitative methods were both more scientific and more helpful to clarify what research subjects actually think. My problem, of course, is that I, along with many other researchers, do not see students or teachers as "subjects," but instead as real live people with concrete experiences that shed light on race and racism in schools. Creating the conditions through which the students and adults I study feel comfortable being who they are is a requirement to share what they think, feel, and see about the world, in their voices. I have clarified how I foster such voice-centered relationships elsewhere (see Knaus, 2011), and my point here is that what is framed as research is often the opposite of the close relationships I try to create as part of the research process.

While narrative-based, voice-centered, and ethnographic methods have been published in research journals, an overarching preference to fund, publish, and support quantitative methods prevails (Borrego, Douglas, & Amelink, 2009; Bryman, 1984; Carey & Swanson, 2003). Many qualitative studies continue to justify choosing nonvalued methods, and in so doing, weaken core aspects of voice. Many qualitative researchers simply ask the wrong questions (while striving for unattainable objectivity that can silence participants), guiding respondents to speak more formally, to answer what they think researchers want. During my research methods courses in graduate school, I was taught to edit narratives for flow, essentially erasing the contours of language so that all respondents sound the same. Tenured professors who received national awards for their research told me to take out swear words, to change contractions, to tone down the passion, to frame my questions less directly. These efforts allow the researcher more control over participants' stories and deny the depth of emotion that is conveyed. Such advice is reinforced by journal editors, publishers, and funders, who generally prefer less risky methods, asking instead for quantitative studies that, in the words of Juquon and Marcelito, "talk but don't say shit."

I have been told by academics (deans, peer faculty, and journal editors) that I should not write about Black men in the way I do in this chapter. When I try to capture African American perspectives on schools, I am told I should focus on positive stories, or more dismissively, to tell readers what "works." A well-respected full professor told me several years ago that only research that captures "what works" to educate Black men should be written because he was "tired of all these sad stories that justify student failure." I argued that being tired is not a reason for others to not express reality, yet the underlying issue is that the majority of educational researchers do not adequately understand why many Black men *choose* academic failure. Those who choose failure are not, by design, being listened to in schools or universities, where "working" and "success" is what Dwele called "paintin' ourselves White."

This point requires further clarification: In a society that values free choice and claims democracy, schools are remarkably intolerant of students who choose to not learn what educators are paid to teach. After reading my first drafts in which I wrote the above line: "many Black men *choose* academic failure," Marcelito offered a clarification:

> It ain't really a choice I make, like I wake up and say, "I wanna fail this class," or like "I want to be stupid today." All of the homies—Juquon and all the cats I kick it with, just about, all of them know what be happenin'. Our momses be knowin'. My cousins, older sisters, aunties. What did Mr. Billings call this? "Common knowledge." The shit Black people know just cause we Black. An' most White people, 'specially teachers I think, they just ain't tryin' to hear that. Bein' in school, stayin' in school, and toleratin' that racist crap is just somethin' a lot of my homies ain't gonna do. Who in they right mind gonna choose to hug on that?

The more I try to center concepts like the one above, particularly in the language that reflects Marcelito's tone and context, the more I am told that points like that are not academia. Faculty colleagues and journal editors and reviewers alike repeatedly dismiss experiences of students like Marcelito as anecdotal. A recent study I conducted captured White school principal preferences for White teachers (Knaus, 2014). I submitted this manuscript to two educational leadership journals, only to be told by the two editors that their journals focused on educational leadership, not race. Yet an editor of a social justice-focused journal (the third journal I submitted the article to) told me that the article was too education focused. None of these three journal editors sent this article out for peer review; instead they exerted their own privilege in denying a race-based study. This experience is the norm for my work: I am continually told by faculty that my work does not really fit in education. But my work also barely fits in traditional ethnic studies departments, which rarely center on applied studies of any kind, much less on the tangible perpetuation of racism in schools.

My research methods attempt to elevate silenced voices, which limits the forums I can publish in. Even race-based journals also perpetuate these biases. In a rejection letter from a race-focused journal, a colleague's study on multiracial Black adoptees was dismissed because a reviewer did not think multiracial people add to the discourse on racism. A recent paper I submitted about African American student experiences was rejected as "not sending the right message about what we want from Black students" (personal communication, August 2013). These examples abound and expand beyond the well-known difficulties of academic journal publication; critical articles on racism, written in the voices of the authors, are simply few and far between precisely because academia is not interested in the voices of those we exclude from our universities. Those who study silenced students and adults are further silenced for trying to record and disseminate oppressed participant perspectives in their own words. This silencing is exacerbated for scholars of color who face daily microaggressions in addition to thinly veiled race-based attacks that seem designed to push them out of universities (Bell, 1998; Bernal & Villalpando, 2002; Ladson-Billings, 1999; Rollock, 2012).

I learned early on as a graduate student that even the academics who most argued for voice presented and spoke at academic conferences in convoluted, verbose ways that directly contradicted their scholarship. At my first academic research conference in education, I sat in the front row, facing five senior scholars of multicultural education, as they each, in turn, read their papers aloud, in monotone choppy voices naming the need for more engaging pedagogy to tap into the cultural context of America's diverse classrooms. I darted my hand into the air the second the moderator asked for questions and asked the panel how they model the teaching they just read about. After some 15 awkward seconds of silence, the moderator asked for another question from the audience, and my challenge to the team of well-published tenured professors was left unacknowledged and unaddressed. Yet after the talk, two of the professors came up to me and told of how they write poetry and facilitate conversations in "the community." They did not, however, feel that modeling multicultural education, through using voice or multiple languages, was accepted—or acceptable—in academic settings, even though they had long ago established themselves as leaders within the field (and received the permanent job protection that comes from tenure at their institutions).

This hypocritical adherence to Freire's (1970/1993) banking system of education came as a shock. "In the banking concept of education," Freire argued, "knowledge is a gift bestowed by those who consider themselves knowledgeable upon those whom they consider to know nothing" (p. 73). Despite that these were the multicultural education and critical pedagogy theorists who introduced me to Freire, their adherence to standardized presentations of "knowledge" confused and angered me. As they read their papers aloud, devoid of passion, creativity, or the very transformative educational approaches they were writing about, I began to question their scholarship as not practical.

This hypocritical introduction to the leaders of the field was reinforced years later at a CRT conference. Three high school students, poet-researchers I had worked with for several years, attended the conference with me. After our performance-based "presentation" was met with a standing ovation, and after invitations to replicate the performance at audience members' host colleges, we fanned out to join other sessions. We met back at the end of the day, and I asked the students about their experience and what they had learned. The students were frustrated. They had begun the day on a high note, with excitement about performing in front of academics who they believed valued student voice and counterstorytelling. They had read these presenters and were excited and honored to meet them. Yet rather than being excited, they were bored out of their minds, frustrated that their expectations of engaging speakers or motivating teaching were not met. Every session that they attended was framed by a PowerPoint slideshow about research processes, which used what these three students referred to as "exclusive White talk." Despite being affirmed by these scholars during our performance, the students left frustrated by the same teaching methods they experienced at school. They left recognizing that while self-proclaimed critical race theorists might value student voices, if they chose to join academia, they would reinforce the very academic norms of Whiteness they claimed they were dedicated to challenging.

The underlying issue for me is that who is allowed to speak within academic (and education) circles tends to embrace the very language of Whiteness that the Black men in this chapter dismiss. How many meetings and efforts at predominantly White colleges "celebrate diversity" without any collective conversation about racism? How many conferences about racism in education are held at exclusive corporate hotels, with PowerPoint after dry speaker pouring knowledge into conference attendees, most of whom are at the conference to present as well? Conference presentations, key to entering academia and gaining tenure, coupled with related airline flights, hotels, and downtown prices, exclude potential faculty who never get past graduate school due to barriers often unacknowledged by critical scholars.

I recently co-facilitated a half-day workshop on CRT for graduate students, and the three faculty co-facilitators wanted to ensure students were not put off by having to confront racism. The three agreed that "race" was a less off-putting frame, despite CRT's foundational assumption of the everyday nature of racism (Ladson-Billings, 1999). Everywhere and all the time, I find most people who claim to be challenging racism to be actually promoting racism by not centering the voices and experiences of oppressed people of color. Underlying the silencing of critical voices and ways of speaking is a notion that "smart" people talk White. Adding a small smattering of street language to remind audience members and readers that the author can code shift is not sufficient to transform the structures of racially exclusive language and does not challenge White definitions of "smart." Yet my personal experiences in academia reinforce that scholars who use normal everyday talk in their writing, who try to write about normal everyday people in their work, are intentionally silenced because they do not embrace or promote stereotypically White academic values.

REDEFINING "SMART"

CRT's answer to the systemic silencing that schools teach, embrace, and ultimately test through standardized assessments is to foster voice, regardless of the consequences. Students and educators must collectively reclaim definitions of "smart" to reflect developing the skills needed to stay alive, make meaningful life decisions, and learn critical, culturally relevant expression. I do not expect academic journals, professors, or anyone aspiring to be validated by elite universities to lead a democratic transformation that fosters divergent ways of speaking, writing, talking, or living. Indeed, the way I define voice, in alignment with poets, musicians, and critical scholars of silenced communities, requires transformation away from what mainstream universities value. Instead, I urge educators to consider ways of developing concrete structures that support student voice and argue that research methods must shift to document how we silence, and could instead support, students learning to recognize and voice who they are.

While there have been efforts to capture some of the structures required to foster voice in schools (Duncan-Andrade & Morrell, 2008; Fisher, 2007; Knaus, 2011; Hill, 2009), little of this has translated into the ways in which K–12 teachers or college faculty are prepared. Indeed, K–12 and higher education policy continually prioritize assessment over voice-focused multicultural education, the hiring of faculty of color, or student of color-integrated curriculum transformation. While efforts must challenge structures, policies, and procedures that maintain the Whiteness of university faculty, who by and large control the preparation of K–12 and college faculty, what is needed ever more deeply is an applied theory to align, guide, and enhance transformative efforts. CRT, with its growing integration into educational research arenas, could be such a lever.

CRT has thus far remained a distanced theory, removed from application in any systematic manner, with benefits mainly going to the academics who write about it and, in some cases, the urban students who are exposed by a practitioner-academic. But CRT was designed for much more; as long as CRT is relegated to a theoretical framework for use in academic articles, racism will continue unabated while individual faculty are rewarded for writing about, but not directly challenging, the structures of oppression. CRT must be applied as a lever for systems transformation, as a means to question, challenge, and ultimately center the voices and experiences of those most excluded by educational design. When CRT becomes an institutional framework for transformation, critical voice becomes central to the daily operation of intuitions.

Two central ways in which I envision CRT being centered include a dramatic shift from policies predominantly created and implemented by White educators, and the development of recurring critical questioning of progress. CRT's focus on voice means that the solutions rest entirely with educators like Mr. Billings, who does not "play the game" because he knows the game is stacked against everyone he cares about. While Mr. Billings cannot solve everything on his own, he, and the tens of thousands of educators like him who have been structurally excluded from the organization of schools, directly informs the underlying racist assumptions that drive education (and educational reform). Policies cannot be made in vacuums that ignore those most impacted by the policies, and CRT should be used as an organizational commitment to centering voice in public decision-making processes. In a literal sense, this means ensuring school boards, elected officials, and educational leaders at all levels interact with, and are responsive to, excluded communities.

While CRT can serve as a useful tool to critique and inform contemporary educational debates and movements (such as tenure, charter schools, assessment, common core, class size, evidence-based decision-making, evaluative processes, and even the purpose of education), it also offers up a continual critique of progress. CRT cautions that educators will want to sing their own praises, wallow in the too-early celebration of not-systemic-enough efforts. What is needed is a foundation to dismiss one-size-fits-all solutions as inadequate to the task of transformation, and that requires using CRT as a means to structure educational organizations. Praxis requires the application of theory to real-world structures, and thus, CRT cannot afford to be limited to academic articles, research, and individual schools. In short, the voices of those most excluded, most oppressed, must directly inform the ways in which educational organizations are structured, operated, and evaluated.

CONCLUSION

At the conclusion of this research and writing, I shared a mostly complete draft with Dwele and Mr. Billings. Just prior to our meeting in Mr. Billings' classroom, one of his students, a relatively close peer of Dwele's, had been murdered by another former student. The first 45 minutes of our meeting was spent discussing the inappropriate responses from the school's administration, which had convened the students for a school-wide assembly. The principal and one of the associate superintendents, both White, apologized that the students had to deal with such violence and told students to "choose to stay away" from "bad influences." Frustrated, many students walked out, resulting in over 40 students being suspended from school. Dwele, one of the few students who had remained, asked Mr. Billings why he wasn't the one speaking to the entire school. And Mr. Billings, defeated, replied, "These White people do everything they can to make sure y'all don't see me as a real teacher, because then they might have to admit that I have something to say." Dwele, incensed, shared these words before he walked out of Mr. Billings' classroom and did not come back to school for two weeks:

This is what I'm sayin', man. This school shit be tellin' the people I look up to that they ain't shit. And they tryin' to get me to talk like them, like I think my people ain't shit. And then you gonna say I need to stay away from my people? Like the only way to save me is to be like you? If that's what school is saying, then I can't be part of this, man. My people, they don't hate us 'cause we troublesome, man, they still love us. Uncon-fucking-ditionally. That's why I am still alive. And then you gonna apologize and shit, like this isn't partially your fault. But it is, man. The kids who be killin' each other, they the ones who left school 'cause you treated them like ass. Someone gotta tell these White teachers and principals and superintendents that they makin' shit worse.

Rather than continue to shush our children, to attempt to soothe pain and suffering by silencing voice, educators must transform our notion of the purpose of schools. We have seen what shushing babies into adulthood does; this is the educational world in which we currently live. Applying CRT as a research tool and educational approach to fostering critical youth voice expands educator notions of young scholars to reveal that another world is indeed possible.

NOTE

1. With the exception of my family, names are participant-chosen pseudonyms to maintain confidentiality.

REFERENCES

Barber, B. (1994). *An aristocracy of everyone: The politics of education and the future of America.* Oxford, UK: Oxford University Press.

Bell, D. (2002). *Ethical ambition: Living a life of meaning and worth.* New York, NY: Bloomsbury.

Bell, D. (1998). *Afrolantica legacies.* Chicago, IL: Third World Press.

Bernal, D. D., & Villalpando, O. (2002). An apartheid of knowledge in academia: The struggle over the "legitimate" knowledge of faculty of color. *Equity & Excellence in Education, 35*(2), 169–180.

Borrego, M., Douglas, E. P., & Amelink, C. L. (2009). Quantitative, qualitative, and mixed research methods engineering education. *Journal of Engineering Education, 98*(1), 53–66.

Brock, R. (2005). *Sista talk: The personal and the pedagogical.* New York, NY: Peter Lang.

Bryman, A. (1984). The debate about quantitative and qualitative research: A question of method or epistemology? *The British Journal of Sociology, 35*(1), 75–92.

Carey, M. A., & Swanson, J. (2003). Funding for qualitative research. *Qualitative Health Research, 13*(6), 852–856.

Delpit, L. (2012). *"Multiplication is for White people": Raising expectations for other people's children.* New York: The New Press.

Duncan-Andrade, J. M. R., & Morrell, E. (2008). *The art of critical pedagogy: Possibilities for moving from theory to practice in urban schools.* New York, NY: Peter Lang.

Everett, G. E., Hupp, S. D. A., & Olmi, D. J. (2010). Time-out with parents: A descriptive analysis of 30 years of research. *Education and Treatment of Children, 33*(2), 235–259.

Fisher, M. T. (2007). *Writing in rhythm: Spoken word poetry in urban classrooms.* New York, NY: Teachers College Press.

Freire, P. (1973). *Education for critical consciousness.* New York, NY: Continuum.

Freire, P. (1993). *Pedagogy of the oppressed.* New York, NY: Continuum. (Original work published 1970)

Fritz, T., Jentschke, S., Gosselin, N., Sammler, D., Peretz, I., Turner, R., Friederici, A. D., & Koelsch, S. (2009). Universal recognition of three basic emotions in music. *Current Biology, 14*(7), 573–576.

Gawande, A. (2009, March 30). Hellhole: The United States holds tens of thousands of inmates in long-term solitary confinement. Is this torture? *The New Yorker.* Retrieved from http://www.newyorker.com/reporting/2009/03/30/090330fa_fact_gawande#ixzz28TCfhLxs

Hill, M. L. (2009). *Beats, rhymes, and classroom life: Hip hop pedagogy and the politics of identity.* New York, NY: Teachers College Press.

hooks, b. (1994). *Teaching to transgress: Education as the practice of freedom.* New York, NY: Routledge.

Jordan, J. (2002). *Some of us did not die: New and selected essays of June Jordan.* New York, NY: Basic Books.

Jordan, J. (1995). Introduction. In L. Muller, S. Bright, G. Chandler, A. Esteva, S. Lewis, S. Rose . . . P. Wilson (Eds.), *June Jordan's poetry for the people: A revolutionary blueprint* (pp. 1–9). New York, NY: Routledge.

Knaus, C. B. (2011). *Shut up and Listen: Teaching writing that counts in urban schools.* New York, NY: Peter Lang.

Knaus, C. B. (2014). Seeing What They Want to See: Racism and Leadership Development in Urban Schools. *The Urban Review, 46*(3), 420–444."

Ladson-Billings, G. (1999). Just what is critical race theory, and what's it doing in a nice field like education? In L. Parker, D. Deyhele, & S. Villenas (Eds.), *Race is... race isn't: Critical Race Theory and qualitative studies in education* (pp. 7–30). Boulder, CO: Westview Press.

Macedo, D. (1994). *Literacies of power: What Americans are not allowed to know.* Boulder, CO: Westview Press.

Macedo, D., & Bartolomé, L. I. (1999). *Dancing with bigotry: Beyond the politics of tolerance.* New York, NY: Palgrave MacMillan.

Muller, L., Bright, S., Chandler, G., Esteva, A., Lewis, S., Rose, S., . . . Wilson, P. (Eds.). (1995). *June Jordan's poetry for the people: A revolutionary blueprint.* New York, NY: Routledge.

Rollock, N. (2012). Unspoken rules of engagement: Navigating racial microaggressions in the academic terrain. *International Journal of Qualitative Studies in Education, 25*(5), 517–532.

Silvera, M. (1989). *Silenced.* Toronto, CA: Black Women and Women of Colour Press.

Smith, L. T. (1999). *Decolonizing methodologies: Research and indigenous peoples*. New York, NY: Zed Books.

Stillwell, R. (2010). *Public school graduates and dropouts from the common core of data: School year 2007–08*. National Council on Education Statistics, NCES 2010341. Washington, DC: Department of Education.

Wa Thiong'o, N. (1986). *Decolonising the mind: The politics of language in African literature*. Portsmouth, NH: Heinemann.

Yosso, T. J. (2005). Whose culture has capital? A critical race theory discussion of community cultural wealth. *Race Ethnicity and Education, 8*(1), 69–91.

CHAPTER 2

RECLAIMING THE INNOCENCE OF LATINO MALES

A Message From Middle School Latino Boys to Their Teachers

Eligio Martinez Jr.
University of Washington

David Fernandez, Isaac Perez, and Guadalupe Montes
Dolores Middle School

Conversations about equity and educational leadership often focus on the experiences of the benevolent teacher or principal that has come to save the day and turn the life around of poor inner-city children who need saving. Program such as Teach for America have exoticized teaching and inner cities as a playground for privileged students to "help" those in need (Heilig & Jez, 2010; Straubhaar & Gottfried, 2014). Educational reform efforts have followed a similar trend, focusing on teachers rather than students, centering research on new innovations or the latest teaching approaches that will help students perform better on standardized tests and improve

Envisioning Critical Race Praxis in K–12 Leadership Through Counter-Storytelling, pages 25–48

student outcomes (Noguera, Hurtado, & Fergus, 2012). Yet in all of these conversations about equity, access, and the achievement gap for Latinos, rarely are Latino students asked to share their opinion about what they think may be working and what practices can educators employ in order to improve the experiences of students of color. The purpose of this chapter is to understand the views that urban Latino middle school students have about teachers, school, and how to improve the quality of their education during middle school. Understanding that middle school is a critical juncture for students in the educational pipeline, this chapter focuses on a composite narrative of three Latino middle school boys and their advice to teachers on how to better engaged Latino students.

LITERATURE REVIEW

Recent research has attempted to understand the performance of Latino male students in an effort to close the gender and achievement gap (Noguera, Hurtado, & Fergus, 2012; Saenz & Ponjuan, 2009). However, the majority of this research focuses on the high school years, a period after the trajectories of most students have already been shaped and students have been placed into different academic tracks (Harper, 2015; Oakes, 1985). The gender gap between Latino males and females continues to widen, with males more likely to drop out of high school, to join the workforce rather than attend college, or leave college before graduating (Gandara & Contreras, 2009; Solórzano, Villalpando & Oseguera, 2005). The lack of research that looks at the critical stage of middle school continues to prevent the development of solutions that can truly change the outcomes for male students.

From a young age, males of color are made to feel inferior to their female and White counterparts, often being marginalized while encountering lower levels of engagement and expectations from teachers (López, 2003; Noguera, 2008). On a regular basis, male students of color are policed, contained, and treated as suspicious in their schools, neighborhoods, and surrounding communities (Cammarota, 2004; Rios, 2011). Females, on the other hand, often encounter schools as more welcoming and supportive (López, 2003; Suárez-Orozco, Suárez-Orozco, & Todorova, 2008). Schools are more likely to classify boys as learning disabled, diagnose them with attention deficit disorder or attention deficit hyperactivity disorder, and place them in special education courses at a much higher rate than female students (Gurian & Stevens, 2005; Noguera, 2008; Saenz & Ponjuan, 2009). These feelings of inferiority can lead to tremendous psychological problems that may go undetected and ultimately lead many students to navigate away from schooling (Pollack, 1998). Knowing that children establish a learning pattern that shapes the course of their entire school career, it becomes more challenging to reengage and motivate them in their later years of schooling if boys become disillusioned with school at an early age (Alexander & Entwisle, 1988).

A challenge with previous research on Latino students is that Latino middle school students have largely been depicted as deficient, troubled, and disrespectful (Carter, 2003; Katz, 1999; Rios, 2011). Compared to their White teenage counterparts who are often viewed as needing an intervention to guide them through their hormone-besieged adolescence, males of color are constructed as being at-risk and a source of danger given the physical changes that males go through (Garcia, 2009; Rios, 2011). As students grow and become more physically imposing compared to their teachers, students are more susceptible to face severe punishment (Gregory, Skiba, & Noguera, 2011; Morris, 2005). When students view teachers as treating them as delinquents, students may internalize some of these notions and develop an oppositional identity to schooling, impacting their self-image and the aspirations that they may develop (Tatum, 2003). Researchers have largely approached Latino students in the same manner, often focusing on their deficiencies rather than the systemic causes (Pizzaro, 2005).

Finn's (1989) theory of school withdrawal further supports this argument as it maintains that identification with school is an important factor in maintaining school involvement and increases participation in school activities. Woolley, Kol, and Bowen (2009) argued that Latino students can also better identify with school through increased teacher support, which was also associated with positive student behavior. Teacher support was also indirectly associated with time spent on homework and academic performance. If students perceive that their teachers are fair and equitable towards them and hold high expectations of them, then they are more likely to remain engaged in their schooling (Liou, Martinez, & Rotheram-Fuller, 2015; Murdock, 1999). Middle school can be a difficult period academically as students are adjusting to a new environment/teaching style, and without proper support, this stage can become a difficult task for students to navigate through alone.

WHY MIDDLE SCHOOL?

The transition from elementary school to middle school, coupled with students' developmental needs, presents several challenges. For example, middle school classrooms, compared to elementary classrooms, are marked by a greater emphasis on student discipline, as well as fewer opportunities for student decision-making and self-management (Midgley & Feldlaufer, 1987), fewer personal and positive student-teacher relationships (Eccles & Midgley, 1989), and an increase in ability grouping (Oakes, 1981; Robinson

& Lubienski, 2011). These practices are likely to emphasize social comparison and competition as well as threaten students' sense of autonomy during a developmental period in which they are most concerned with peer relationships and need a greater sense of control. According to Eccles et al. (1993), the fit between middle school students' developmental needs and the educational environment plays an important role in students' self-perceptions and motivation to succeed academically. Given the nature of middle school, males of color can be at greater risk during this stage as they may be placed into lower academic tracks (Oakes, 1985; Werblow, Urick & Duesbery, 2013).

Additionally, middle school plays a key role in determining the social hierarchy within schools as students are made aware of the role that race plays in their schooling, placing males of color at the bottom of the hierarchy (Katz, 1999; Morris, 2005). Teachers also see White and Asian American students as being more committed to school than African American and Latino students, and they are more willing to engage with them academically than students from other backgrounds. Tatum (2004) argues that it is during middle school when issues of race and difference occur. In particular, she notes the self-selection of friendship groups developed by students based upon race in search of solidarity with their peers. Through this self-selection process, many more differences become apparent that carry over into the classroom and impact the experience of students.

Middle school is also the place where many students distance themselves from schools and are more likely to leave school early. Wigfield, Eccles, Schiefele, Roeser, and Davis-Kean (2006) argue for the importance of achievement motivation among students and the role of motivation in students' failure to remain engaged in school as they progress from middle school to high school. Osterman (2000) contends that in order for students to be successful in school, they have to psychologically develop a sense of belonging to the school community. This in turn impacts motivation, school behavior, and performance. She argues that students who experience acceptance by peers and teachers are more highly motivated and engaged in learning and more committed to school. Higher levels of commitment and engagement, in turn, are linked closely to students' performance and to the quality of student learning.

Disciplinary issues increase for young men of color during this stage with increased expulsion for verbal confrontations with teachers and school staff (Skiba, Horner, Chung, Rausch, May, & Tobin, 2011). Latino male students, along with other male students of color, face stricter disciplinary practices from teachers and other adults that lead to the criminalization of youth of color (Lewis, Butler, Bonner, & Joubert, 2010; Rios, 2011). Excessive punishment can be a major cause for academic failure among Latino students as constant punishment can lead to more time outside of the classroom, which can cause students to fall behind academically (Losen & Skiba, 2010; Skiba et al., 2011). Middle school, in particular, is a stage in which increased suspension rates occur for students, primarily due to behavioral issues related to disrespectful conduct towards other students and authority figures (Kaufman et al., 2010).

Perhaps the most significant characteristic about middle school is the role that it plays in the development of career aspirations and educational opportunities for students. Cabrera and La Nasa (2000) identified three critical steps that students face in their path to higher education: acquiring the necessary academic qualifications for college work, securing a high school diploma, and applying and enrolling in a four-year institution of higher education. Of these steps, they identified the first step as being the most critical in laying the foundation for success, believing that the acquisition of college qualifications begins as early as 8th grade. Cabrera and La Nasa (2000) argue that students who begin to prepare for college in 8th grade enter high school ahead of their peers, are more prepared to apply for college, and are more likely to attend college compared to peers who may not be aware of the college admissions process at this stage. Lack of knowledge about college planning and the development of academic aspirations leaves students ill prepared to successfully transition into high school (Kao & Tienda, 1998).

Further, previous research demonstrates how inner city boys' post-secondary expectations are highly sensitive to contextual factors, making it critical for them to develop a sense of belonging in middle school (Cook, Church, Ajanaku, Shadish, Kim, & Cohen, 1996). Eighth grade boys appear to begin to understand restrictions placed on them by social structures and develop career aspirations that are perceived as the most realistic given their social status (Cook et al., 1996; Gottfredson, 1981). Latino students, in particular, seem to have the least stable educational aspirations compared to any other racial and ethnic group (Hill & Torres, 2010; Kao & Tienda, 1998; Mau, 1995). Failure to adapt to middle school and develop realistic expectations for the future can leave Latino males at a severe disadvantage moving forward in their educational trajectories.

New approaches that seek to understand how young Latino males come of age and are socialized through the school system are necessary in order to improve the educational outcomes of these students. School leaders must begin to look at the role that their institutional practices play in shaping the experiences of students rather than simply passing the blame onto students and their families. School leadership must be deliberate in their hiring practices, curriculum design, and development of support services, taking into account the needs of their diverse student populations.

Educational researchers must work closely with school leadership to shift the focus away from outcomes and instead focus on the root causes that are disenfranchising young men of color during the early stages of the pipeline. Research should differentiate and highlight the uniqueness of Latino males and demonstrate how it differs from their female and White counterparts. Most importantly, school leaders and K–12 researchers must listen to students and understand their needs from the student perspective.

THEORETICAL FRAMEWORK

Critical race theory permits researchers to understand the experience of Latino middle school males from their perspective, allowing them to dictate the direction of the conversation and create a space for their voices to be heard (Solórzano & Yosso, 2002). Through CRT, students are able to discuss what issues matter to them and share their perspective on schools and teachers. CRT allows for the experience of these students to come to the center of the discussion in order to truly understand how they perceive their raced and gendered social identities (Howard, 2008; Ladson-Billings & Tate, 1995). More importantly, it validates their voices and experiences by placing value on them and showing students that their experiences do matter and can contribute to the educational system (Solórzano, 1998; Solórzano & Yosso, 2002).

In using CRT as a framework, I turn to the centrality of experiential knowledge, a critical tenet of critical race theory in education (Solórzano, 1998). By focusing on personal narrative, critical race theory scholars assert and acknowledge the importance of the personal and community experiences of people of color as a source of knowledge (Dixson & Rousseau, 2006). CRT allows for the emergence of a voice for students about their reality and perceptions of school, community, and the surrounding environment, including how race, gender, ethnicity, and class impact their lived experiences. As Dixson and Rousseau explain,

> CRT scholars believe and utilize personal narratives and other stories as valid forms of "evidence" and thereby challenge a "numbers only" approach to documenting inequity or discrimination, which tends to certify discrimination from a quantitative rather than a qualitative perspective. Critical Race Theory places the students and their experiences in the center of the analysis. (p. 35)

Therefore, CRT challenges traditional research methodologies by placing the narratives of people of color and their experiences as central to the research, showing the uniqueness and variance in their experiences.

Storytelling and counterstorytelling are additional tools that I employ to name one's own reality and create an avenue for the expression of one's voice. Counterstorytelling provides a mechanism for capturing the voices of the marginalized people of color to emerge from the boundaries and challenge dominant discourses. As Yosso (2006) discusses:

Critical race counterstorytelling is a method of recounting the experience and perspectives of racially and socially marginalized people. Counterstories reflect on the lived experiences of People of Color to raise critical conscious-ness about social and racial injustice ... counterstories do not focus on trying to convince people that racism exist. Instead, counterstories seek to docu-ment the persistence of racism from the perspectives of those injured and victimized by its legacy. (p. 10)

While race and racism are prevalent in the educational experience of stu-dents in middle school, counterstorytelling allows for students to share their perspective and vantage point on schooling. It permits students to cri-tique the educational system and provide accounts of how they are counter-ing stereotypes that have been placed upon them. As Delgado (1998) adds, "Counter-stories can quicken and engage conscience. Their graphic qual-ity can stir imagination in ways in which more conventional discourse can-not" (p. 260). Counterstories become a means for empowering students and building a collective consciousness. Using counterstorytelling will allow themes to emerge from participants and not from the preconceived no-tions of what we believe is important during that stage of the educational pipeline. In short, naming one's own reality with stories about one's expe-riences can affect school practices by informing teachers, counselors, and school administrators how everyday practices serve to marginalize Latino students (Ladson-Billings & Tate, 1995; Yosso, 2005).

SCHOOL CONTEXT

The co-authors of this chapter attended a middle school in the Pacific Northwest, which I have given the pseudonym of Dolores Middle School. The school was located in a predominantly White community that has seen a large influx of Latino, Russian, and South Asian immigrants over the past 10 years. Since 2001, the population of Latino students at Dolores Middle School more than doubled from 11.7% to 26.1%, becoming the middle school with the largest concentration of Latino students in the district. This can be partially attributed to the working-class communities of color adjacent to the southern part of the city of Joburg (pseudonym). Dolo-res Middle School has a very diverse student body compared to rest of the schools in Joburg, with 39.6% of its students being Caucasian, 21.4% Asian/ Pacific Islander, 4.7% African American, 0.8% Native American and 7.3% multiracial. In terms of social class, 48.6% of the students qualify for free or reduced lunch (Office of Superintendent of Public Instruction, 2012). While the demographics of the school have changed, very few changes in personnel have occurred during this same time period. Of the 36 teachers on staff, only five are faculty of color. Two of them, the Spanish teacher and a reading instructor, are the only Latino faculty members.

Discipline was a major problem at the Dolores Middle School with data following national trend as Latino students represented a significant number of the disciplinary cases. In 2009, Latino students constituted 22% of the school population, yet they accounted for 33% of the out-of-school suspensions and 66% of the in-school suspensions, with more recent data expected to show a higher rate of discipline for Latino boys (Office of Superintendent of Public Instruction, 2012).

METHODS

Using counterstorytelling as a method, a composite narrative was created that weaved the voices of the participants into one singular voice. As defined by Delgado and Stefancic (2001), "A counterstory is writing that aims to cast doubt on the validity of accepted premises or myths, especially ones held by the majority" (p. 144). A composite narrative of the three students was employed in the writing of this chapter. A composite narrative is more than a definition or series of statements about a phenomenon, but rather it is a reflective story that draws upon the experiences and stories of participants (Todres, 2008; Wertz, Nosek, McNiesh, & Marlow, 2011). Three students participated in the writing process, in which they wrote and shared their experiences at Dolores Middle School. After discussing their experiences, students collectively wrote a narrative that addressed what they felt was the Latino experience at school. At the time of the writing of this chapter, the three students were enrolled in 8th grade and belonged to various clubs and sports at Dolores Middle School.

FINDINGS

The following narrative comes from an afterschool conversation with three Latino middle school students. Students were asked to share their opinions of teacher treatment of Latino students and the Latino male student experience. Focusing on personal accounts, students created counterstories about their school experience. The student counterstories centered around five main themes: (1) students' value of education, (2) the significance of race at school, (3) the role of supportive teachers, (4) the perception that teachers developed about Latino students, and (5) the value of teacher encouragement and support of students.

The Student Experience

Interviewer: So I have been at school for a while now and I have seen how you guys interact with teachers, but I want to get your opinion about your views on teachers. What perception do you believe that teachers have about Latinos? What are some things that cause teachers to think this way?

Students: We feel that some people believe that us Latinos don't care about education but to them, we'd say what was their reason to say something like that? That some people may act as if they didn't care about school, but just because a few Latino boys act bad or don't care about school, it shouldn't in any way mean that every single Latino doesn't value education. We know that some teachers treat us different because they think that all Latinos won't do anything with their education, so they don't give us a chance and focus on helping White students or Asian students.

Interviewer: With that said, what value do you guys place on education?

Students: Education is important for us because we try to look through all the racism and try to forget about all that to be successful in life and be full of education. In our cases, our siblings and us will probably be the first to be a college grad and to our parents it would be really important and we'd feel good about ourselves. Some people, mainly Latinos and African Americans, don't have opportunities to have a good job that can keep food on the table for them to be a strong family, but instead those resources are stolen from them because of race relations in our society.

Graduating from high school and going to college will show that we're not just another failure to society and we'd be as educated as any other American and it would bring joy to our families' lives. Education isn't just for one to gain knowledge, it's also for one to know things to get into a good actual job that is good for one to help maintain their family in a healthy shape and to keep it together. We know that education walks along with the growing technology, so if we want to get a good job that will get us the money to support our families, we're going to have to get a job that trains us in the most updated technology.

Interviewer: Okay, so I see that education is valuable to all of you, but it seems that race is a factor in your experience. I have observed how you guys interact with your teachers, but what do you guys think about your interactions with them. What role

do you believe that race plays in your education and how
have you seen race be a factor?

Students: One thing that we see in class is that, we Latinos are viewed
in a different way than other races. For example, when we
were in class once, the teacher asked a question and one
of our friends that's Latino raised his hand and then a girl
raised her hand, to be honest, she's really smart, and the
teacher called on her, even though our friend raised his
hand first. We kinda see this as if the teacher was racist, because well our friend is Latino and the girl is Asian and just
because she's smart, the teacher didn't give him a chance,
we seen this a lot of times at school.

Interviewer: So why do you guys think that teachers may think less of you?

Students: We think it's the stereotypes that they have about Latinos,
like one stereotype about Latinos is that we all use drugs.
Like we know that some students do, but that's not all of us.
Like there's been a few times that people get stopped in the
morning by teachers when the Latinos enter school with
their eyes red, but what they really don't know is that the
night before those students spent the whole night without
sleeping studying so they don't fall behind, so they can be
considered educated.

Interviewer: Do teachers ever say things to you guys that makes you think
that they believe in stereotypes?

Students: Yeah. Teachers often tell us who to be around and what
kind of friends to hang out because they think they know
what's best for us. We don't think it's right for teachers to
tell us who to be around because even some though they're
bad influences, we don't follow up with what they do. A lot
of people say Hispanic people are irresponsible or they're
unsuccessful but everyone is different and we give effort to
try to be successful. Sometimes teachers will tell us, don't
hang out with "those kids," but what they really meant was
don't hang out with those Mexicans. They might think that
the Latinos have a bad influence but it's up to you to make
the choice to be good or bad.

Interviewer: So how does being treated because of race make you guys feel?

Students: How teachers treat us based on race makes us feel like
to them we're just another wetback, including all Latino
Americans. It's all bad they don't see how it affects us but it
does, they may call us another typical dropout. When we are
treated this way we feel mad and sad. Mad because we feel
like they think we are lower than others when we were just as

equal! And sad because they don't give us a chance to show them our potential.

Sometimes teachers would ask us a question in class and they would immediately think we were wrong before we even answered the question and even if we had the right answer they would find the smallest mistake and tell us we were wrong and quickly turn to the smart kid in the group and nicely asked him to answer the question. This makes us feel stupid and like we couldn't answer a question correctly. After this, we don't even want to continue participating in that same class, we feel discouraged.

Interviewer: So how do you guys respond to how teachers treat you?

Students: For teachers who think that we are all bad, we try to show them and prove them that we are more than they speak of us and tell them that we're better than they say. We show them that White students aren't the only ones that can graduate.

Interviewer: Do all teachers treat you guys this way?

Students: Nah, not the good teachers.

Interviewer: So what does a good teacher do?

Students: Good teachers won't do that. Good teachers will help and push you, like when you answered a question and you got it wrong, they would give you another question and see if we could answer the second one. Then they would show us different ways to get the answer of the question and give us the steps to success. When they do this, it makes us feel like we could keep trying and finally would reach the answer without feeling discouraged.

Interviewer: So okay, you say that good teachers push you and challenge right? Can a White teacher be a good teacher?

Students: While we see teachers be biased based on race, we also know that there are also White teachers that do give you a chance, even if you're not that smart. For example, our algebra teacher, even though we're not the smartest kids in class, she always calls on us when we raise our hand, even if we get the wrong answers, she still thanks us for trying and she's really nice. Even through we're not the same color, she still helps us and respects us, we think that more teachers should be like her, she doesn't care about color, if a student is smart or not, she treats them equally and she gives us, the Latinos more options to progress in school and in life.

Interviewer: So are there other good teachers. And what else do good teachers do?

Students: We've seen many of our teachers show they care for their students beyond the classroom. For example, we play soccer for our school and here one teacher takes time out of his schedule to play soccer with us and our team. He takes time and makes an effort to go to some of our games. We really appreciated that because our team is mostly Latinos. When we see that, we start thinking that some teachers do care about their students outside of the classroom.

Interviewer: So not all White teachers are bad then?

Students: No. Some teachers do treat us the same as everyone else. They call us to tell us that we are missing work and tell us when it would be a good time to work on it with the teacher. If we had more Latino teachers it would be different for us Latinos because then I think we would interact more with the teachers. Like there's this one teacher who we don't have him anymore, but every day he would check some of our grades and if we're missing something in a class, he tells us to turn it in and helps us do the assignment. Just seeing him do that, when we don't even have him as a teacher, gives us a reason to keep our grades up and be good in school. He's a big motivation to us and tells us that we can succeed in life if we try. There should be more teachers like him, that actually care about their students, not just here at our school but throughout other school too.

Interviewer: What other things do good teachers do that help you guys in school?

Students: Some teachers help us prove some of the stereotypes wrong, like one teacher incorporated things about Latinos in his class. Reading about people like us in class made us feel that at least some teachers understand us and we're not just being ignored, like talking about Latinos helps to educate other students as well. It also makes us feel motivated to learn and try harder because we feel like we can relate more to the material. Like hearing the negative stuff about Latinos and then reading positive things helped motivate us and try to make a difference for Latinos.

Interviewer: So it feels like you're saying that White teachers can be good teachers too, but it seems that you guys feel that having more Latino teachers would be better for you guys, right? How do you think having more Latino teachers would change your school experience?

Students: Having more Latino teachers would be different because they would probably understand our responsibilities we have at home or parent issues/family problems. We would see how as a Latino would take time to become teacher and it would show us that they care and that I should too. They would tell us things like try hard to overcome to be equal and tell us that we can succeed as a Chicano and have the determination to prove the people that dragged them down wrong.

Interviewer: So what can teachers do that can help you guys be more engaged in school?

Students: There are three main keys in life that one needs to succeed—motivation, determination, and to be supported, and if teachers don't support you it's hard to stay focused. The way teachers treat us is a way you would treat little kids. The teacher's attitude impacts us in a way that we don't really want to engage during class. The reason why we either want to be respectful to a teacher or not is based on how they treat us.

When teachers respond positive to us, it makes us feel the complete opposite and shows us that they care about us and don't care about the darker shade of brown differences. They care about our education and futures as well as any other human being. It makes us and other Latino brothers know that they care more than one thinks and that they're here to help us when we need them and that they will motivate us too.

Interviewer: What else can teachers do to motivate you guys and how can this impact your lives at school?

Students: In order to motivate us, teachers should call on Latinos more because they don't call on us most of the time. They should stop focusing on us, they're just on us to see if we are doing something wrong but they don't focus on other students who are doing wrong also. I think the teachers do care about us and they help us but they don't praise us for the good things that we do. For example, when Latinos do something good they just say good job but when we do something bad, they give us a long lecture.

If we had the support of our teachers the way a regular American would have, we would not only just have good grades but our attitude as well, but our life would change in a positive way. Us, the Latinos, we need more supportive teachers because some of us were not born here and we face more obstacles compared to other students that were born here and that don't face as many obstacles. For us Latinos, it's not that we don't want to learn, it's that sometimes we don't get the chance from teachers and other adults. Just because English isn't our first language and because we're not as smart as Asian or white kids, we should be left behind.

Us, as Latinos, soccer is a big part of our lives and as a soccer season comes, we get our grades up to play soccer, but in this school, were just seen as soccer players that bring pride to the school, but it's not just that, we as students, we wanna be seen as more than just soccer players because we're actually working hard in school and trying to have a better life in the future and now. We want more chances to prove that were trying and that we can be better than what we are right now.

DISCUSSION

Middle school marks a critical stage as it can either hinder or enhance the aspirations that students may have. For Latino male students, this is greater as children of immigrants largely enter the school system with low levels of social capital and higher aspirations. As a result, these students often rely more on teachers and staff members to help them maintain their college and career aspirations (Taylor, Kochhar, Livingston, Lopez, Morin, & Fry, 2009). The students in this narrative begin to give us insight about how teachers can work with students and attempt to understand their experiences rather than placing judgment on students based on preconceived notions about Latino males.

To begin, teachers must understand that Latino students do place a high value on education, as discussed in the narrative, as students recognize that a good education will allow them to have a better life in the future. One of the challenges that students may face is the lack of information and access to resources that can prevent them from accomplishing their academic goals. Despite the negative perceptions that teachers may develop about them based on select disruptive behavior, Latino students largely remain positive and use negative experiences as motivation to help counter negative perceptions that teachers may have of them. Latino students do make an effort to participate in class discussions as much as possible but need teachers to be encouraging to them and allow them to participate.

While Latino males may have high aspirations, they recognize that they may have different obstacles because of their background and socioeconomic standing, but they remain optimistic about being able to go to college and become successful. Latino students understand that in order for them to have a better quality of life and be able to provide for their families when they get older, they must obtain a college degree that can better prepare them to enter the job force as adults. Further, students are also cognizant of the growing demand of high-skilled labor and recognize that they may have to pursue careers in high-tech fields in order to remain competitive in the job market.

During middle school, students can become increasingly sensitive to race-based treatment from teachers that can create tension between students from different communities. As discussed by the Latino males, preferential treatment for students can be discouraging as it can impact their motivation and desire to become engaged academically if they feel that their teachers will not give them an equal opportunity to participate in class discussions. As the students demonstrate here, teachers' attitudes towards them have an effect, but they remain optimistic given the value they place on education. Latino male students welcome teachers calling upon them to participate in class discussion and are willing to engage more academically if teachers provide an avenue for them.

As race-based treatment becomes more salient during middle school, students can begin to internalize the racial microaggressions perpetuated by teachers, which can have a significant impact on their psychological well-being. This behavior by teachers can lead to students feeling alienated and can cause them to begin to distance themselves from school and school agents. Rather than discouraging students, teachers must find ways to encourage and engage students outside of the traditional classroom setting. Seeing how critical middle school is in the educational trajectory of students, teachers can begin to foster positive relationships with students by encouraging and being supportive of students. Instead of dismissing students, teachers can push students to think further and more critical in order to increase participation in class and help students build self-confidence. White teachers can play a key role in improving engagement by looking for similarities with their Latino male students. Engaging students in the activities that they are interested in, such as soccer, can demonstrate to students that teachers are interested in them beyond their classroom.

One of the recommendations from students was increasing the number of teachers who come from the same background as them. Having teachers of similar backgrounds to students can be beneficial as students can relate to them because of their shared lived experiences. Seeing someone who looks like them, speaks their language, and can relate to their home life and culture can serve as an example for students to follow and learn from. Increasing the number of teachers of color can increase the number of people who can advocate on behalf of Latino students as well.

White teachers, however, can also become allies and be supportive of Latino males by showing Latino males that they have the same capacity as other students. Teachers who develop long-lasting relationships with students, even far after the student is no longer is enrolled in their classes, can be instrumental in developing a support system for Latino males that can allow them to develop a sense of belonging at school. These long-term relationships can also demonstrate to students that teachers are concerned for their overall well-being and allow them to have someone that they can trust, just as students discussed in their narrative. This can also impact the motivation that students have and help improve their outlook on school.

Teachers can also help increase engagement by revamping the curriculum to make it more culturally relevant to the lives of Latino students. By incorporating the Latino experience into class discussions and readings, teachers can help educate students and other teachers about the Latino community and some of the contributions that they have had in society. More importantly, it can positively affect the attitude of Latino male students towards their classes, and they can become more engaged and enthusiastic about their school work. Reading about the experience of other Latinos can also open the possibility to new careers and allow students to explore other fields that they may of not have considered before.

Students often feel that Latino students need to be supported more and encouraged to participate during class rather than being left alone. Positive teacher engagement through encouragement and calling on them during class can lead to improved academic outcomes for Latino males, which in turn can lead to decreased disciplinary issues. Throughout my time at Dolores, I witnessed several teachers limiting the opportunity for students to be engaged and participate in class. Few teachers recognized that Latino students learn and engage differently than others and became creative and purposeful in their teaching approach in order to engage more Latino students, and in particular, the Latino males.

Instead of focusing on the negative behavior of students, teachers can provide encouragement by encouraging participation of all students and reinforce how valuable their contributions can be during class discussions. Although students recognize that they may have some barriers because of their difficulties with the language, this should not be a reason for students to be disregarded, but rather, teachers should recognize the needs of students and attempt to find additional resources for students who may need them.

RECOMMENDATIONS

Teachers need to understand how to connect with students at their level. Even though students may be of a different background than their teachers, that should not prevent them from being able to connect with their students. Teachers must find a common ground with their students in order to engage and continue to support their students. Relating to students can lead to increased notions of belonging and feeling accepted, which can boost academic performance among students. The following are recommendations for critical race practitioners based on the experiences of the students and my observations working with students at Dolores Middle School.

Listening to the Student Voice

One of the challenges that educational leaders face when addressing issues of race is the lack of engagement from teachers and school personnel in discussing the issue. Rather than engaging in dialogue, teachers and school leadership view the topic as a personal attack and become defensive. When discussing race, school leaders and teachers must stop being defensive about their position and be open to engaging in dialogue about race. When students bring up the issue of race, it does not signify that students are accusing teachers of being racist, but they are instead expressing a key factor in their educational experience. School leaders must not silence students when they express their opinion and instead listen to them in order to understand how particular school practices shape their educational experience. During fieldwork at Dolores, a group of teachers engaged in discussions about race at school and attempted to create a focused space for Latino male students to discuss their experiences openly.

While many veteran teachers have been in classrooms for decades, they must realize that their teaching styles and engagement must change as the demographics of schools change, such as what took place in Dolores. What might have worked in the past may not work with classrooms that are becoming increasingly diverse. Teachers and school leaders must continuously ask themselves whether their teaching approach is effective and must recognize when they are not capturing students, rather than expecting students to keep up with a curriculum that they may not understand.

One such example of adapting to student needs is one of the teachers mentioned by the Latino male students in the narrative. Although their teacher was a White male, he made the effort to get to know his students beyond the classroom, often coming to soccer games, spending time after school to play soccer with the Latino males, and asking them questions about how they felt about the game and how their families were doing. This teacher would also often ask me what he was doing right and how he could be more sensitive to the students' needs.

Improving Language and Teaching Practices

Language is critical to the school experience. How we speak about and refer to students influences their attitudes towards school and can either engage or alienate them. Teachers and administrators must be more sensitive and careful with the language they use to refer to and address particular groups of students. Language arts teachers in particular at Dolores Middle school actively attempted to engage students. When a student answered a question wrong, the teachers often prodded a little more to make the student think critically about the question until they would get the right answer. When a student was stuck, instead of dismissing the student, teachers would ask the class, "Who can help your classmate out?" This practice allowed students to feel like their comments were valid and encouraged them to keep participating in class discussions.

Students generally felt that even when they got the wrong answer, teachers would help them find the answer and would thank them for being engaged. Students enjoyed being in their language arts classes and very few disciplinary issues came from these classes. The same thing can be said in the sciences classes. Teachers were more engaging and often asked questions to students as a follow-up. Again, how teachers engaged students in class materials would reflect on the attitude that students adopted when they were in class, with many of them actively participating in class. Language arts and science teachers were often among the most popular teachers with students because of their ability to connect with and engage all students, regardless of their background. Even with the science teacher, who struggled a bit with class management, students felt that he cared about them because on multiple occasions they saw him in his classroom late at night setting up labs and working on other materials in preparation for class. Students saw this commitment and reciprocated it by trying to do better in class and completing their work.

Schools can learn from teachers who do a good job at engaging students by observing their teaching style and approach to working with Latino male students. Although the 7th grade language arts teacher was a White male, he constantly looked for ways to connect with students either through his personal experiences or through student interests, often asking them questions about their soccer games or by attending soccer games and practices. Students recognized his efforts and were more receptive to his approaches. When teachers do a better job at connecting and engaging their students, fewer disciplinary issues can arise and students can develop a sense of belonging with their teachers that can improve school outcomes.

Expanding Opportunities for Engagement

Schools and school personnel must take the initiative to engage students outside of their academic space. Although the middle school context does not traditionally lend itself to increased engagement as much as the high school environment that may have numerous student clubs, teachers must find ways to become active participants in the education of their students.

Afterschool programs and services, as an example, provided a critical form of engagement for students that allowed them to stay after school long after the school day ended and after teachers left for home. Yet, what happens when there is no buy-in from teachers to support these programs or create programs of their own? Teachers and schools cannot pass on the responsibility to outside organizations to ensure the safety and wellbeing of their students, but rather, they must make an effort to become invested in their students. Athletics is a major form of engagement for many young men of color, but often athletics are left to outside coaches or individuals who do not have the necessary credentials to support students academically (Broh, 2002; Fraser-Thomas, Côté, & Deakin, 2005).

Soccer/athletics and other extracurricular activities are critical to the success of Latino students, and these must be further explored as a form to engage students and improve their academic outcomes. Teachers' interest in student activities, and in particular athletics, allowed teachers to bring some of the experiences from the soccer field into the classroom by discussing leadership and sportsmanship issues that they saw during soccer games. This allowed teachers to build off of the activities that students were already engaged in and demonstrate to students that they shared similar interests.

A major positive accomplishment at Dolores Middle School was the creation of the Latino Boys Club created by one of the counselors. The group provided a space for students to learn more about their identity and develop cultural pride through a school-sanctioned activity. By bringing different speakers with whom students identified culturally and whose stories resonated with the students' lives, students were able to think critically about their future aspirations and use other peoples' stories in order to navigate through the school environment. Further, the Latino Boys Club served as a way to validate the experiences of Latino males and let them know that they mattered at school.

Additional forms of extracurricular activities that promote cultural awareness must be provided continuously to expose not only Latino students to their culture, but also other students so that they can learn about each other's cultures. Teachers must play a critical role in creating and supporting new activities to show students that they are interested in their wellbeing outside of the classroom space. As demonstrated by the student narrative, teacher engagement impacts the perception that students develop about individual teachers and causes some students to be more receptive to listen to teachers and complete their work.

Diversifying and Training Teachers and Staff

Lack of hiring of teachers of color prevents students from finding someone that they can relate to at school. Hiring practices must be deliberate and target the recruitment of new teachers and staff from diverse backgrounds that can match the demographics of Dolores Middle School. However, the problem with engagement is not solved simply by hiring a more diverse teaching staff, but rather by showing teachers of all backgrounds how to care about their students.

Cultural competency trainings can also help improve the relationship between teachers and students and prepare teachers to be better suited to work and engage with diverse student populations. Showing teachers how to incorporate new material that students can relate to can serve not only as a way to attract student interest, but also to validate students' cultural experiences in the classroom. As demonstrated in the student narrative, incorporating materials that discuss the experiences of people of color can have a positive effect on student attitude and lead to increased engagement in class materials. These new approaches can lead to positive self-imaging by students and help improve student outcomes.

CONCLUSION

This chapter contributes new understandings of the school experiences of Latino males in middle school. Their racialization and their treatment in the schools by teachers and other school personnel based on preconceptions of their home lives, abilities, and cultural values, in turn, influences how the students perceive themselves and interact with teachers and peers. More importantly, it highlights the student voice. Fostering a new learning environment that allows Latino males to become engaged in course discussions and supporting their personal interest can help improve the outcomes for Latino males.

The significance of the narrative is that the educational experiences of middle school males are far more complex than previously documented. The study challenges the notion that oppositional behavior is the only behavioral form for male students of color by demonstrating the value that all Latino students, not just males, place on education and the significance that it can have for their future. Attention specifically to the struggles of Latino males reveals many of the challenges of growing up in a multicultural society when one is a member of a minority ethnic group. For middle school males, the academic goals remain high, but practices that alienate and disenfranchise Latino males can discourage them from being active participants in class.

This study also proved how students begin to deviate during middle school and become disengaged by the time that they reach high school. Additional research is necessary on the middle school experience in order to understand how to meet the needs of students during this stage that can ensure that they are prepared and can successfully transition into high school. In order to close the opportunity gap, researchers and practitioners must pay attention to all of the segments of the educational pipeline and follow students through each stage in order to address the problems that create wide differences in school completion among racial and ethnic groups. As researchers and practitioners, listening to students, observing their behavior from a non-deficient perspective, and implementing practices that are culturally inclusive, respectful, and fair are necessary approaches that can change the school culture and better support middle school students in achieving educational success.

REFERENCES

Alexander, K. L., & Entwisle, D. R. (1988). Achievement in the first 2 years of school: patterns and processes. *Monographs of the Society for Research in Child Development, 53*(2), 1–157.

Broh, B. A. (2002). Linking extracurricular programming to academic achievement: Who benefits and why? *Sociology of Education,* 69–95.

Cabrera, A. F., & La Nasa S. M. (2000). Three critical tasks America's disadvantaged face on their path to college. *New Directions for Institutional Research, 2000,* 107.

Cammarota, J. (March 01, 2004). The gendered and racialized pathways of Latina and Latino youth: Different struggles, different resistances in the urban context. *Anthropology & Education Quarterly, 35*(1), 53–74.

Carter, P. L. (2003). "Black" cultural capital, status positioning, and schooling conflicts for low-income African American youth. *Social Problems, 50*(1), 136–155.

Cook, T. D., Church, M. B., Ajanaku, S., Shadish, W. R., Kim, J. R., & Cohen, R. (1996). The development of occupational aspirations and expectations among inner-city boys. *Child Development, 67*(6), 3368–3385.

Delgado, R. (1998). Storytelling for opposition and others. In R. Delgado & J. Stefancic (Eds.), *The Latino/a condition: A critical reader* (pp. 259–270). New York, NY: NYU Press.

Delgado, R., & Stefancic, J. (2001). *Critical race theory: An introduction.* New York, NY: NYU Press.

Dixson, A. D., & Rousseau, C. K. (2006). And we're still not saved. In A. D. Dixson & C. K. Rousseau (Eds.), *Critical race theory in education: All God's children got a song* (pp. 31–54). New York, NY: Routledge.

Eccles J. S., & Midgley, C. (1989). Stage/environment fit: Developmentally appropriate classroom for early adolescence. In R. E. Ames & C. Ames (Eds.), *Research on motivation in education* (Vol. 3, pp. 139–186). New York, NY: Academic Press.

Eccles, J. S., Midgley, C., Wigfield, A., Buchmanan, C. M., Reuman, D., Flanagan, C., MacIver, D. (1993). Development during adolescence: The impact of stage-environment fit on young adolescents' experiences in schools and in families. *American Psychologist, 48*(2), 90–101. doi:10/1037/10254-034

Fraser-Thomas, J. L., Côté, J., & Deakin, J. (2005). Youth sport programs: An avenue to foster positive youth development. *Physical Education & Sport Pedagogy, 10*(1), 19–40.

Finn, J. D. (1989). Withdrawing from school. *Review of Educational Research, 59*(2), 117–142.

Gandara, P. C., & Contreras, F. (2009). *The Latino education crisis: The consequences of failed social policies.* Cambridge, MA: Harvard University Press.

Garcia, L. (2009). "Now why do you want to know about that?": Heteronormativity, sexism, and racism in the sexual (Mis)education of Latina Youth. *Gender and Society, 23*(4), 520–541.

Gottfredson, L. (1981). Circumspection and compromise: A developmental theory of occupational aspirations. *Journal of Counseling Psychology, 28,* 545–580.

Gurian, M., & Stevens, K. (2005). *The minds of boys: Saving our sons from falling behind in school and life.* San Francisco, CA: Jossey-Bass.

Gregory, A., Skiba, R. J., & Noguera, P. A. (2010). The achievement gap and the discipline gap: Two sides of the same coin? *Educational Researcher, 39*(1), 59–68.

Harper, S. R. (2015). Success in these schools? Visual counternarratives of young men of color and urban high schools they attend. *Urban Education, 50*(2), 139–169.

Heilig, J. V., & Jez, S. J. (2010). Teach For America: A review of the evidence. *Education Policy Research Unit.*

Hill, N. E., & Torres, K. (2010). Negotiating the American Dream: The paradox of aspirations and achievement among Latino students and engagement between their families and schools. *Journal of Social issues, 66*(1), 95–112.

Howard, T. (2008). Who really cares? The disenfranchisement of African American males in preK–12 schools: A critical race theory perspective. *The Teachers College Record, 110*(5), 954–985.

Kao, G., & Tienda, M. (1998). Educational aspirations of minority youth. *American Journal of Education, 106*(3), 349.

Katz, S. R. (1999). Teaching in tensions: Latino immigrant youth, their teachers, and the structures of schooling. *Teachers College Record, 100*(4), 809–840.

Kaufman, J., Jaser, S., Vaughan, E., Reynolds, J., Di, D. J., Bernard, S., & Hernandez-Brereton, M. (2010). Patterns in office referral data by grade, race/ethnicity, and gender. *Journal of Positive Behavior Interventions, 12,* 1, 44–54.

Ladson-Billings, G., & Tate, W. F. I. V. (1995). Toward a critical race theory of education. *Teachers College Record, 97*(1), 47–68.

Liou, D. D., Martinez, A. N., & Rotheram-Fuller, E. (2016). "Don't give up on me": Critical mentoring pedagogy for the classroom building students' community cultural wealth. *International Journal of Qualitative Studies in Education, 29*(1). 1–26.

Lewis, C., Butler, B., Bonner II., M., & Joubert, M. (February 01, 2010). African American male discipline patterns and school district responses resulting impact on academic achievement: Implications for urban educators and policy makers. *Journal of African American Males in Education. 1*(1), 7–25.

López, N. (2003). *Hopeful girls, troubled boys: Race and gender disparity in urban education.* New York, NY: Routledge.

Losen, D. J., & Skiba, R. (2010). *Suspended education: Urban middle schools in crisis.* Montgomery, AL: Southern Poverty Law Center.

Mau, W. (1995). Educational planning and academic achievement of middle school students: A racial and cultural comparison. *Journal of Counseling and Development, 73,* 518–526.

Midgley, C., & Feldlaufer, H. (1987). Students' and teachers' decision-making fit before and after the transition to junior high school. *The Journal of Early Adolescence, 7*(2), 225–241.

Morris, E. W. (March 1, 2005). "Tuck in that shirt!" Race, class, gender and discipline in an urban school. *Sociological Perspectives, 48*(1), 25–48.

Murdock, T. B. (1999). The social context of risk: Status and motivational predictors of alienation in middle school. *Journal of Educational Psychology, 91*(1). 62–75.

Noguera, P. (2008). *The trouble with Black boys: And other reflections on race, equity, and the future of public education.* San Francisco, CA: Jossey-Bass.

Noguera, P., Hurtado, A., & Fergus, E. (2013). Invisible no more. *Understanding the Disenfranchisement of Latino Men and Boys.* New York, NY: Routledge

Pizarro, M. (2005). *Chicanas and Chicanos in school: Racial profiling, identity battles, and empowerment.* Austin, TX: University of Texas Press.

Oakes, J. (1981). Limiting opportunity: Student race and curricular differences in secondary vocational education. A study of schooling in the United States. Technical Report Series, No. 28. Dayton, OH: Institute for Development of Educational Activities.

Oakes, J. (1985). *Keeping track: How schools structure inequality.* New Haven, CT: Yale University Press.

Office of Superintendent of Public Instruction. (2012). *Washington State Report Card.* Retrieved from www.reportcard.ospi.k12.wa.us

Osterman, K. F. (2000). Students' need for belonging in the school community. *Review of Educational Research, 70*(3), 323–367.

Pollack, W. S. (1998). *Real boys: Rescuing our sons from the myths of boyhood.* New York, NY: Random House.

Porter, A., McMaken, J., Hwang, J., & Yang, R. (2011). Common core standards the new U.S. intended curriculum. *Educational Researcher, 40*(3), 103–116.

Rios, V. M. (2011). *Punished: Policing the lives of Black and Latino boys.* New York, NY: NYU Press.

Robinson, J. P., & Lubienski, S. T. (2011). The development of gender achievement gaps in mathematics and reading during elementary and middle school examining direct cognitive assessments and teacher ratings. *American Educational Research Journal, 48*(2), 268–302.

Saenz, V., & Ponjuan, L. (2009). The vanishing Latino male in higher education. *Journal of Hispanic Higher Education, 8*(1), 54–89.

Skiba, R. J., Horner, R. H., Chung, C. G., Rausch, M. K., May, S. L., & Tobin, T. (2011). Race is not neutral: A national investigation of African American and Latino disproportionality in school discipline. *School Psychology Review, 40*(1), 85–107.

Solórzano, D. (1998). Critical race theory, race and gender microaggressions, and the experience of Chicana and Chicano scholars. *International Journal of Qualitative Studies in ducation, 11*(1), 121–136.

Solórzano, D., Villalpando, O., & Oseguera, L. (2005). Educational inequities and Latina/o undergraduate students in the United States: A critical race analysis of their educational progress. *Journal of Hispanic Higher Education, 4*(3), 272–294.

Solórzano, D. G., & Yosso, T. J. (2002). Critical race methodology: Counter-story-telling as an analytical framework for education research. *Qualitative inquiry, 8*(1), 23–44.

Straubhaar, R., & Gottfried, M. (2014). Who joins Teach For America and why? Insights into the "typical" recruit in an urban school district. *Education and Urban Society,* Online ahead of print. DOI: 10.1080/03050068.2014.884823

Suárez-Orozco, C., Suárez-Orozco, M. M., & Todorova, I. (2008). *Learning a new land: Immigrant students in American society.* Cambridge, MA: Harvard University Press.

Tatum, B. D. (2003). *"Why are all the Black kids sitting together in the cafeteria?": And other conversations about race.* New York, NY: Basic Books.

Tatum, B. D. (2004). Family life and school experience: Factors in the racial identity development of Black youth in White communities. *Journal of Social Issues, 60*(1), 117–135.

Taylor, P., Kochhar, R., Livingston, G., Lopez, M. H., Morin, R., & Fry, R. (2009). *Between two worlds: How young Latinos come of age in America.* Washington, DC: Pew Hispanic Center.

Todres L. (2008). Being with that: The relevance of embodied understanding for practice. *Qualitative Health Research, 18*(11), 1566–1573.

Werblow, J., Urick, A., & Duesbery, L. (2013). On the wrong track: How tracking is associated with dropping out of high school. *Equity & Excellence in Education, 46*(2), 270–284.

Wertz, M. S., Nosek, M., McNiesh, S., & Marlow, E. (2011). The composite first person narrative: Texture, structure, and meaning in writing phenomenological descriptions. *International Journal of Qualitative Studies on Health and Well-Being, 6*(2), 463–475.

Wigfield, A., Eccles, J. S., Schiefele, U., Roeser, R., & Davis-Kean, P. (2006). Development of achievement motivation. In N. Eisenberg (Ed.), *Handbook of child psychology: Vol. 3. Social, emotional, and personality development* (6th ed., pp. 933–1002). New York, NY: John Wiley.

Woolley, M. E., Kol, K. L., & Bowen, G. L. (2009). The social context of school success for Latino middle school students: Direct and indirect influences of teachers, family, and friends. *Journal of Early Adolescence, 29*(1), 43–70.

Yosso, T. (2005). Whose culture has capital? A critical race theory discussion of community cultural wealth. *Race, Ethnicity & Education, 8*(1), 69–91.

Yosso, T. J. (2006). *Critical race counterstories along the Chicana/Chicano educational pipeline.* New York, NY: Routledge.

CHAPTER 3

FITTING "OUT"

How American Indian Students Make Sense of School Success

Stephanie Zywicki
Purdue University

In many ways, this story began decades ago, as I tried to make sense of my own experiences as an American Indian student trying to navigate my elementary and middle school classrooms. Unfamiliar with the landscape of racial identity and politics, I had no words to describe how disconnected I felt from the other students in the class, yet I was acutely aware of feeling like I did not fit in with in with my peers. It was through this process of sense making that led to my research on American Indian students, particularly those attending mainstream middle schools. This work, which began in the halls of my own middle school, serves to give voice to American Indian students trying to navigate their own experiences in school.

Drawn from a larger qualitative study, this chapter focuses on the experiences of five 8th grade American Indian students who attended a public middle school (not tribally affiliated) in a rural Midwestern community and how they made sense of what it means to be successful in their school.

Envisioning Critical Race Praxis in K–12 Leadership Through Counter-Storytelling, pages 49–68
49

Using the lenses of critical race theory (CRT) and tribal critical race theory (TribalCrit), I present two different narratives on student success. The first narrative, serving as the master narrative, describes how the school operationalizes "success" in terms of behaviors and attitudes. The second narrative, serving as the counterstory, describes how American Indian students see themselves within this construction of student success. The purpose of this chapter is to "shatter complacency, challenge the dominant discourse on race, and further the struggle for racial reform" (Solórzano & Yosso, 2002, p. 32) by illustrating how notions of student success are often defined using dominant cultural values and how this is problematic for American Indian students who do not share those cultural values.

While there is no universal definition on what makes a student successful, there are several factors often mentioned when school leaders discuss student success. Some researchers argue student achievement occurs through a combination of intellectual ability, social identity, self-motivation, social (family, community, peers) support, and culturally relevant learning environments (Gentry & Fugate, 2012; Parrish, Klem, & Brown, 2012; Pewewardy, 1998; Sanders, 1987; Van Hamme, 1995; Warikoo & Carter, 2009). However, the research on success in American Indian students points to different factors. In several studies (Deyhle, 1995; Lipka 1994; Platero, Brandt, Witherspoon, & Wong, 1986) conducted with American Indian student high school dropouts, White administrators and staff reported that what prevented students from being successful was the lack of familial support, poor academic skills and performance, home and family problems, and lack of personal interest in school. It is important to note that in this study, the White administrators and teachers never cited factors associated with the school environment, racial mistreatment, and school interactions as important to a student's success (Deyhle & Swisher, 1997).

There are many reasons that this research is important for school leaders. For one, American Indian students lag behind their peers in academic achievement (National Center for Education Statistics [NCES], 2011). The U.S. Department of Education first called attention to this trend in 1991 when it commissioned a task force to address the growing divide in academic achievement between American Indian students and their peers. The task force report (U.S. Department of Education, 1991) found several issues that existed in educating American Indian students such as failure to nurture intellectual development, lack of support for native language development and use, unfriendly school climate that fails to promote holistic development, Euro-centric curriculum, low expectations, and overt and subtle forms of racism. Unfortunately, many of these issues remain in place today. Reflected in the 2011 National Indian Education Study (NIES; NCES, 2011) is the continued divide in academic performance between American Indian students and their non-American Indian peers. According to the

NIES, American Indian students in eighth grade scored thirteen points lower than non-American Indian students on the reading portion of the National Assessment of Educational Progress (NAEP), with 78% of students performing at "basic" or "below basic" levels (NCES, 2011, p. 15). In math, eighth-grade American Indian students scored 19 points lower on average than their non-American Indian peers. Eighty-three percent of students performed at "basic" or "below basic" on the NAEP (NCES, 2011, p. 29). While standardized test scores do not represent the whole of the student experience, their usage in measuring the achievement of American Indian students requires attention.

Another reason this research is important for school leaders is that as more students from diverse backgrounds enter classrooms, teachers must modify their teaching to accommodate the new learners. These types of modifications require challenging teachers' sociocultural awareness, that "one's worldview is not universal but is profoundly shaped by one's life experiences, as mediated by a variety of factors, chief among them race/ethnicity" (Villegas & Lucas, 2002, p. 27). However, without studies that ask diverse students about their experiences, people can never learn where and how the system both benefits and fails these students. My study places American Indian students, a group rarely studied within this topic, at the center in order to uncover how American Indian students experience schools.

LITERATURE REVIEW

For the purpose of this study, I focused on the cultural differences between majority students and American Indian students as well as the factors that contribute to student success and the barriers that limit student success. These factors were most relevant in the construction of student success at Leaf Lake Middle School and contributed to my understanding of how certain elements of the schooling experience position American Indians students as "outsiders" in the schools.

Cultural Differences

There are two types of cultural differences American Indian students experience when they enter educational environments. The first difference occurs in the cultural models American Indian communities employ when approaching education. Fryberg and Markus (2007) attempt to explain the difference in the educational experiences of American Indian students and their White peers using a cultural model of education framework. Fryberg and Markus define "cultural model of education" as "the patterns of ideas and practices relevant to schools, teachers, and self that mediate and regulate behavior in the academic domain" (p. 213). They found that American Indian models of education diverged from the mainstream models: American Indian students "were more likely to view education as a tool for individual *and* community success, to give negative associations to education and teachers, and to put family and community concerns ahead of academic concerns when the two domains were in conflict" (p. 238). This supports earlier research that found that, starting with sixth grade, many American Indian students became withdrawn, sullen, resistant, and frustrated by their experiences in school (Sanders, 1987). Scholars link this to several aspects of the school experience including treatment by peers and school personnel, connection to the curriculum, and academic ability (Deyhle & Swisher, 1997; Huffman, 2010; Little Soldier, 1985, Sanders, 1987).

The second difference American Indian students encounter is a values difference between American Indian students and their White peers. Students experience schooling in their own unique way and their experiences can be influenced by many factors, including students' cultural perspectives and values. Key then to understanding the positionality of American Indian students in schools is acknowledging that American Indian students do not often share the same cultural values as their dominant group peers. As Little Soldier (1985) writes, "Education is an institution within society and thus an instrument of that society, with schools reflecting prevailing values and attitudes" (p. 185). For mainstream schools, those prevailing values and attitudes reflect dominant group perspectives. Given that there are over 560 recognized tribes in the U.S., American Indian people represent diverse and culturally nuanced communities, and therefore not every American Indian person espouses or practices the same values attributed to American Indian people in educational settings. However, Sanders (1987) argues that "although each tribe is different because of tribal structure and geography, there are prevailing basic, consistent values and attitudes held by American Indian people that transcend and cut across tribes as well as across reservations and urban areas" (p. 82). For example, one value commonly held throughout American Indian communities is the desire to remain culturally independent from the mainstream culture of White America and to resist against assimilation or acculturation.

Other value differences also exist between American Indian cultures and White culture. Based on work conducted by Sanders (1987) and Deyhle (1995), there are three distinct areas where one can observe the differences between American Indian students and White students: speaking, participation, and interactions with others. White students tend to speak loudly and faster than their American Indian peers, who tend to speak more softly and slowly. In fact, American Indian students often do not speak in class, preferring to listen. White students, on the other hand, address people directly and interrupt when necessary.

There are also differences in participation. American Indian students often have delayed responses when asked questions, sometimes not answering at all. When placed in groups to work, American Indian students emphasize cooperation and put the needs of the group over their need to be right. American Indian students may also encourage sharing within the classroom. White students, on the other hand, provide immediate responses to the teacher, even when not called on. They are also more likely to focus on competition between groups and consider their personal goals more important than the group goals.

Lastly, American Indian students and White students engage in interactions with other students in ways that reflect cultural values. White students often need to control and affect other students and have little trouble with their self-expression and disclosure. White students are concerned mostly with facts and can be viewed as aggressive in their interactions. This differs from American Indian students who value privacy and noninterference in their personal lives, exercise self-discipline when it comes to others, and exercise patience when working with others.

While I recognize these types of values comparisons can essentialize both White students and American Indian students, schools are structured in ways that reward White values over American Indian values (regardless of how essentialized they are). Throughout my conversations with school administrators, White values were routinely described as "important" for school success.

Student Success Factors and Barriers

Scholars argue that students are most successful and motivated in school when they feel that schools support their cultural identity (Little Soldier, 1985; Sanders, 1987). However, mainstream schools, which reflect White culture and not American Indian culture, do not always support the cultural identity of American Indian students (Castagno & Brayboy, 2008). For some students, mainstream schools represent a tension between enculturation and acculturation. Enculturation is the process in which students learn about their home culture. For American Indian students, schools are not places of enculturation given the way the curriculum represents American Indian culture (Chandler, 2010). This means that for some American Indian students, being successful in schools requires them to go through the process of acculturation, which occurs when American Indian students acquire the behaviors of White students in order to "fit in" or feel a sense of belonging (Little Soldier, 1985). This differs from White students, who can often see their culture reinforced throughout their schooling experience.

Another factor related to student success in school is the level of parental involvement. Gentry and Fugate (2012) identified the following as helpful parental behaviors: parenting, communicating, volunteering, learning at home, decision-making, and collaboration with school administrators. In the same study, American Indian parents identified barriers to their involvement in schools. Those barriers included feeling unwelcome, negative experiences in their own educational history, lack of cultural sensitivity, and different communication styles from school personnel.

The third factor related to student success in schools is the quality of relationships students have between their teachers and their peers. The student–teacher relationship is important for increased student achievement, increased learning, and decrease in disruptive behaviors (Gentry & Fugate, 2012; Sanders, 1987). For American Indian students, positive student–teacher relationships require an acknowledgement and recognition of American Indian values and worldviews (LaFromboise, Trimble, & Mohatt, 1990). Although there is limited research on the influence of peer relationships on American Indian student success in schools, peers who share the same values can positively affect academic efficacy (Gentry & Fugate, 2012). In addition to shared values, another influence on peer dynamics in the classroom is different attitudes toward classroom behaviors such as group work or participation (Gentry & Fugate, 2012).

One of the most significant barriers American Indian students experience in schools is the use of the cultural deficit model (Deyhle & LeCompte, 1994; Deyhle & Swisher, 1997). Solórzano and Yosso (2001) argue that the cultural deficit model "contends that minority cultural values, as transmitted through the family, are dysfunctional, and therefore cause low educational and occupational attainment" (p. 6). This type of deficit thinking leads to subtle forms of oppression levied against American Indian students by those "trying to help." The "help" offered manifests itself in the patronizing attitude emphasizing lowered expectations for success and behavior for American Indian students (LaFromboise et al., 1990). Additionally, deficit thinking leads to White paternalism and limited expectations (Sanders, 1987). For example, rather than appreciate the richness of American Indian culture, teachers may treat American Indian culture as backwards and insufficient.

THEORETICAL FRAMEWORK

In order to understand the dominant narrative of student success, including the experiences of American Indian students within this narrative, I relied on several theoretical perspectives. The first two perspectives are critical race theory and tribal critical race theory. Critical race theory (CRT) emerged from critical legal studies as a reaction to the role the legal system played in legitimizing systemic oppression (Yosso, Parker, Solórzano, & Lynn, 2004). Critical race scholars "theorized, examined, and challenged the ways in which race and racism shape schooling structures, practices, and discourses" (Yosso et al., 2004, p. 3) in education. CRT interrogates societal structures while providing space for individual knowledge construction. Solórzano (1997, 1998) identified key aspects of CRT as intercentricity of race and racism with other forms of subordination, challenges to dominant ideology, commitment to social justice, centrality of experiential knowledge, and transdisciplinary perspective. The first tenet begins with the notion that embedded in the U.S. systems is racism in a way that makes it normal, natural, and fundamentally necessary to the functioning of U.S. society. It acknowledges the intersectionality of racism with other subordinated identities. Secondly, CRT challenges dominant ideologies by refuting claims that schools provide equal opportunities to students. Claims of objectivity serve to protect the power and privilege of dominant groups (Solórzano, 1997). Thirdly, CRT embodies a commitment to social justice by exposing interest convergence. Interest convergence occurs when policies, procedures, and/or laws that favor racial minorities in the United States pass only when they are mutually beneficial to Whites. The fourth tenet of CRT recognizes the importance of storytelling to "analyze the myths, presuppositions, and received wisdoms that make up the common culture about race and that invariably render blacks and other minorities one-down" (Delgado, 1995, p. xiv). Educators should introduce students to narratives from people not like themselves, but also provide space for students to share their own experiences with race and racism. CRT highlights the exclusion of minoritized voices from the dominant discourse and seeks to include them again. Lastly, CRT is an important tool for the "deconstruction of oppressive structures and discourses, reconstruction of human agency, and construction of equitable and socially just relations of power" (Ladson-Billings, 1998, p. 9) because it challenges the meaning and value of Whiteness outside the realm of education. Acknowledging the impact race has requires acknowledging the power in being White.

Related to CRT is tribal critical race theory (TribalCrit) (Brayboy, 2005), which also provides a macrostructural lens to use in analyzing narratives of student success. Within TribalCrit, two positions emerge. The first position is that ideas around culture, knowledge, and power take on new meanings when analyzed through the lens of American Indian identity. Given the power inherent in student success narratives, recognizing how American Indian students understand these narratives offers greater insight into disrupting the narrative. The second position of TribalCrit links the goals of mainstream education to assimilation. By describing how the construction of school success reflects assimilation practices, it allows researchers to consider different ideas on how to create culturally responsive environments. Lastly, TribalCrit as an analysis tool links together the practices of school with larger structural explanations for low academic achievement.

The third theoretical perspective that informed my analysis is cultural discontinuity theory. Although I find cultural discontinuity theory problematic in its application in school environments, it has strongly influenced the research conducted with American Indian students in K–12 schools (Huffman, 2010). The premise of cultural discontinuity theory stipulates that "much of the frustration in the nature and consequences of American Indian educational endeavors to opposing Native and mainstream cultural patterns especially those in the form of communication and interaction styles" (Huffman, 2010, p. 23). Cultural discontinuity theory argues that the communication styles, learning styles, and behavioral expectations used by teachers and staff in the school reflect White values, placing American Indian students at a disadvantage when entering mainstream schools. Lack of American Indian success then becomes about this cultural mismatch between their culture and the dominant group culture.

Critics of cultural discontinuity theory, however, argue that by focusing solely on individual and micro-level interactions, this theory detracts from systemic analysis of macrostructural factors contributing to the lack of American Indian success in schools (Ledlow, 1992). In a study conducted by Wilson (1991) on the experiences of American Indians in mainstream schools, she reported that the limitations in academic achievement were connected to macrostructural factors such as school policies and practices. Wilson also argued that American Indian students reported high levels of frustration and isolation in mainstream schools. Lastly, mainstream personnel lacked awareness of the seriousness of cultural conflict occurring in school. Wilson's (1991) approach represents the treatment of cultural discontinuity as generalized cultural conflict, not just culturally based communication misunderstandings. Her findings speak to the arguments raised by CRT and TribalCrit by highlighting the voices of American Indian students and arguing against assimilation as an appropriate path to success.

METHODOLOGY

In the 2011–2012 school year, I conducted a qualitative case study (Merriam, 2002; Yin, 2009) in Leaf Lake Middle School (all names of people and places are pseudonyms). Leaf Lake School District is located in a town of approximately 5,000 people in a Midwestern state. It is a rural community located near the Leaf Lake American Indian reservation, although the population of Leaf Lake is predominately White. At the time of my study,

305 students enrolled at Leaf Lake Middle School, with 92 students in the eighth grade. Within the eighth-grade population, 10 students identified as American Indian.

Located on the Leaf Lake Indian Reservation is the Leaf Lake Tribal School. According to the school personnel I interviewed, interesting tensions existed between the Leaf Lake School District and the Leaf Lake Tribal School. Enrollment policies allow American Indian students to move freely between schools, and this commonly occurs within any given year. The participants in my study had attended school in the Leaf Lake School District since first grade. While they attended preschool and kindergarten at Leaf Lake Tribal School, their families felt Leaf Lake School District schools provided better educational opportunities than Leaf Lake Tribal School. An initial challenge in gaining access to the families of my participants was the fear that my study sought to diminish the education at Leaf Lake Middle School in favor of the education provided at Leaf Lake Tribal. School choice is a complicated issue for most families; the families of my participants were adamant in their belief that Leaf Lake Middle School was a better, more appropriate environment for their children. When asked why, the most information I received related to academic level—Leaf Lake Tribal School was two years behind Leaf Lake Middle School. I could not verify this information (Leaf Lake Tribal School never replied to my messages); however, verification is unimportant since the families believe it to be true.

I spent three months at the site, using ethnographic research methods (Esterberg, 2002) to understand the experiences of American Indian students in mainstream schools. After meeting with the superintendent, principal, assistant principal, and community elders (parents), it made the most sense to research eighth grade students and limit my study to one specific grade and one specific classroom. According to school data, the eighth grade contained the greatest number of American Indian students. Community elders felt the eighth grade students would enjoy participating in this opportunity. Based on my own interest in social studies curriculum and the veteran status of the eighth grade social studies teacher, I agreed to conduct in-depth observations in the social studies classroom.

Recruiting participants presented several challenges. While I secured permission from the appropriate school officials to conduct my study in the middle school, federal regulation prevented the school from sharing racial demographic information. In order to gain participants, I worked closely with community gatekeepers (school administrators, teachers, and parents) to introduce myself to students eligible to participate. I also presented my research to each social studies class period and solicited volunteers through that approach. Once students expressed interest in participating, I worked with their families to secure permission.

Overall, my study consisted of eight participants: five students and three school personnel. The five eighth-grade students were Melita, Gertie, Lara, Freddie, and Grace. Melita and Gertie lived in Leaf Lake, while Lara, Freddie, and Grace lived on the Leaf Lake Reservation. All of the student participants were involved in activities at school. Melita, Gertie, Lara, and Grace played basketball and ran track. Freddie was active in art-based activities. All five of the students had plans to attend college.

The three school personnel were Mr. Longley, principal of Leaf Lake Middle School; Mr. Hanson, 8th grade social studies teacher; and Mr. Ravenwood, the education aide. Both Mr. Longley and Mr. Hanson are White, while Mr. Ravenwood is the only staff person who identified as American Indian. Both Mr. Longley and Mr. Hanson attended college in the Midwestern state where Leaf Lake is located and stayed there throughout their teaching careers. They both found the position at Leaf Lake intriguing because of their desire to work with diverse student populations. At the time of my study, Mr. Longley was in his second year as principal at Leaf Lake Middle School, while Mr. Hanson was in his 20th year of teaching. Mr. Ravenwood was in his first year as the education aide at Leaf Lake Middle School and had no formal training in education.

FINDINGS

As I conducted my research and began analyzing the data, what emerged were two different stories that reflected the perceptions of student success at Leaf Lake Middle School. The majoritarian story, told through school policies, teacher reflections, and student perceptions, served as the foundation for which administrators, teachers, and students measured their success. The counterstory, told through the voices of my participants and teachers, served to illustrate how American Indian students were excluded, by themselves and their teachers, from being recognized as successful students.

What Successful Students Do At Leaf Lake Middle School

Throughout the time I spent at Leaf Lake Middle School, I had the opportunity to learn the explicit and implicit ways in which school administrators, teachers, and students communicate what made a "successful" student. Oftentimes successful students are not those who earn the highest grades, but rather those who follow a prescribed set of behaviors (Hatt, 2012). Students have little power to change the perception of their success in school, which often reflects the assumptions of school personnel, teachers, and peers rather than actual behavior or academic performance. At Leaf Lake Middle School, there were three different ways I felt the school communicated what it meant to be a successful student. The first way was the student success matrix, which were the written expectations for students and their behavior on school property. The second way was through the attitudes and behaviors that teachers and students felt that successful students exhibited. The third way that the school used in determining student success related to the perception of family involvement.

Students initially receive information about what makes a student successful from the student success matrix. This document outlined expectations for students based on specific settings, which included classrooms, the bus, playground, and school hallways. In addition to settings, the matrix divides those expectations into three categories: respect, responsibility, and relationships. It is understood that these are the behaviors students should exhibit, and the school expects students to follow these guidelines throughout the school day. When teachers or administrators observe students going "above and beyond" the stated expectations, students receive a green ticket, which they can turn in for prizes. There is no record of who receives green tickets; therefore, there is no way to track which students go "above and beyond" expectations.

Due to the nature of my study, I did not observe students on the bus or playground. However, the expectations for respect in the classroom and hallway are the same—students are to follow and respond appropriately to directions and use appropriate language and tone with teachers and others. With regard to the classroom, students demonstrate responsibility by knowing and following classroom rules, owning their actions, coming to class prepared, and applying their best effort. Within the hallways, students act responsibility when they avoid being distracting, pick up trash, admire hallway displays with no touching, and sign in and out when leaving the hallway. Lastly, the expectations for relationships in the classroom ask that students be considerate of others' feelings, listen to the other person's side, respond politely to people, and work collaboratively. In the hallway, students should focus on their own conversations, be courteous to others, and report any problems to adults. The student success matrix is located throughout the school and is available within the handbook. Students understand how teachers and staff use the matrix to determine positive behavior in the school. Throughout the duration of my study, none of my study participants received any green tickets.

In addition to collecting the student success matrix, I asked the student participants as well as Mr. Longley (the school principal) and Mr. Hanson (social studies teacher) to articulate what made successful students at Leaf Lake Middle School. The student participants identified four behaviors that successful students exhibited—listening to the teacher, doing homework, paying attention, and understanding the material in class. Mr. Longley echoed these sentiments in stating:

> Successful students are obedient students. The culture of our building has been in the past that if you sit, you do your homework, you turn it in, and you'll be okay. If you are obedient to the adults in the school then you are successful.

Both the students and Mr. Longley shared the same ideas about how success was defined at Leaf Lake, which mirrored those established in the student success matrix. Successful students are those who follow the rules, pay attention, and do not challenge adults.

Mr. Hanson, on the other hand, defined student success as those students, who at the end of the school year, "have a smile on their face," which to him meant students who were generally happy with their experience. However, during my observations of Mr. Hanson's classroom, he conveyed a much different message of student success. During one lesson, Mr. Hanson tells the class that students will be more successful if they use deductive reasoning to problem solve. He follows this by saying, "You're methodological thinkers . . . well, some of you are. Some of you are quiet in class because you're scared." On a different day, when helping students prepare for an upcoming test, Mr. Hanson asked the students if they considered themselves studious. When one student asked what studious meant, Mr. Hanson replied, "It means being smart. Being a student. She's always been smart. But now she's also attentive." Mr. Hanson often times used sarcasm to get his point across regarding behavior. During one class period, in response to students asking him to repeat the instructions for the assignment, Mr. Hanson replied, "The smarter we are, the more questions we have to ask." In each of these examples, Mr. Hanson communicated several things about what he considered appropriate behavior. First, he communicated that good students participated in class and those who did not did so because they were afraid or fearful. Second, smart students were those students who were attentive to the teacher and listened. Third, Mr. Hanson communicated that smart students were those who listened and did not need to ask clarification questions.

What American Indian Students Do at Leaf Lake Middle School

American Indian students, however, considered themselves "outsiders" in relation to their understanding of what successful students did at Leaf Lake. Even though the participants could articulate what successful students did at Leaf Lake, they did not believe this extended to their own academic experience.

One of the ways in which American Indian students felt like outsiders in their school was based on how teachers treated American Indian students as compared to White students. Gertie felt that teachers provided more support to White students than American Indian students. She argued, "Ah, American Indians might not get the same help...like, the teacher may help them, but maybe not with the same kind of information as the other [White] students." Lara believed that all teachers viewed American Indian students as "troubled children" who are "probably going to start using drugs and alcohol." Lara felt that teachers internalized stereotypical messaged they received about American Indians, despite the fact that "none of us here even do drugs or drink alcohol." Another way that American Indian students felt different from their White peers was based on how teachers treated their in-class participation. The participants in my study felt discouraged from participating in class because when they asked questions, the teachers accused them of not paying attention. Throughout my observations, I witnessed several of these exchanges. When White students asked questions, Mr. Hanson engaged with the students. If American Indian students asked questions (which rarely happened), they were ignored or Mr. Hanson would tell the students he went over the material already. When I confronted Mr. Hanson about this during our interview, he admitted this occurred.

> I'm guilty of that [accusing students of not paying attention when they ask questions]. I catch myself doing that. I jumped all over Freddy earlier about not paying attention and just because I was just, we had just gotten out of a meeting and it's the first hour and I was just mad and jumped all over him and there he is, poor kid, is just standing there, not knowing what's going on, sitting their crying and he was just sitting there trying to decipher these directions.

This type of negative reinforcement experienced and witnessed by the American Indian students contributed to their beliefs that they were not successful in the same way as their White peers.

In addition to feeling like outsiders, the participants in my study did not believe that American Indian students could be as successful as their White peers could. During my interviews with students, it was evident that participants did not have a vision that American Indian students are successful at school. The statements made by Grace and Lara illustrate this point.

> I don't really blend in, I feel like. Like, with the crowd. Cause they're like all smart and I'm not that smart to participate in discussions or whatever and to listen that much. I don't understand what's going on. I pay attention, I just don't know that's going on. Cause I always get second thoughts about things. (Grace)

Um, I guess, the schooling [when asked about the differences between American Indian students and White students]. Um, in academic ways. I see a lot more White kids that have better grades and like not much American Indians have good grades. Like, you see that some of the American Indians need more help, like the academic awards tonight, there are more White kids than Native kids going. (Lara)

Despite feeling that they did not belong academically, my participants often engaged in behaviors that served as self-preservation. The participants offered reasons as to why they did not exhibit successful student qualities. For example, when describing their behaviors as opposite of those of successful students (for example, not paying attention, daydreaming, not doing work), they relabeled that work as boring, frustrating, or unimportant. Grace shared, "They [teachers] never have anything important to say, it's always the same old stuff."

At the same time, these acts of academic self-preservation masked fear of judgment for not fitting in as well as judgment on being an American Indian at school. Grace offers this as one reason why students choose not to participate in class:

Because I guess they're more afraid that they'll get judged upon their traditions and what they do and their skin color maybe. And I guess they're scared what to say, if they say the wrong thing, because usually nowadays if you're a different color you have to say all the right things and wear all the right clothes just to be in with the group. I'm scared to say things out loud, because I'm scared to be wrong, so I usually don't participate. But I'm just scared to, like, raise my hand to, and question someone, or say the answer, because I'm scared to be wrong.

Grace was not the only student to have those fears. Lara shared that she does not participate in class "because there's a lot of students there and I don't feel comfortable talking in front of a lot of people. And some of the stuff I don't really get so I'm afraid of saying the wrong answer." It was easier to stay silent than risk being seen as more different from their peers.

Another example of academic self-preservation was the desire to work in groups with other American Indian students. During one of our interviews, Melita described this need as important because of shared understanding. According to her, if American Indian students worked together, "we can help each other understand more because, the other kids [White kids], they'll confuse us, and from there we'll be confused." In her opinion, working in groups with American Indian students allowed for greater success because "we learn the same way and we understand everything the same way." However, because teachers placed students in groups without their friends, the American Indian students did not have shared connections with other students in their group. Lara argued that this became problematic because the White students in the group wanted to complete the task their way with no consideration of other solutions. Rather than challenge those students, Lara said she simply stopped talking.

DISCUSSION

My research presents two different narratives present in Leaf Lake Middle School—the first narrative serves as the major narrative in the school on success and offers insight into how teachers and administrators view student success. The second narrative centers on the feelings of exclusion held by American Indian students, contributing to the lack of confidence in their ability to be successful, which leads to acts of self-preservation. These competing narratives place American Indian students at odds with their White peers and can contribute to the creation of school spaces that further marginalize American Indian students.

What the literature tells us about school success is that students are most successful in environments where their cultural values are recognized and strong relationships between teachers and peers. Based on my findings, none of these factors existed at Leaf Lake Middle School for American Indian students. The master narrative of school success, which emphasized behaviors such as using appropriate language and tone, following and responding to directions, paying attention, understanding the material, following the teacher, and actively participating in the class do not, at first glance, seem rooted in any particular set of cultural values. However, school administrators and teachers determine what an acceptable demonstration of that behavior is. One example of a successful student behavior is active participation in class. Yet American Indian students and White students differ in their participation patterns in the classroom, based on a set of cultural values. American Indian students are less likely to speak or raise their hand, and they often provide a delayed response to questions asked as compared to their White peers. However, the type of participation rewarded is based on the White American values of immediacy and focused, direct communication. Shared values is one of the reasons the American Indian students wanted to work in groups with other American Indian students— they shared a common value system for participation, collaboration, and communicating with each other.

Another factor that contributes to a student's success is strong relationships with teachers and peers. Although this particular analysis did not delve deeply into peer-to-peer interactions, the participants spoke at length about their relationships with teachers. American Indian students felt that their teachers treated them differently by not offering the same type of help as White students were offered, by reinforcing stereotypes of American Indians as substance abusers, and by ignoring them or reprimanding them for asking questions in class. According to the American Indian model of education (Fryberg & Markus, 2007), American Indian students are more likely than their White peers to view teachers and the educational system negatively. Yet the experiences of the students in this study indicate why those negative views might exist. The perceptions held by American Indian students are that they are treated poorly by their teachers.

One of the barriers to American Indian student success in schools is the use of cultural deficiency models such as the cultural discontinuity theory. These theories argue that American Indian students are not as successful as their White peers because their American Indian culture prohibits them from accessing the White cultural behaviors and norms rewarded in schools. Unfortunately, the American Indian students in this study applied a cultural deficit model to their own success at Leaf Lake Middle School. By using phrases such as "not as smart as the White kids," and "not as academic as the White kids," and "White kids get better grades than us," the participants replicate the notion that American Indian students, by default, as less academically successful than their White counterparts.

Taken together, the experiences of American Indian students do not mirror the narrative presented on successful students. Analyzing inequity in educational settings requires "challenging claims of neutrality, objectivity, color-blindness, and meritocracy" (Ladson-Billings & Tate, 1995, p. 56) present in current discourse on race and education in the U.S. School leaders sometimes struggle in their understanding of race because they adhere to the "colorblind" ideology. Colorblind ideology takes on different forms in schools—in this situation, school leaders assumed the constructed narrative of school success had no racial implications. Even when school leaders think their actions are "colorblind," research indicates their behaviors and practices demonstrate recognition of racialization (Schofield, 2007; Yosso et al., 2004). Acting "colorblind" ignores the reality of minoritized students' experiences (Schofield, 2007). Using CRT as a frame for understanding the experiences of American Indian students allows for interrogation of current schooling practices and exposes the existence of the oppressor/oppressed relationship present in education.

Policies toward American Indians students historically represented the belief that American Indian students' success depended on their ability to assimilate to the majority culture. In all the ways that CRT and TribalCrit challenge the White-centered emphasis in schools, the continued use of cultural discontinuity theory reflects the deficit model paradigm (Valencia, 2010), supporting assimilation and/or acculturation as the "best" way for American Indian students to succeed in education. The use of cultural discontinuity theory aligns most closely with this paradigm. It argues that the reason American Indian students do poorly in school (compared to White peers) is due to the mismatch between the cultural heritage of American Indian students and the White-dominated culture of school. Despite the lack of empirical evidence to support this theory, it continues to persist in the conversation on American Indian education, much to the detriment of American Indian students' success in schools.

Given this, what remains is how school leaders might employ CRT and TribalCrit to include American Indian students in school spaces. The first step school leaders can take is to find and disrupt practices that reflect the dominant ideology. There are several ways to do this. School leaders can ask American Indian teachers or parents to evaluate school policies for cultural representation and modify when necessary. School leaders can also have conversations with teachers about cultural discontinuity theory in relation to the stereotypes associated with American Indian communities. These conversations can help inform teachers as they work with American Indian students.

The second step school leaders can take is recognizing that American Indian students bring different types of knowledge and values to the school environment and creating ways to demonstrate that these values are equal to those of White students. One of the main tenets of TribalCrit is acknowledging how problematic assimilation policies are for American Indian students. Fighting against this assimilation requires school leaders and teachers to recognize and support American Indian student values. Teachers can support these cultural values by redefining what classroom participation entails, or by encouraging American Indian students to work with other American Indian students.

CONCLUSION

This work is a beginning conversation on American Indian students and their experiences in middle school, and I hope that scholars continue to study American Indian issues in education and focus on the inclusion of American Indian students in school environments without the implicit or explicit expectation of assimilation. One way that school leaders can support the inclusion of American Indian students is by using CRT and TribalCrit as lenses of analysis when determining how school policies and teacher practices may influence the success of American Indian students. By evaluating school policies and practices through the lens of race, school leaders can begin to understand how and why the experience of American Indian students differ so greatly from those of White students, even when these policies seem objective and colorblind. CRT and TribalCrit provide useful tools for school administrators to understand their complicity in the reproduction of racism and to determine steps school leaders can take to reduce this racism.

Too often, research with American Indian students occurs at tribally controlled schools, despite the fact that over 90% of American Indian students attend mainstream public schools. This chapter is my contribution to the goal of increasing equity in education for American Indian young people. My research suggests that while oppressive practices toward American Indians students continue to occur, educators have the power to disrupt the practices that inhibit American Indian students from participating equally in the school environment. It is time for schools to stop "killing the Indian"—our students deserve better.

REFERENCES

Brayboy, B. (2005). Toward a tribal critical race theory in education. *The Urban Review, 37*(5), 425–446.

Castagno, A., & Brayboy, B. (2008). Culturally responsive schooling for Indigenous youth: A review of the literature. *Review of Educational Research, 78*(4), 941–933.

Chandler, P. (2010). Critical race theory and social studies: Centering the Native American experience. *The Journal of Social Studies Research, 34*(1), 29–58.

Delgado, R. (1995). *Critical race theory.* Philadelphia, PA: Temple University Press.

Deyhle, D. (1995). Navajo youth and Anglo racism: Cultural integrity and resistance. *Harvard Educational Review, 65*, 403–444.

Deyhle, D., & LeCompte, M. (1994). Cultural differences in child development: Navajo adolescents in middle schools. *Theory Into Practice, 33*(3), 156–166.

Deyhle, D., & Swisher, K. (1997). Research in American Indian and Alaska Native education: From assimilation to self-determination. In M. W. Apple (Ed.), *Review of Research in Education, 22*, 113–194.

Esterberg, K. (2002). *Qualitative methods in social research.* Boston, MA: McGraw Hill.

Fryberg, S., & Markus, H. (2007). Cultural models of education in American Indian, Asian American, and European American contexts. *Social Psychology of Education, 10*, 213–246.

Gentry, M., & Fugate, C. M. (2012). Gifted Native American students: Underperforming, under-identified, and overlooked. *Psychology in the Schools, 7*, 1–16.

Hatt, B. (2012). Smartness as a cultural practice in schools. *American Education Research Journal, 49*(3), 438–460.

Huffman, T. (2010). *Theoretical perspectives on American Indian education: Taking a look at academic success and the achievement gap.* Plymouth, UK: AltaMira Press.

Ladson-Billings, G. (1998). Just what is critical race theory and what's it doing in a nice field like education?. *International Journal of Qualitative Studies in Education, 11*(1), 7–24.

Ladson-Billings, G., & Tate, W. F. (1995). Toward a critical race theory of education. *Teachers College Record, 97*, 47–68.

LaFromboise, T., Trimble, J., & Mohatt, G. (1990). Counseling intervention and American Indian tradition: An integrative approach. *The Counseling Psychologist, 18*(4), 628–654.

Ledlow, S. (1992). Is cultural discontinuity an adequate explanation for dropping out? *Journal of American Indian Education, 31*(3), 21–36.

Lipka, J. (1994). Language, power, and pedagogy: Whose school is it? *Peabody Journal of Education, 69,* 71–93.

Little Soldier, L. (1985). To soar with the eagles: The enculturation and acculturation of Indian children. *Childhood Education, 61*(3), 185–191.

Merriam, S. (2002). *Qualitative research in practice: Examples for discussion and analysis.* San Francisco, CA: Jossey-Bass.

National Center for Education Statistics. (2012). *National Indian Education Study 2011 (NCES 2012–466).* Institute of Education Sciences, U.S. Department of Education, Washington, D.C.

Parrish, M. S., Klem, J. L., & Brown, D. R. (2012). Diversity in learning: A comparison of traditional learning theories with learning styles and cultural values of Native American students. *Ideas and Research You Can Use: VISTAS 2012, 1,* 1–9.

Pewewardy, C. (1998). Fluff and feathers: Treatment of American Indians in the literature and the classroom. *Equity & Excellence in Education, 31*(1), 69–76.

Platero, P., Brandt, E. A., Witherspoon, G., & Wong, P. (1986). *Navajo students at risk: Final report for the Navajo area dropout study.* Window Rock, AZ: Navajo Nation.

Sanders, D. (1987). Cultural conflicts: An important factor in the academic failures of American Indian students. *Journal of Multicultural Counseling and Development, 15*(2), 81–90.

Schofield, J. W. (2007). The colorblind perspective in school: Causes and consequences. In J. Banks & C. M. Banks (Eds.), *Multicultural education: Issues and perspectives* (pp. 271–295). Hoboken, NJ: Wiley & Sons.

Solórzano, D. (1997). Images and words that wound: Critical race theory, racial stereotyping, and teacher education. *Teacher Education Quarterly, 24,* 5–19.

Solórzano, D. (1998). Critical race theory, racial and gender microaggressions, and the experiences of Chicana and Chicano scholars. *International Journal of Qualitative Studies in Education, 11,* 121–136.

Solórzano, D. G., & Yosso, T. J. (2001). From racial stereotypes and deficit discourse toward a critical race theory in teacher education. *Multicultural Education, 9*(1), 2–8.

Solórzano, D. G., & Yosso, T. J. (2002). Critical race methodology: Counter-storytelling as an analytical framework for education research. *Qualitative Inquiry, 8*(1), 23–44.

U.S. Department of Education. (1991). *Indian nations at risk: An educational strategy for action.* Washington, DC: US Government Printing Office.

Valencia, R. R. (2010). *Dismantling contemporary deficit thinking: Educational thought and practice.* New York, NY: Routledge.

Van Hamme, L. (1995). American Indian cultures and the classroom. *Journal of American Indian Education, 35*(2). Retrieved from http://jaie.asu.edu/v35/V35S2ame.htm

Villegas, A. M., & Lucas, T. (2002). *Educating culturally responsive teachers: A coherent approach.* Albany, NY: State University of New York Press.

Warikoo, N. & Carter, P. (2009). Cultural explanations for racial and ethnic stratification in academic achievement: A call for a new and improved theory. *Review of Educational Research, 79*(1), 366–394.

Wilson, P. (1991). Trauma of Sioux Indian high school students. *Anthropology & Education Quarterly, 22,* 367–383.

Yin, R. (2009). *Case study research: Design and methods.* Thousand Oaks, CA: Sage.

Yosso, T. J., Parker, L., Solórzano, D., & Lynn, M. (2004). From Jim Crow to affirmative action and back again: A critical race discussion of racialized rationales and access to higher education. *Review of Research in Education, 28,* 1–25.

PART II

LEADERSHIP

CHAPTER 4

THE BURDEN OF ADMISSION

Profile of an African American Female Educational Leader

Rachelle Rogers-Ard
Oakland Unified School District

Isolation.
No one to trust; no one to hear.
Tired.
Tired of fighting to be heard, fighting for a spot at the table, fighting to be seen.
Invisible . . . except when you control the money; then everyone sees you as an opportunity.
What you create is a "program"; an "initiative"; a "pilot."
What they create is "infrastructure"—
Even when it's exactly the same thing you've been doing for years.
When you are passionate and vocal, you are labeled as "angry" and "territorial."
When you are silent, you are labeled as "angry" and "not a team player."
When you are happy and smiling, you are hiding something.
When you are sad and despondent, you are unstable and emotional.
When you dress well you are showing off.
When you dress down you are too casual.
And, whatever you do, don't say the word "racism"—
"Playin' the race card."
Tired of the game; tired of the same.

Yet, you continue to put on the mask making sure it's firmly in place.
Show up early so no one can accuse you of being late.
Leave late so no one can accuse you of leaving early.
Nod appreciatively when your ideas are taken and implemented—
Or better yet, when you're asked to help "support" someone implement your ideas,
your innovations, your designs . . .
But sometimes the mask gets too heavy.
Sometimes the mask stays in place for so long it begins to meld itself to your face.
How long has it been since you've been real at work?
Do you even know?
Tired. Isolated. No fight left.
Who is this person?

What does it mean to be a black female leader within urban educational structures? What is the cost of admission, and is it too high to pay? This chapter uses narrative methodology to shed light on one leader's journey within educational structures and to provide a counterstory to much of the current research about African American female leaders. The use of narrative is intentional, allowing readers to be drawn into the story while identifying recurring themes. Because this work is framed around race, sexism, and historical stereotypes against the backdrop of institutional racism, it provides a deeper level of insight into situations surrounding black women's authentic identity as leaders.

Narrative inquiry allows reflection in the midst of research and is extremely powerful in constructing new knowledge. Through several vignettes, separated by bullets and written in italics, the author connects theory to practice in a meaningful way. Answers to questions around race and gender lie deep; it is difficult to excavate past the superficial way we present ourselves, especially within the work environment. However, digging for those connections and delving into the ways in which one person's stories can enlist, enlighten, and even enrage is particularly insightful and meaningful for us all.

The narrative reflections in this chapter are a composite of the author's experiences as a leader in several different educational systems, including urban school districts and nonprofit organizations. Borrowing heavily from Knaus (2011), the author's narratives are based upon a compilation of interrelated experiences and conversations that have been recorded over time in a number of journals, online blogs, and other posts. While not taken word-for-word, these reflections mirror the tone, attitude, and context of the actual conversations.

FRAMEWORK

One hundred years past what was supposed to be the emancipation of slaves, the legacy and vestiges of slavery continue to impact thoughts and actions of Africans in America, dictating conscious and unconscious decisions for making changes in language, dress, dialect, tone, hair, smiles, laughter, family, and demeanor towards the goal of assimilation into dominant society (Giddings, 1984; Jones & Shorter-Gooden, 2003; Thomas, 1999).

Black female leaders must navigate between being Black enough for peers and authentic enough for community stakeholders, while not appearing to be "too Black" for White superiors. African American women make great personal changes because of the "double-negative" associated with being Black and female in the United States (Jones & Shorter-Gooden, 2003). For those who are leaders in educational institutions, the cost of changing and modifying the ways in which they present themselves is extremely high.

African American female educational leaders must constantly grapple with the notion of the authentic self without succumbing to the stereotypical ways in which African American women have been historically viewed. Many people see African American women either as loud, brassy, pushy women with their hands on their hips, neck swiveling, constantly in charge and telling others what to do (think any African American woman on a "Housewives" or other reality show), or as an overly motherly "mammie" character whose main job is to take care of others (think Aunt Jemima or Oprah). Equally as important, making attempts to become less "threatening" so White colleagues feel more comfortable might also seem like "selling out," which could lead to alienating African American coworkers, both male and female. Hence, the burden.

One month into my new job, Billie, the only other African American person in the department, indicated she was leaving the organization. In a tearful exit, Billie indicated that my White boss, Heather, had denigrated her to such an extent that she would no longer be able to work there. As she was walking out of the door, she asked to speak to me.

"Rachelle, I just wanted you to know that I was really hurt about the way you have been treating me. When you first came here, I thought you would be cool, but you have really disrespected me."

"Wow, Billie; I'm really confused. I certainly never meant to disrespect you—when exactly did I offend you?"

"You know...the way you look at me, and when you asked me to do a newsletter, your tone was bad..."

"I'm really sorry, Billie; I had no idea."

I had asked Billie to put together a monthly newsletter as a way to ensure better communication with our teachers. I did not take into consideration how she would feel being "bossed" by a woman much younger. I had disrespected her by my tone and actions from a younger Black woman to an older Black woman, while trying to be effective in my new role. I needed to learn to watch my tone, not just with White folks, but with all folks.

While many Black women in leadership positions struggle with notions of identity and the intersection of race, gender and class, for Black females in positions of leadership within educational organizations the role is particularly difficult. First, educational institutions are inherently racist structures (Jones et al., 2009; Knaus & Rogers-Ard, 2012). Second, as with most racist structures, the further up the ladder one climbs, the fewer folks of color there are breathing the rarified air—hence the sense of isolation. Finally, because education was historically one of the only careers available for educated African American women after World War II (Zinko, 2007), many baby boomers found themselves as teachers and later, principals. The retirement of many of these women coincided with a move towards younger White women as predominant carriers of knowledge in our school systems. Currently, 85% of the nation's teachers are White (Knaus & Rogers-Ard, 2012).

My framework (Appendix A) represents this struggle and relies heavily on Bell and Nkomo's work (2001) around the notion of black women and their struggle for professional identity. The authors intersect race, gender and class in their framework; I am intersecting race, gender/sexism and historical stereotypes for this work. The three elements are all represented equally although historical stereotypes may seem larger because it encompasses so much; in fact, any one element may loom larger at any given point in the women's lives depending on numerous societal and/or personal factors. The three elements ultimately affect the way in which a Black woman presents herself as a leader, versus the way in which a Black woman perceives herself to truly be, and results in a fragmented and ever-shifting identity.

Webster defines race as "a group of people united or classified together on the basis of common history, nationality, or geographic distribution" (1976, p. 950). I prefer Bell and Nkomo's (2001) definition: "Race is no longer a concept used to classify groups of people based on physical traits such as skin color, but rather denotes the meanings given or attached to phenotypical differences among people" (p. 17), although Guinier and Torres define race as "a social and political construct that has been used for both good and evil" (2002, p. 34).

Identity is the "distinguishing character or personality of an individual" (Webster, 1996, p. 568). For African American women, the issue of identity doesn't just deal with personality traits that make women intrinsically different; identity is about those characteristics that have been placed upon Black women by a society that still views them in the same way they were viewed during slavery (Giddings, 1984). In fact, one theory is that Black women must reject all notions of whatever characteristics have been placed upon them by the dominant society (head of family, hard worker, mother to all) because those same characteristics were used and are still being used to demean Black women (Hill-Collins, 2000).

HISTORICAL STEREOTYPES

Historically, Blacks as a group were considered inferior from the time of their enslavement in the 1620s, which was used to justify slavery (Davis, 2000; Jackson, 1996; Thomas, 1999). African women had a particularly difficult time during slavery because of a triple burden: They were expected to work in the fields, work at home, and bear children to continue the labor force (Giddings, 1984; Jackson, 1996). Repeated rapes and molestation were problematic during the slavery period as well (Jackson, 1996). To ease White guilt, many cultural stereotypes of Black women were generally accepted as the norm in post-slavery days (Bell & Nkomo, 2001; Davis, 2000; Jackson, 1996).

The first image, "Mammy," is based upon a domestic figure who was happy working in the master's home, taking care of the master's children, and cooking meals. Because she was overweight and dark, she was not seen as someone in whom the white man would have an interest, and therefore she was safe to have around the house as a desexualized woman. The Mammy was always smilingly submissive to her master. This image was used to convince Whites that African American Mammies were happy in their subservient roles (E. L. Bell, 1992; Davis, 2000; Jackson, 1996). While "Mammy" was the caretaker for the master's children, she would often look at her own family members with disdain. She felt like she belonged to the White family and frequently developed some aspects of self-hatred for her people (Pilgrim, 1999). The Mammy/mother image of the large, dark-skinned Black woman plays an important role in how that type of woman is viewed when at work in a leadership position: "White women view the Mammy as an advocate of other blacks in the company" (Bell & Nkomo, 2001, p. 245).

I had been told that my federally funded program designed to recruit and retain teachers of color was being moved to another department. As I prepared for my meeting with my new director, I began thinking about the ways in which I could share my vision for the entire district.

After exchanging pleasantries, we began discussing her vision for a new unit: one that would ultimately recruit and retain teachers of color—the same as my "pilot program." At first, I thought I would be asked to lead this "new" unit, but I was told that someone else (a man with two fewer degrees than I) would be the director, and I was being "strategically placed" to support him.

"So, I will be reporting to Maceo?"

"Yes. I know he does not have the traditional educational background that you do, but he does have the institutional knowledge that is important in this work, and he has great ideas!"

I didn't understand. I was not being given the opportunity to even apply for the position, even though I had been doing this work for the past four years. What was even more frustrating was the notion that I would somehow be happy supporting this person as he worked to build a unit around our program. If I did not act supportive, I would be labeled as not a "team player," and I knew White folks hate that.

Perhaps the most frustrating element was that I was supposed to be really excited about this move; having someone else expand the work I had been doing for four years for which I had secured funding was supposed to make me happy. I had to grin, smile, and take my overweight, dark-skinned self into the big house to help raise Massa's children.

In addition to the mammy stereotype, the "tragic Mulatto" stereotype portrayed a very light-skinned woman who looked White. This type of woman would usually "pass" for White because of her hatred for her Blackness and for the way in which she was sired (Pilgrim, 1999).

The Jezebel image is more prevalent today (Pilgrim, 1999). It is similar to the Mulatto except that Jezebel was brazen and wonton about her sexuality and desire for a White man, and she was not necessarily light-skinned (Pilgrim, 1999). From numerous prostitutes in the 1970s films (Pilgrim, 1999), to Halle Berry's Oscar-winning role in *Monster's Ball*, Black women continue to be seen as highly sexualized characters with few other redeeming qualities. It is difficult to be taken seriously if constantly viewed as sexually promiscuous; female leaders must take stereotypical images into consideration. A nurturing, caring leader is reminiscent of the Mammy image; likewise, a sexually confident female brings the Jezebel image to mind.

Somewhere in between Jezebel and Mammy is the Sapphire image, which originated from the enormously popular "Amos and Andy" radio shows in the 1930s and 40s (Davis, 2000). Sapphire, while not large like Mammy, is brown-skinned, loud, brash, and opinionated about everything. Most importantly, she emasculates the African American male by arguing with and ridiculing him at every turn (Pilgrim, 1999). Some theorists argue that the Sapphire image is nonthreatening to Whites because she is not sexual; her loudness and excessive talking is barely tolerated by her own men, much less Whites (Davis, 2000; Jones & Shorter-Gooden, 2003). However, others indicate that Sapphire can be harmful to African American females because White people don't know how to handle a dramatic, bossy Black woman. Many times, Sapphire is characterized as being aloof and/or rude; White co-workers feel that she might take everything "personally," responding in a hostile manner to anything racial with an "attitude." Of course, this prevents Sapphire from moving ahead in the company because

White superiors and co-workers don't know how to handle her and feel her personality is too volatile (Bell & Nkomo, 2001).

I had been working in the district for about three years and had successfully grown the program and found funding. I was excited about meeting with the new department head because I knew she frequently discussed working with a sense of purpose around race in educational systems. As we began to talk, however, I was confused about some of her comments.

"When you meet with cabinet, be sure to watch your tone; sometimes, it can come off as harsh."

"Um . . . ok."

"Also, don't disagree with folks outright; take some time to frame things so people won't feel like you're not a team player."

"Well . . ."

"Remember that your facial expressions tell a whole different story . . ."

"Um . . . thanks for this feedback; but I'm not sure how to take it. I'm constantly looking towards advancement . . ."

"I didn't know you wanted to be a leader in this district!"

"Well, I do have a doctorate in educational leadership. . . ."

"Yes, but . . . I didn't know".

"Why?"

"Well. . . . if you really want to go into district leadership, you will need to work on some things. . . ."

The message was clear; I could not be authentic (which might mean calling out some things—like race) if I was to be a leader. I could not be seen as aloof or rude, or have an attitude or take things personally. I could not be seen as being territorial or caring or display any passion that might make white folks feel uncomfortable.

The question was: Was being fake worth it, and if so, how long could I keep that façade in place?

The Sapphire image is the most media-apparent of all of the stereotypical images. Almost every African American television comedy has a "Sapphire" image: Florence from *The Jeffersons*, Winona from *Good Times*, Kim from *Moesha*, Maya from *Girlfriends*, and any movie or stage play involving the "Madea" character. It is the same image that drives Black mothers to tell their little girls to speak quietly and to sit unnoticed. As adults in the workplace, African American female leaders may have to quiet their voices and demeanor so as not to channel this image (Jones & Shorter-Gooden, 2003).

Living under the spectrum of historical stereotypes can be difficult, but for those in leadership positions, it is even more pronounced because those who are in subordinate or authoritative positions may already have a stereotypical perception of Black women in their minds. For example, White folks who have been exposed to the many Mammy media images may expect an overweight, dark African American woman to be nurturing in the workplace. When she does not conform to this role, tensions may occur because the White person doesn't know what to expect and, therefore, how to control this woman. White women, especially, tend to be confused when faced with managing African American female leaders. Therefore, the burden of admission means that African American women have to "coach up" their White colleagues and managers to help them feel more comfortable with leading a strong African American woman. This coaching takes time and effort and may not always yield results, but it is totally necessary when White folks are confronted with an African American woman who defies stereotype.

SEXISM/GENDER ROLES

One's personal life, deep understanding of oneself, empathy, and perspective all meld together to form one's identity. Therefore, how one perceives oneself matters to leadership. Granted, there is a body of literature that speaks to differences in leadership styles of men and women (Hamilton, 2004; Northouse, 2004; Waring, 2003). These researchers highlight relationship building—an intrinsic part of female leadership versus the task-oriented style of men (Waring, 2003), but there is still a lack of theoretical knowledge about the uniqueness of African American female leaders. Perhaps that lack of knowledge about differences in the conceptions of leadership could be linked to the role that sexism has played in Black women's lives. The civil rights movement was started by a woman, yet men received and continue to receive a great deal of the credit (Allen, 1996). For almost all African American women, there was never a choice of taking care of family versus doing one's job; doing both was simply what was done from slavery times to the present (Giddings, 1984; Jackson, 1996), which is why African American women did not empathize nor become part of the women's movement in the 1970s (Giddings, 1984). Most African American women worked too hard for their bras to burn them. While many White women were finding out they could work outside of the home and no longer had to emulate Donna Reed, Black women simply continued to work.

As sung in a 1970s perfume commercial: "I can bring home the bacon, fry it up in a pan, and never, never let you forget you're a man . . . 'cause I'm a woman...Enjoli." The song played a "bad-to-the-bone" jazz rift while a White woman in a business suit sang the lyrics and did a pseudo-striptease. This was obviously aimed at White women with the newfound independence of working outside the home (Giddings, 1984). For Black women, who had been working outside the home since slavery, the commercial couldn't have been less relevant (Giddings, 1984).

For women in leadership positions, reaching across racial barriers is hard, but it is also difficult to reach across gender barriers, even for the same gender. Black women and White women have a longstanding history of mistrust dating back to slavery (Bell & Nkomo, 2001).

Race and gender climates are often chilly and frozen in the workplace, particularly between Black and White women. Black women in a position of leadership understand that they will never truly fit in with their White counterparts, but they are technically part of the team. Thus, they have what Patricia Hill-Collins refers to in Bell and Nkomo's work (2001) as "outsider-within status." Black female leaders have membership in the club without all of its social privileges.

Racist experiences with White women are a common factor for African American educational leaders. Bell and Nkomo (2001) suggest that because White women have had such limited contact with Black women in positions of leadership, they have no context with which to participate in dialogues with Black women. If the only contact a White woman has had with Black women has been in subordinate situations, then White women are hard-pressed to respond correctly to Black female peers, and can become condescending. Therefore, for the African American woman, sexism comes both from men and white women. The only way to truly bridge those gaps is for both parties to understand and acknowledge race/gender politics, work together to forge true, authentic relationships based on honesty, and agree to call out sexist behavior when it happens.

My manager, a White woman, had a conversation with me:

"Rachelle, I've received several comments from folks in our department about you. People are saying that you're unapproachable, and sometimes you don't say hello. What we're talking about is the ability to create a good workspace with others. I know that this may be difficult, but I'm willing to work with you and coach you so you can recognize when these things are happening."

"Penelope, I like myself and feel fine. I don't need to be coached about speaking to people."

"Well, as your manager, I want you to make sure that you at least speak to Sandy. I don't want people in my department not speaking to each other."

"So, you're making me speak to another co-worker with whom I have very little interaction?"

"Yes. And she was really hurt that you didn't invite her to your program's end of the year celebration."

"She's not part of our program."

"Her feelings were also hurt when she took all weekend to paint the office space, but when you moved in, you repainted it white."

"I don't like yellow, and she's not even in this office!"

"It doesn't matter. I want you to speak to her so her feelings won't be hurt."

The conversation above centered on White people feeling hurt about an African American woman's behavior. At no time were the African American woman's feelings brought into the conversation; rather, it was assumed that (1) not speaking to someone in another department led to tensions; (2) the African American woman's lack of speaking was a problem that merited coaching; (3) the problem was a large enough to be brought to the attention of the White manager; and (4) we want to ensure that White folks' feelings are not hurt. This is highly reminiscent of discussions around respect, particularly in the Jim Crow south. African American folks were not allowed to look directly at White folks; to do so was a form of disrespect. Similarly, to not speak to a White person, to not invite a White person to an event, and to repaint one's own office could lead to tensions and disrespect within the department. Here, depending on the level of trust with the White female manager, the African American woman had the option of coaching the White manager, or, if trust was not developed, choosing to alter her behavior to navigate office politics.

It was my first social outing with the department. When I arrived at the restaurant, most of my co-workers were already there. At one table sat four of the African American female teachers I had hired that year. At another table sat three White women: my boss, the office manager, and a board member. I moved towards the table with the four Black teachers, but as I was getting ready to sit down, my boss come over to me and said loud enough for everyone to hear, "Rachelle, why are you sitting there?" As she guided me away from the instructors, she said as an aside to me, "You don't want to send a message that all of the Black people sit together at the same table."

I wanted to respond right away, but it was the wrong time and the wrong place. However, I fumed all night long about this situation.

The next day, I said, "Heather, can I talk to you? I was confused about last night. You indicated that I don't want to send a message about all of the Black people sitting together at the same table, yet you were seated at the all-White table—didn't that send a similar message?"

"What are you talking about? Last night? Oh...I just wanted you to sit with me and the board members; they were boring me to death!"

I just looked at Heather; I couldn't believe she had played me like that. Clearly, I had a lot to learn.

IDENTITY

Given the negative effects of stereotypes, racism, and sexism, Black women have to "play the role" or put on a mask for economic survival (Bell & Nkomo, 2001) which begins with their personal search for identity as young children. It is difficult for many African Americans to develop their own identity without taking on the roles given to them by White people. African Americans search to "be themselves" or "say it loud: I'm Black and I'm proud" because they are constantly viewed negatively by the dominant society. Race, then, becomes a major part of the identity struggle for African American people; for African American women, race and gender are two major elements that define who they are. Unlike other disenfranchised groups, Black women can do little to change the way they were born and must therefore deal with prejudice and racism in ways that White women who are lesbian do not, for example. Black women, whether educated or not, all have their skin color in common, which is usually the first thing people see when they walk into a room. For many Black women, the issue of skin color preempts the issue of gender because White women can still move in their privilege. Because African American women conduct their search for identity through the lens of race, historical stereotypes, and gender roles, Black women's identity is a concept that continually changes. Jones and Shorter-Gooden (2003) introduce the notion of "shifting" to explain this phenomenon.

Black women, as mentioned at the beginning of this chapter, constantly change their hair, dress, speech, and demeanor to fit into society. This is extremely present within the workplace and is a huge part of the landscape when in a position of leadership. Jones and Shorter-Gooden (2003) indicate that women change not just for work, but also to placate White colleagues, Black men, and other community members. Indeed, the authors postulate that this shift is such a part of these women's lives, it is totally natural:

> From one moment to the next, they change their outward behavior, attitude, or tone, shifting 'White' then shifting 'Black' again, shifting 'corporate', shifting 'cool'. And shifting has become such an integral part of Black women's behavior that some adopt an alternate pose or voice as easily as they blink their eyes or draw a breath—without thinking, and without realizing that the emptiness they feel and the roles they must play may be directly related. (Jones & Shorter-Gooden, 2003, p. 7)

How do women shift? They change their hair, dress, walk, and most importantly, their speech:

> For an African American woman, perhaps no act is as critical to successfully counteracting the myths and stereotypes that swirl around her as changing the way she speaks. The pitch of her voice (whether it is deemed too loud or just right), the rhythm of their speech (undulating like the blues or popping in a crisp staccato), and the vocabulary she uses (calling a coworker 'trifling' as opposed to 'irresponsible') can mean the difference between acceptance and rejection. (Jones & Shorter-Gooden, 2003, pp. 95–96)

Jones and Shorter-Gooden (2003) have identified strategies African American women use as they try to navigate racial, gender, and stereotypical situations. First, some women choose to "battle the myth" by altering their behavior in order to disprove the historical stereotypes that are always present. Second, many Black women try to deal with being in a racist society by monitoring how their movements are perceived at every turn through second-guessing each and every movement made by the "other" in the workplace. Another strategy some African American women use as a means of shifting their identity is to block their feelings of inferiority that happen around White folks. Although they may not acknowledge their own way of handling racism, building a wall around it or denying its presence could be affecting these women's health through elevated blood pressure and other diseases. Of course, many Black women deal with the workplace shifting dance by seeking spiritual and emotional support. Sororities, community and civic organizations, and faith-based congregations provide a means for African American women to handle the pressures of everyday life. Ultimately, many African American women tire of the dance and choose to fight back against the oppressive system to overturn racist and sexist practices.

I went to a predominantly White elementary school, but when I got to 7th grade, I found a whole new reality: I went to a predominantly African American school, and the dynamics were totally different. I was called an "Oreo" (black outside and white inside) and was accused of "talking white."

I began to change the way I dressed: more hip, with a lot more flava. I also began using a lot of slang, curse words, and dropped the endings of my words. However, my mother wasn't having it: she made it clear that I needed to "speak proper English" at home. I began two live two distinct dialects; one spoken at home and the other at school with my friends.

Years later, as an African American leader, I found myself in the exact same situation. For my White superiors and co-workers, I maintained a constant flow of educational buzz words and SAT words that would cement my level of intelligence. However, for African American classified staff, it was necessary to prove that I was not "uppity" by code-switching frequently.

The African American custodian came into my office late one evening.

"Hello," she said.

"How are you?" I replied, with a smile.

"Fine," she said, with her head bowed.

"Good. You know, I really like your braids."

She smiled, came closer, and said, "Really? I like your twists."

"Girl, these are so old!"

We went on in that vein, discussing hair styles. Finally, she said, "You know, I've been cleaning your office for a while. I saw your nameplate and saw that you are a doctor, so I asked someone who you were. I thought you must have been one of those uppity folks 'cause you got a piece of paper . . . but you're really down to earth. God bless you."

I was so touched, first, because it was necessary to disabuse her of the notion that all black folks with a little education were "uppity," but also because I had learned that it was necessary to prove to those without that level of education that I still knew where I came from. After that exchange, we began talking, sharing stories, and became friends. I was glad I took the time to break down that barrier.

It is clear that African American women deal with their issues of identity through shifting each day, but at what cost do the women shift? What is the burden of admission to leadership positions within educational systems? Perhaps the largest lump sum payment comes at the expense of each Black woman's ability to be whole. The price of constantly changing perspectives; feeling isolated; second-guessing decisions; and navigating past historical stereotypes, racism, and sexism can ultimately be too high to pay for a long period of time.

The price tag includes a huge identity battle that comes from the notion of being true to oneself—the need to find balance and be authentic within work-related situations. Tatum (1997) likens race to "smog in the air"; I would include the identity struggle as being so prevalent, Black female leaders have to develop coping mechanisms.

Currently, I am in the midst of this struggle. I continue to pay the cost in hopes that the work I do makes a difference. I provide structure for other disenfranchised educators of color to share their stories, while I silently seethe on the sidelines. As an African American female leader, I commiserate with teachers and Black female leaders, nodding in assent as we discuss the ways in which we all code switch and navigate the system, but in my mind, I'm always thinking, "When will we dismantle the system so we can have the chance to truly affect change?"

As I continue in a leadership position, watching as many older African American female leaders are silenced, placed in subservient positions where their voices can no longer be heard, or encouraged into early retirement, I wonder how long I will be able to wear the mask. How long and how much will I have paid when I can no longer stand to be silenced? When I finally leave the mask on the stage where it belongs, what image will I see in the mirror?

APPENDIX A
Burden of Admission Framework

Burden of Admission Framework

Educational Organizations

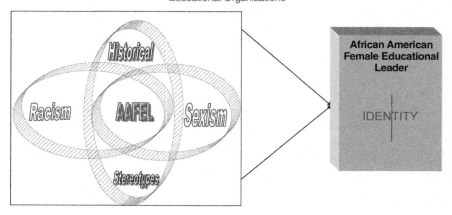

© 2015 Rachelle Rogers-Ard

REFERENCES

Allen, Z. (1996). *Black women leaders of the civil rights movement.* New York, NY: Franklin Watts.

Bell, E. L. (1992). Myths, stereotypes, and realities of Black Women: A personal reflection. *Journal of Applied Behavioral Science, 28,* 363–376.

Bell, E. L., & Nkomo, S. M. (2001). *Our separate ways: Black and white women and the struggle for professional identity.* Boston, MA: Harvard Business School Press.

Davis, R. L. (2000). *Popular art and racism: embedding racial stereotypes in the American mindset – Jim crow and popular culture.* Retrieved from www.jimcrowhistory.org/resources/lesson plans

Giddings, P. (1984). *When and where I enter.* New York, NY: Perennial.

Guinier, L., & Torres, G. (2002). *The miner's canary.* Cambridge, MA: Harvard University Press.

Hamilton, K. (2004). The best is yet to come. *Black Issues In Higher Education, 20,* 60–63.

Hill-Collins, P. (2000). *Black feminist thought: knowledge, consciousness and the politics of empowerment.* New York, NY: Routledge.

Jackson, K. A. (1996). *America is me.* New York, NY: HarperCollins.

Jones, C., & Shorter-Gooden, K. (2003). *Shifting.* New York, NY: HarperCollins.

Knaus, C. (2011). *Shut up and listen.* New York, NY: Peter Lang.

Knaus, C., & Rogers-Ard, R. (2012). Educational genocide. *ECI Interdisciplinary Journal for Legal and Social Policy, 2*(1).

Northouse, P. G. (2004). *Leadership theory and practice.* Thousand Oaks, CA: Sage.

Pilgrim, D. (1999). *Jim Crow Museum.* Retrieved from http://www.ferris.edu/news/jimcrow/menu.htm

Tatum, B. D. (1997). *Why are all the black kids sitting together in the cafeteria?* New York, NY: Basic Books.

Thomas, H. (1999). *The slave trade: The story of the Atlantic slave trade: 1440–1870.* New York, NY: Simon and Schuster.

Waring, A. L. (2003). African-American female college presidents: Self-conceptions of leadership. *Journal of Leadership & Organizational Studies, 9,* 31–45.

Webster, M. (1976). *Webster's New Collegiate Dictionary.* Springfield, MA: G & C Mirriam Company.

Zinko, C. (2007, September 25). WWII Meant Opportunity for Many Women; Oppression for Others. *San Francisco Chronicle.*

CHAPTER 5

EDUCATIONAL LEADERSHIP

A Critical, Racial, and Theoretical Examination of the "We-Need-More-Leaders-of-Color" Discourse

Nicholas D. Hartlep
Illinois State University

Aza A. Baylor
University of Wisconsin-Milwaukee

We use tenets of critical race theory, such as "counterstorytelling" (Solór-zano & Yosso, 2001, 2002), "whiteness as property" (Harris, 1993), and "white interest convergence" (Bell, 1980) to argue that *pushing* for more educational leaders of color must be more nuanced than what is currently being advocated for by traditional educational leaders—recruitment and retention issues. We discuss the need for educational leaders of color to be members of the communities in which they serve and the importance of differentiating leaders of color by their personal and professional commitments, not just if they are people of color.

Envisioning Critical Race Praxis in K–12 Leadership Through Counter-Storytelling, pages 87–105

BACKGROUND

We start by reviewing the literature on the underrepresentation of leaders of color (LEAP, 2012; Tewell & Trubowitz, 1987), especially Asian and African Americans within educational contexts (Cole, 1986; Rong & Preissle, 1997). The concept of a "bamboo/glass ceiling" (Ong, 2003), a term that describes the barrier that Asian Americans confront when becoming leaders within organizational and educational settings, is touched upon in the chapter. A result of this barrier is that there is a shortage of educational leaders who are Asian American (Bracey, 2001). Black women are also visibly underrepresented as school principals (Bloom & Erlandson, 2003); therefore, the "glass ceiling" is not exclusively an impediment for the Asian American community, but also for African American women.

The introduction of our chapter describes the need for more educational leaders of color, whose work demonstrates an understanding of the sociopolitical needs of the community in which they serve. Additionally, we point out why underrepresentation is not uniquely a racial issue (Duarte, 2000). We focus on the importance of educational leaders possessing "communal" and "cultural" experiential knowledge (Yosso, 2005). After describing how we envision traditional educational leadership discourses—like the tropes of Asian model minority and the "Black Bourgeoisie"—align with certain tenets of critical race theory (CRT), we share our own personal counterstories which counter these pre-established stereotypes within the traditional educational leadership discourse.

The first counterstory pushes back against the myth that Asian Americans are "model minorities" who do not experience discrimination, such as "bamboo ceilings" (Lee, 2002; Sakamoto, Takei, & Woo, 2012; Woo, 2000). Hartlep's counterstory describes the importance of Asian American leaders who are from the community to be trained to become educational leaders. Hartlep explains how CRT informs the approaches he uses when leading in the classroom and the community. Racialized as "passive" people (Littlewood, 2000), Asian Americans are not considered to have the qualities necessary to lead in educational environments, but Hartlep believes otherwise. He shares his own experience of being the first Asian American leader of the Graduate Student Council (GSC), a standing committee of the American Educational Research Association (AERA). He also explains how this experience shaped how he teaches at Illinois State University.

Baylor, an African American doctoral candidate at the University of Wisconsin–Milwaukee, an "Urban 13" research university, provides this chapter's second counterstory. Her autobiography addresses the limitations of the widely accepted "Black Bourgeoisie" stereotype, which labels successful Black leaders as "uppity" and/or "disconnected" from the larger Black community. As a Black woman educator, her counterstory tells of a "politicized mothering" approach within a system where an unspoken expectation to accept and adhere to White middle-class values were commonplace. Baylor's experiences being a caseworker for child welfare, an early childhood and elementary teacher, and a curriculum coordinator demonstrates her strong dedication to the wellbeing of urban children.

As a leader of color, Baylor developed a "politicized mothering" perspective, stressing the development of a critical consciousness as the most vital element of success for her urban students, and ultimately the community as a whole. Baylor's counterstory shares specific details about her racialized experiences being a Black woman educator and how those experiences shaped her leadership style, which focused sharply on planting seeds of "critical consciousness" (Freire, 2000, p. 183). Freire (2000) argues for a problem-posing method of teaching and learning, one in which the relationship between the teacher and student should be cultivated by engaging in dialogue and critical reflection in order to make meaning. This method of education is believed to lead to critical consciousness, through which students acquire a critical awareness to overcome oppression and a critical view of their sociocultural reality. Critical consciousness, then, is believed to, in this context, lead to a transformative pedagogy whereby students gain the critical thinking skills to transform their sociocultural reality (Freire, 2000).

Purpose of Our Chapter

In our chapter we argue that the Asian model minority and "Black Bourgeoisie" discourses—different, albeit at times similar—are problematic since they limit individuals who do not fit the narrow stereotype. The stereotypes of "nerdy" Asians and "uppity" African Americans promote racist thoughts and beliefs that define leaders of color in inaccurate ways. We believe that these race-based stereotypes of educational leaders are relevant to the discourse that informs educational leadership itself. What we identify as "the-need-for-more-leaders-of color" mantra needs to be subjected to a more nuanced form of analysis: an analysis wherein communal approaches and sociocultural, political, and economic understandings are deemed essential for educational development and leadership (Yosso, 2005).

"Black Bourgeoisie" Discourse

According to Woodson (1933),

It may be of no importance to the race to be able to boast today of many times as many "educated" members as it had in 1865. If they are of the wrong kind the increase in numbers will be a disadvantage rather than an advantage. The only question, which concerns us here, is whether these "educated" persons are actually equipped to face the ordeal before them or unconsciously contribute to their own undoing by perpetuating the regime of the oppressor. (p. xvii)

W. E. B. Du Bois (1903b) maintained that the "Talented Tenth" should stimulate social change by educating the Black community. "From the very first" he exclaimed, it "has been the educated and intelligent of the Negro people that have led and elevated the mass, and the sole obstacles that nullified and retarded their efforts were slavery and race prejudice" (Du Bois, 1903b, para. 3). Unlike the "Black Bourgeoisie," coined by Franklin Frazier (1957), which assumes that successful educated Blacks have an elitist attitude and consequently are disconnected from the Black community as a whole, Du Bois focused on uplifting the Black race. Frazier believed that since the older generation of the Black Bourgeoisie had embraced White values and standards for behavior and beauty, while the new Black Bourgeoisie sought recognition through their education and money, something that set them apart from the Black masses. As a result, the Black Bourgeoisie placed importance on obtaining an education because it symbolized White cultural capital.

According to Frazier, nothing is to be expected from the Black middle class other than self-indulgence, while others insist that the role of educated Blacks is to improve the oppressive conditions demonstrated through discriminatory educational practices (Du Bois, 1903a, 1903b; Frazier, 1957; Kronus, 1971; Landry, 1987). Highly criticized, some viewed Du Bois' "Talented Tenth" address as being elitist and an attempt to create an aristocracy in which the masses were neglected and ruled by the Talented Tenth (Battle & Wright, 2002). However, this interpretation is incorrect, especially since Du Bois discussed his meaning of the Talented Tenth more thoroughly during the Nineteenth Grand Boule Conclave Memorial Address in 1948. In fact, Du Bois (1903a) stressed the importance of in-depth scientific study of the issues facing Blacks in order to adequately address those problems.

Taking a CRT position, we believe that it is imperative that educational leaders have a "communal" approach when leading in order to counteract the systematic disenfranchisement that people of color face in urban schools today (Yosso, 2005). Indeed, if they do not possess such a responsibility, then the mis-education that Carter G. Woodson described in 1933 is even more important for today's people of color than ever before. When leaders are unaware of race, class, and/or gender oppression, they in many ways further mis-educate minorities by maintaining a school climate that lacks cultural relevance.

The same educational process, which inspires and stimulates the oppressor with the thought that he is everything and has accomplished everything worthwhile, depresses and crushes at the same time the spark of genius in the

Negro by making him feel that his race does not amount to much and never will measure up to the standards of other people. (Woodson, 1933, p. xiii)

If school leaders do not possess such a responsibility, then the mis-education that Woodson described in 1933 is even more important for today's people of color than ever before.

"Model Minority" Discourse

Similar to Black Bourgeoisie discourse, which distinguishes between types of Blacks, the model minority discourse *Orientalizes* certain Asians (mostly East Asians), while systematically excluding others, such as South Asians (Chae, 2004; Hartlep, 2014; Mayeda, 1999). According to Chae (2004), "The *model minority discourse*, like most discourses about race, multiculturalism and diversity, reinforces uni-dimensional and static notions of identity and culture" (p. 70, italics added) which is the highest form of Asian essentialism. This kind of essentialist discourse needs to be replaced with more authentic discourses, which allow for accurate understandings of the experiences of Asian American educational leaders.

The statistics are revealing: Not only are Asian Americans lacking in positions of K–12 educational leadership, they are also missing in higher education as well in positions such as president and chancellor. Renu Khator, an Asian Indian woman, and president of the University of Houston and chancellor of the University of Houston System has commented on the Asian "bamboo ceiling" that exists for Asians in the United States. This partially explains why Khator (2010) encourages her fellow Asian American colleagues to consider becoming university presidents, stating, "There are many Asian students on American campuses today, so you might consider doing it for them, if not for yourself" (p. 31).

If Asian Americans are truly overachievers, as the discourse of the model minority suggests, then they should be highly qualified and represented in the ranks of university presidents. But the reality is that Asian Americans are extremely underrepresented in such positions. According to Khator (2010), statistics indicate that Asian Americans are nearly absent from the ranks of university presidents.

Our chapter concludes by offering several recommendations for leadership education in terms of the need to shift the discourse from the need to increase numbers of educational leaders of color to stressing the importance that those leaders of color should be dedicated to the communities that they claim to serve. We also believe that traditional educational leadership discourses should consider institutional, communal, and linguistic and ethnic diversity, rather than perseverating on racial diversity. It is not enough that an educational leader is a *racial or cultural minority* (ethnoracial inclusivity). We believe that schools, educational institutions, and society need educational leaders of color who possess a sociocultural, political, and economic understanding of the communities they serve.

PROBLEM STATEMENT

There is a documented shortage of Asian and African American educational leaders, including PK–12 teachers. According to Toldson (2011), "Today, of the more than 6 million teachers in the United States, nearly 80 percent are White, 9.6 percent are Black, 7.4 percent are Hispanic, 2.3 percent are Asian, and 1.2 percent is another race" (p. 183). Although there are 114,209 Asian female teachers (1.89%), a meager 27,557 are Asian males (0.46%). Similarly, there are 467,689 Black female (7.74%) teachers but only 109,483 Black male (1.81%) teachers.

Solutions for Shortage and the "We-Need-More-Leaders-of-Color" Narrative

The traditional educational establishment perpetuates the narrative that the shortage of leaders of color can be ameliorated by leadership preparation programs such as those by the Broad Foundation (2014), whose mission statement is "Strong Leadership: Identifying, Preparing and Supporting Successful Leaders of Public School Systems." A significant problem with programs run by the Broad Foundation, and similar nonprofit groups such as Teach for America (TFA), is that they are extremely elitist and far removed from the communities they supposedly serve (Heilig, 2010; Vetri, 2010).

Some TFA educators are graduates of Ivy League colleges and universities and teach only long enough to pad their resumes in order to gain admission into a law, professional, or graduate school program. Frequently these TFA leaders hold oppressive attitudes toward their students—the majority who are minorities—while maintaining deficit ideologies since they do not come from the communities where they teach (Anderson, 2013).

Contradistinctively, local "grow-your-own" teacher programs tend to employ more "justice-oriented" (Westheimer & Kahne, 2004) frameworks than the programs previously mentioned. The nature of the problem is not the low number of leaders of color, but rather the commitments that each leader of color makes to the community in which she or he serves. The current set of circumstances—lack of leaders of color, and issues of recruitment and retention—will not improve as a function of the number of minority leaders that our nation has (Haberman, 1989); however, it will improve if each leader of color is committed to her or his community and is dedicated to staying in her or his community (Duncan-Andrade, 2000). As Anyon (1997) opined: "Attempting to fix inner city schools without fixing the city in which they are embedded is like trying to clean the air on one side of a screen door" (p. 168). In order for leaders to be effective, it makes sense that they come from the communities that need them; they are insiders. However, traditional educational leadership trends demonstrate a seemingly different attitude toward community representation in leadership roles.[1]

The following two counterstories push back against traditional educational leadership discourse. Hartlep's counternarrative is shared first, followed by Baylor's.

COUNTERSTORIES TO TRADITIONAL EDUCATIONAL LEADERSHIP NARRATIVES

I Refuse to Be a Pawn for Whiteness: A Counterstory about Asian American Leadership

The stock story that I would like to counternarrate is that Asian Americans are "model minorities" (Hartlep & Porfilio, 2015; Lee, 1991; Li & Wang, 2008; Qin, Way, & Mukherjee, 2008). Ironically, despite all of their perceived *positive* characteristics, the mainstream establishment does not consider Asian Americans to be leadership material. This, in a way, leads to the concentration of Asian Americans in technical jobs, rather than leadership positions, within industry, corporate, and higher education America (Eguchia & Starosta, 2012; Lawler, 2000; Ono & Pham, 2009).

In reality, it is my belief that Asian Americans make excellent leaders (Hirahara, 2003). Although Asian Americans bump up against a "bamboo" ceiling, some have pierced it and have gone on to hold major leadership positions in some of the most successful companies (domestically and internationally). According to Zweigenhaft and Domhoff (2011), by December 31, 2010, twenty Asian Americans had been corporate executive officers (CEOs) of *Fortune* 500 companies. For a company to be considered a *Fortune* 500 company, it must appear in the list of the top 500 U.S. public corporations ranked by *Fortune* magazine according to their gross revenue.

Zweigenhaft and Domhoff's (2011) data support the argument that we are making in this chapter, that in addition to an increase in racial diversity, "educational" and socioeconomic diversity is also needed. Of the twenty Asian American CEOs, the majority were educated in elite colleges and universities. For instance, in 1986, Gerald Tsai became the first Asian American to be a CEO of a *Fortune* 500 corporation; he attended Wesleyan University, an elite liberal arts university in Middletown, Connecticut. Similarly, Andrea

Jung, CEO of Avon, went to Princeton. Koichji (Ko) Nishimura, CEO of Solectron, and Jerry Yang, co-founder of Yahoo, both attended Stanford University. Wayne Inouye, CEO of Gateway, and Indra Nooyi, CEO of Pepsi, both graduated from Yale. Lastly, Vikram Pandit, CEO of Citigroup attended Columbia University. While it is rewarding to see successful Asian American CEOs, it is also important to recruit Asian American leaders who come from less prestigious colleges and universities because this contributes to diversity of education, experiences, and environment.

What could account for so few Asian American leaders? According to a survey conducted by the Committee of 100 (2001)—a committee of 100 top Asian American leaders—23% of Americans are uncomfortable voting for an Asian American to be President of the United States. This is in contrast to 15% compared with an African American candidate, 14% compared with a woman candidate, and 11% compared with a Jewish candidate. These findings should not be surprising: The United States re-elected President Obama, the first African American to hold the office.

When will the United States have its first Asian American President? This question comes at a time when Asian Americans are constructed to be unworthy of affirmative action since they are racialized to be overtaking some of the most selective colleges and universities. MIT no longer stands for Massachusetts Institute of Technology, but "Made in Taiwan," and UCLA no longer stands for the University of California, Los Angeles, but "United Caucasians Lost Among Asians" (Hartlep, 2014)

Consequently, my counterstory aims to problematize the "masterscripting" (Kim, 2008; Poon & Hune, 2009) that causes Asian Americans to not be considered good leaders, and that Asian Americans come from stable families and possess a "do-not-rock-the-boat" mentality that leads to their educational success. I am interested in better understanding whom the "we-need-more-leaders-of-color" narrative benefits? What is the *cui bono* of the current set of circumstances that Asian American leadership finds itself? Poon and Hune (2009) write that the "*master narratives* of Asian Americans as '*model minority*' and 'perpetual foreigner' bring a certain level of visibility to them, but in the end these narratives also render Asian Americans invisible and silent in [educational leadership], marginalizing their perspectives and the issues they deem important" (p. 100, italics added).

I Was Adopted

I was adopted from Seoul, South Korea in 1984. I was born in Nowongu's Kongneung-dong, Gongneung-dong (the particular region of Seoul), on November 25, 1983. My biological father was an alcoholic and very angry. He was angry about life: his familial, educational, and socioeconomic circumstances.

As a transracial adoptee, I had White adoptive parents and grew up in predominantly White communities. As a result of growing up in milieus where "White" was "right" and also the norm, I had to remind myself that there were alternative ways of seeing the world. I held this belief to myself quietly, reminding myself that at the opportune time, I would unleash it for the benefit of other people of color who were fighting for racial and socio-economic justice. What does this mean?

In college, when studying to become an elementary school teacher, I served on many educational leadership boards. I was the President of Kappa Delta Pi, an educational honor society for education majors.[2] I also served as a regional vice president for the National Society of Collegiate Scholars (NSCS), a reputable undergraduate honor society. As a Korean who was high achieving and holding positions of leadership, as early as college and in what can only be labeled spaces of Whiteness, some may have perceived me being a "model minority." Although elected to these positions of leadership and influence, I still was not able to "act" in ways that I wished to— which later changed as a result of my empowerment.

Empowered to Lead

Not until I was a doctoral student did I become empowered enough to speak out about the lack of Asian American leaders. In my second year of doctoral studies I was elected the chair-elect of the American Educational Research Association's (AERA) Graduate Student Council (GSC). As the chair-elect, I was able to rub shoulders with many powerful and influential national and international educational leaders. I finally had a platform in which to express my desires and own passions related to leadership. As leader of the GSC, I organized panels on issues of importance for people of color, especially Asian Americans, whom I understood to be invisible in the academy. The GSC leadership experience for me was extremely unique considering that I was the first Asian American to hold the position.

I quickly understood that I led in ways that were different from most Anglo- and androcentric models of leadership. I chose to listen to others and to allowed less privileged people to join in on the discussions. I also stressed that institutional diversity is a strength, not a weakness for AERA and the GSC, meaning that we needed to ensure people from different universities were at the table when key topics in education we being discussed. My experience being the "only" Asian American was something that I have experienced frequently as a Korean adoptee. This pattern of being the "only" continued until I was a teacher in a suburban first-grade classroom and later in an urban second-grade classroom. There were no Asian American male early childhood teachers in these schools; I was the only one.

Cumulatively, these experiences caused me to feel that I needed to be a critical role model for other Asian Americans. I certainly did not have an

Asian American role model while I was an elementary school teacher. As a doctoral student, I took it upon myself to counsel fellow Asian American graduate students and encourage them to be politically active and to fight the stereotype that we do not wish to "rock the boat" and that we are unqualified to be educational leaders.

My Leadership Heritage

When I found my biological Korean father and was reunited with him for the first time since our fateful separation 28 years ago, I learned immediately that leadership runs in my family's heritage. My biological father is a minister in the world's largest church, Yoido Full Gospel Church, and does social justice work throughout Korea and in other countries (see Hartlep, 2012, p. 188). Yoido has roughly one million church members and is so well attended that the church has seven Sunday services of worship and prayer that are translated into 16 different languages. In addition to his pastoral and missionary work, my father is a well-respected author, having published two books: 꼴통 목사의 전도 행전, 조임생 편저, 쿰란 출판사 (Gloss: *Weird Pastor's Mission Work, Part I*, 2007) and 꼴통목사의 전도행전 2, 고봉준 목사, 나뷔출판사 (Gloss: *Weird Pastor's Mission Work, Part II*, 2008).

My counterstory about Asian American leadership is an important one considering traditional educational leadership discourse, which believes that Asian Americans lack the qualities to be effective leaders.

The truth is that Asian Americans have a rich history of leadership and advocacy within education. It was not until I learned for myself that I was already a great leader did I fully understand why dismantling the masterscript that Asian Americans are "model minorities" was so important (Poon & Hune, 2009). My counterstory should be convincing: Asian Americans are already able to be effective educational leaders. It is not just that we need more racial representative leaders (which we desperately need), but we need to question the backgrounds and social commitments of the few leaders of color we currently have. By refusing to be a pawn for Whiteness, I disrupt "white interest convergence" (Bell, 1980, p. 528) and avoid becoming what Delgado (2009) labels as a good "role model."

Mothering of the Mind: A Politicized Mothering Counterstory

The following counterstory is grounded in a politicized mothering ideology. As I situate my counterstory within this discourse, it illuminates how mothering in the Black community supports and provides leadership within school communities, directly countering the commonly accepted Black Bourgeoisie stereotype of disconnecting from the community. Additionally, this counterstory addresses two CRT tenants, "Whiteness as property" and "White interest convergence" discussed in the analysis section.

My upbringing in a small Mississippi town, where fewer than eight thousand residents lived, nestled in the dense foliage of kudzu vines, which the elders say were used as camouflage during the Civil War. The splendor of the Mississippi countryside fostered my childhood. Blithe warm days were spent in play yards where bright red clay became chalk, as I played school underneath the esteemed beauty of magnolia trees. My memories of schooling begin with Head Start,[3] a natural transition into schooling, not because of the program but because of the Black women who occupied the learning space in each classroom. The building sat about two blocks "across the tracks"[4] and was home to my mother and father's segregated high school.

Although the *Brown v. Board of Education* decision was determined in 1954, my parents' segregated high school did not close until 1969. Funny, as a six-year-old, the history of the old segregated Booker T. Washington School building was subtly brought into vision as I transitioned to first grade. More than 10 years later, the history of resistance could be felt as I prepared for first grade with an unspoken understanding that Whites would dominate my learning experience from that point forward. No longer would I walk into the classroom greeted by hugs or teachers humorously saying, "them Bonnie Ruth legs there honey," speaking of how my shapely legs resembled those of my paternal grandmother. Or being asked about my maternal grandmother: "How Ms. Louiser doing? I haven't seen her in a good while." And almost always a comment of my beauty and comparison to my mother: "Hey pretty girl, you know you look just like Dottye Pearl with your hair pulled up like that." Ultimately, comments such as these brought warmth and comfort. The school environment felt like an extended family and embodied a sense of safety, similar to that felt when surrounded by family. All adults were respected as community leaders who wanted the children of the community to grow into sharp critical thinkers in an effort to further develop a strong community.

Unlike the community-centered Head Start center where my mother was the center director and my paternal grandmother and other women from the community were the teachers, the integrated (1st–6th grade) elementary school was noticeably different. The major distinction at face value was in the unfamiliar White faces of the majority of the teachers, who clearly were not from the Black community. I remember distinctly Ms. Lucas, my sixth grade teacher, the first Black teacher in my experience at the school. She reminded me of home—her style, finesse, and overt display of caring. I was home in her classroom. From that point forward when I went into a classroom where there was a Black teacher, I had a sigh of relief. "Home," I thought. Her classroom was a place in which I was free to talk about issues important to me, where I could question and be disciplined from a place of love. The lack of Black teachers and school leaders throughout my schooling experience became clearer as I matriculated through secondary school and on to college.

My southern upbringing framed my understanding of race relations and its connection to Black communities and Black education. As a school leader, I embodied characteristics that aligned with the notion of the "Talented Tenth," yet I maintained a pedagogical approach that is reflective in both Tamara Beauboeuf-Lafontant's (1997) "politicized mothering"[5] and what bell hooks (1984) describes as "engaged pedagogy." [6] Being driven by such beliefs, I was often faced with expectations that were misaligned with my belief system. I worked alongside other school leaders who were overwhelmingly interested in teaching rote basic skills without any connection to the historic and community needs of the children they served. In addition, many of the school leaders I worked with focused more on their personal career goals as a departure point for school leadership and expected the same of me. It became abundantly clear that my interest in aiding in the development of critical thinkers among the students was an unwelcomed position. Too often I was criticized for being "attached" to the children. I was even told that I needed to focus more on academics as opposed to developing relationships with the students and the families. Needless to say, my colleagues did not understand that my engagement approach was in fact an avenue to allow students to take ownership in their academic success.

My counterstory rejects the expectation of detachment and maintains one that values a maternal stance, engaged pedagogy, and critical consciousness development. Politicized mothering stance is distinguishable by characteristics that are maternal, political, and embodying of a moral understanding of education as one that cultivates critical consciousness. The Black Bourgeoisie theory, as stated above, views education attainment and White middle-class values as cultural capital in our society. Therefore, utilizing engaged pedagogy and politicized mothering as school leadership tools has been widely overlooked in the experience described above. As we continue the discourse of "we-need-more-leaders-of-color," we should widen our perspective and embrace those who aim to cultivate community by aiding in the development of a critical consciousness among students in an effort not only to improve academic achievement, but to plant seeds of awareness in the minds of students.

CONNECTING OUR COUNTERSTORIES TO WHITENESS AS PROPERTY

The idea of "Whiteness as property" and its absolute right to exclude is symbolized in the actual closing of many Black schools during the 1960s. The closing of these schools left many Black teachers and administrators jobless, at the mercy of White school administrators for employment (Horsford & McKenzie, 2008). The remnants of this exclusion are ever-present in the lack of diversity in the current teacher population. What is the underlying reason for traditional educational policy discourse to want to address the shortage of teachers of color? The fact remains: It is an issue of retention as much as it is one of recruitment. Furthermore, many state policies exist that lead to the exclusion of Black teachers from the teaching profession in the form of biased teacher certification exams (e.g., Delpit, 1997; Ladson-Billings & Darling-Hammond, 2000).

The history of hegemonic political and economic domination in United States history is heavily connected to property rights and consequently segues to racial inequality. Cheryl Harris (1993), in her extensive examination of Whiteness as property, demonstrates the construction of Whiteness as high commodity with rights of disposition, rights to use and enjoyment, reputation and status property, and the absolute right to exclude.

CONNECTING OUR COUNTERSTORIES TO INTEREST CONVERGENCE

The counterstories above demonstrate that the principle of "we-need-more-leaders-of-color" discourse is reflective of interest convergence. In describing the flaws of the *Brown* decision, Bell (2004) argues two points related to interest convergence. First,

> [T]he interest of blacks in achieving racial equality will be accommodated only when that interest converges with the interest of whites in policymaking positions. This convergence is far more important for gaining relief than the degree of harm suffered by blacks or the character of proof offered to prove that harm. (p. 6)

And second, "Even when the interest convergence results in an effective racial remedy, that remedy will be abrogated at the point that policy makers fear the remedial policy is threatening the superior societal status of whites" (p. 69).

In Hartlep's counterstory, he told of his experiences of being an educational leader within AERA, the world's premier educational research association. His counterstory pointed to how he refused to be used by the dominant society to maintain the status quo. Rather, he shifted the need for racial representation to other important facets of diversity, such as institutional diversity.

Within Baylor's counternarrative, she addresses the expectation of leadership from a Black Bourgeoisie position. Baylor's experience noted that personal career interests among White school leaders were of greater importance than the needs of the school community. In fact, a disregard for the needs of the school community was commonplace, while rote basic skills were valued over aiding in the development of critical thinking.

Research indicates a commonality among Black women educators in regard to implementing othermothering practices. It has been noted that "exemplary African American women educators use the familiar and familial mother-child relationship as a guide for their interactions with students" (Beauboeuf-Lafontant, 2005, p. 74). This level of advocacy is formed in most cases due to the fact that many Black women educators often see themselves as "othermothers," or women who feel accountable for and therefore commit themselves to the social and emotional progression of all children in the community (Collins, 1991; Irvine, 2009). Overall, the guiding force of othermothering is clear-sighted attachment resulting from childhood memories of being "watched both by maternal figures and by community figures" (Case, 1997, p. 36). According to Beauboeuf-Lafontant (2005), analyses of exemplary Black educators overwhelmingly demonstrate a maternal approach. Beauboeuf-Lafontant explains, these educators "view the maternal as a profound commitment to the well-being and survival of Black children and Black people" (p. 76).

SUMMARY

This chapter has asserted that "majoritarian" educational leadership discourses, such as the "model minority" stereotype and the "Black Bourgeoisie," serve to fuel the "we-need-more-leaders-of-color" rhetoric. In reality, the larger question that the educational community has not asked itself is what commitments do these leaders have for themselves, others, and the wider community?

In this chapter we have attempted to use CRT in order to counternarrate the "masterscripts" (Poon & Hune, 2009) that imply that increasing the numbers of leaders of color is the most important issue facing education. The tenets of "counterstorytelling" (Solórzano & Yosso, 2001, 2002), "whiteness as property" (Harris, 1993), and "white interest convergence" (Bell, 1980) were called upon in order to argue that the *push* for more educational leaders of color must be more nuanced than what is currently being advocated for by the "mainstream" educational leadership establishment.

Asian and African Americans can be mentored and promoted to positions of leadership in more socially just and inclusive ways. Concordia University–Saint Paul's Southeast Asian Teacher[7] (SEAT) Program and Clemson University's Call Me MISTER[8] (Mentors Instructing Students Toward Effective Role Models) initiative are ways that the progressive educational establishment can recruit and grow the numbers of Asian and African American leaders while simultaneously fighting "whiteness as property" (Harris, 1993). Additionally, culturally relevant leadership trainings are needed to address ways in which race and culture influence professional development, recruiting, and promotion and retention practices. It is imperative that the classroom teacher to school leader pipeline include educators of color. Not just educators of color, but educators who possess an acute understanding of sociopolitical issues and a drive to counter the ill effects of a historically racist system.

NOTES

1. Headlines of articles such as "WANTED: 2 million teachers, especially minorities" (Duarte, 2000) illustrate that what is emphasized is whether or not a teacher/leader is a person of color.
2. Website that still references my presidency President—Nick Hartlep—Winona State University, http://studentclubs.winona.edu/kdp/President.htm
3. President Johnson's attempt to wage war on poverty resulted in the development of the Economic Opportunity Act of 1964, which established the Office of Economic Opportunity (OEO) where the idea for early childhood education for the poor in the form of Head Start programs to improve early child development were established in 1965 (Steiner, 1976).
4. Term used to distinguish a boundary marked by railroad tracks dividing White and Black communities
5. Politicized Mothering examines caring beyond the cultural aspect, and hones in on the political awareness that shapes the maternal approach of Black women teachers. This type of caring is characterized as authentic caring, a "trans-historical and communal vision of social change that sustains their commitments to children" (Beauboeuf-Lafontant, 1997, p. 258).
6. Engaged pedagogy: The teacher's role is not simply to empower students but to "care for their souls" and to grow as a result of their relationships with students (hooks, 1984, p. 13).
7. http://www.csp.edu/seat/
8. http://www.clemson.edu/hehd/departments/education/research/callmemister/

REFERENCES

Anderson, A. (2013). Teach for America and the dangers of deficit thinking. *Critical Education, 4*(11), 28–47. Retrieved from http://ojs.library.ubc.ca/index.php/criticaled/article/down load/183936/184137

Anyon, J. (1997). *Ghetto schooling: A political economy of urban school reform.* New York, NY: Teachers College Press.

Battle, J., & Wright, E. (2002). W. E. B. Du Bois's talented tenth: A quantitative assessment. *Journal of Black Studies, 32*(6), 654–672.

Bell, D. A. (1980). *Brown v. Board of Education* and the interest-convergence dilemma. *Harvard Law Review, 93*(3), 518–533.

Bell, D. A. (2004). *Silent covenants: Brown vs. Board of Education and the unfulfilled hopes for racial reform.* New York, NY: Oxford University Press.

Beauboeuf-Lafontant, T. M. (1997). *Politicized mothering among African-American women teachers: A qualitative inquiry* (unpublished doctoral dissertation). Harvard University, Cambridge, MA.

Beauboeuf-Lafontant, T. (2005). Womanist lessons for reinventing teaching. *Journal of Teacher Education, 56*(5), 436–445.

Bloom, C. M., & Erlandson, D. A. (2003). African American women principals in urban schools: Realities, (re)constructions, and resolutions. *Educational Administration Quarterly, 39*(3), 339–369.

Bracey, G. W. (2001). Why so few Asian American teachers? *Phi Delta Kappan, 83*(1), 14–16.

Broad Foundation. (2014). Retrieved from http://www.broadeducation.org

Brown v. Board of Education, 347 U. S. 483 (1954).

Case, K. I. (1997). African American othermothering in the urban elementary school. *The Urban Review, 29*(1), 25–39.

Chae, H. S. (2004). Talking back to the Asian model minority discourse: Korean-origin youth experiences in high school. *Journal of Intercultural Studies, 25*(1), 59–73.

Cole, B. P. (1986). The Black educator: An endangered species. *The Journal of Negro Education, 55*(3), 326–334.

Collins, P. H. (1991). On our own terms: Self-defined standpoints and curriculum transformation. *NWSA Journal, 3*(3), 367–381.

Committee of 100. (2001). American attitudes towards Chinese Americans and Asian Americans. Retrieved from http://archive.adl.org/misc/american_attitudes_towards _chinese.html

Delgado, R. (2009). Affirmative action as a majoritarian device: Or, do you really want to be a role model. In E. Taylor, D. Gillborn, & G. Ladson-Billings (Eds.), *Foundations of critical race theory in education* (pp. 109–116). New York, NY: Routledge.

Delpit, L. (1997). Foreword. In M. Foster (Ed.), *Black teachers on teaching* (pp. ix–xii). New York, NY: The New Press.

Duarte, A. (2000). WANTED: 2 million teachers, especially minorities. *Education Digest, 66*(4), 19–23.

Du Bois, W. E. B. (1903a). *The souls of Black folks.* New York, NY: Dover Publications.

Du Bois, W. E. B. (1903b). The talented tenth. Retrieved from http://teachingamericanhistory.org/library/index.asp?document=174

Duncan-Andrade, J. M. R. (2009). Note to educators: Hope required when growing roses in concrete. *Harvard Educational Review, 79*(2), 181–194.

Eguchia, S., & Starosta, W. (2012). Negotiating the model minority image: Performative aspects of college-educated Asian American professional men. *Qualitative Research Reports in Communication, 13*(1), 88–97.

Frazier, E. F. (1957). *Black bourgeoisie.* New York, NY: Free Press.

Freire, P. (2000). *Pedagogy of the oppressed* (30th anniversary edition). New York, NY: Continuum.

Haberman, M. (1989). More minority teachers. *Phi Delta Kappan, 70*(10), 771–776.

Harris, C. I. (1993). Whiteness as property. *Harvard Law Review, 106*(8), 1707–1791.

Hartlep, N. D. (Ed.). (2014). *The model minority stereotype reader: Critical and challenging readings for the 21st century.* San Diego, CA: Cognella Publishing.

Hartlep, N. D. (2014). Black Mormonism as an example of model minority discourse. In N. W. Arnold & M. C. Brooks (Eds.), *Critical perspectives on Black education: Spirituality, religion, and social justice* (pp. 59–86). Charlotte, NC: Information Age.

Hartlep, N. D. (2012). Two letters from my lost father: A transracial adoptee shares his heart. In L. Yue & V. Katagiri (Eds.), *Where are you from: An anthology of Asian American writing* (pp. 173–189). Portland, OR: Thymos.

Hartlep, N. D., & Porfilio, B. (Eds.). (2015). *Killing the model minority stereotype: Asian American counternarratives and complicity.* Charlotte, NC: Information Age Publishing.

Heilig, J. V. (2010). *Teach for America: A review of the evidence.* Boulder, CO: Education and the Public Interest Center. Retrieved from http://nepc.colorado.edu/files/PB-TeachAmerica-Heilig.pdf

Hirahara, N. (2003). *Distinguished Asian American business leaders.* Westport, CT: Greenwood Press.

hooks, b. (1984). *Feminist theory: From margin to center.* London, UK: Pluto Press.

Horsford, S. D., & McKenzie, K. B. (2008). "Sometimes I feel like the problems started with desegregation": Exploring Black superintendent perspectives on desegregation policy. *International Journal of Qualitative Studies in Education. 21*(5), 443–455.

Irvine, J. J. (2009). Culturally relevant pedagogy. *Teaching Tolerance, 36,* 40–44.

Khator, R. (2010). Breaking the bamboo ceiling. *Presidency, 13*(2), 28–31.

Kim, L. S. (2008). Continuing significance of the model minority myth: The second generation. *Social Justice, 35*(2), 134–144.

Kronus, S. (1971). *The Black middle class.* Columbus, OH: Merrill.

Landry, B. (1987). *The new Black middle class.* Berkeley, CA: University of California Press.

Ladson-Billings G., & Darling-Hammond L. (2000). *The validity of national board for professional teaching standards (NBPTS)/interstate new teacher assessment and support consortium (INTASC) assessments for effective urban teachers: Findings and implications for assessments.* Washington, DC: National Partnership for Excellence and Accountability in Teaching.

Lawler, A. (2000). Silent no longer: 'Model minority' mobilizes. *Science, 290*(5494), 1072–1077.

LEAP. (2012). *2012 API representation on fortune 500 boards.* Los Angeles, CA: Leadership Education for Asian Pacifics. Retrieved from http://www.leap.org/docs/2012_LEAP _F500_FullReport.pdf

Lee, J. K. (2002). Where the talented tenth meets the model minority: The price of privilege in Wideman's "Philadelphia Fire" and Lee's "Native Speaker." *NOVEL: A Forum on Fiction, 35*(2/3), 231–257.

Lee, T. (1991). Trapped on a pedestal: Asian Americans confront model-minority stereotype. In J. A. Kromowski (Ed.), *Racial and ethnic relations* (pp. 95–98). Guildford, CT: Duskhin Publishing Group.

Li, G., & Wang, L. (Eds.) (2008). *Model minority myth revisited: An interdisciplinary approach to demystifying Asian American educational experiences.* Charlotte, NC: Information Age.

Littlewood, W. (2000). Do Asian students really want to listen and obey? *ELT Journal, 54*(1), 31–36.

Mayeda, D. T. (1999). From model minority to economic threat: Media portrayals of major league baseball pitchers Hideo Nomo and Hideki Irabu. *Journal of Sport and Social Issues, 23*(2), 203–217.

Ong, E. (2003). Transcending the bamboo and glass ceilings: Defining the trajectory to empower Asian Pacific Islander American women in politics. In D. T. Nakanishi & J. Lai (Eds.), *Asian American politics: Law, participation, and policy* (pp. 331–354). Lanham, MD: Rowman and Littlefield.

Ono, K. A., & Pham, V. N. (2009). Threatening model minorities: The Asian American Horatio Alger story. In K. A. Ono & V. N. Pham (Eds.), *Asian Americans and the media* (pp. 80–96). New York, NY: Polity Press.

Poon, O. A., & Hune, S. (2009). Countering master narratives of the "perpetual foreigner" and "model minority": The hidden injuries of race and Asian American doctoral students. In M. F. Howard-Hamilton, C. L. Morelon-Quainoo, S. D. Johnson, R. Winkle-Wagner, & L. Santiague (Eds.), *Standing on the outside looking in: Underrepresented students' experiences in advanced-degree programs* (pp. 82–102). Sterling, VA: Stylus.

Qin, D. B., Way, N., & Mukherjee, P. (2008). The other side of the model minority story: The familial and peer challenges faced by Chinese American adolescents. *Youth & Society, 39*(4), 480–506.

Rong, X. L., & Preissle, J. (1997). The continuing decline in Asian American teachers. *American Educational Research Journal, 34*(2), 267–293.

Sakamoto, A., Takei, I., & Woo, H. (2012). The myth of the model minority myth. *Sociological Spectrum, 32*(4), 309–321.

Solórzano, D. G., & Yosso, T. J. (2001). Critical race and LatCrit theory and method: Counter-storytelling. *Qualitative Studies in Education, 14*(4), 471–495.

Solórzano, D. G., & Yosso, T. J. (2002). Critical race methodology: Counter-storytelling as an analytical framework for education research. *Qualitative Inquiry, 8*(1), 23–44.

Steiner, G. (1976). *The children's cause.* Washington, DC: The Brookings Institution.

Tewell, K. J., & Trubowitz, S. (1987). The minority group teacher: An endangered species. *Urban Education, 22*(3), 355–365.

Toldson, I. (2011). Diversifying the United States' teaching force: Where are we now? Where do we need to go? How do we get there? *The Journal of Negro Education, 80*(3), 183–186.

Vetri, B. T. (2010). *Learning on other people's kids: Becoming a Teach for America teacher.* Charlotte, NC: Information Age.

Westheimer, J., & Kahne, J. (2004). What kind of citizen? The politics of educating for democracy. *American Educational Research Journal, 41*(2), 237–269.

Woo, D. (2000). *Glass ceilings and Asian Americans: The new face of workplace barriers.* Walnut Creek, CA: AltaMira Press.

Woodson, C. G. (1933). *The mis-education of the Negro.* Chicago, IL: African American Images.

Yosso, T. J. (2005). Whose culture has capital? A critical race theory discussion of community cultural wealth. *Race Ethnicity and Education, 8*(1), 69–91.

Zweigenhaft, R. L., & Domhoff, G. W. (2011). *The new CEOs: Women, African American, Latino, and Asian American leaders of fortune 500 companies.* Lanham, MD: Rowman & Littlefield.

CHAPTER 6

IGNORED BY THE BOARD

Disrupting School Closure and Illuminating White Racism Through Counterstorytelling

Antonette Aragon
Colorado State University–Fort Collins

I sat in my kitchen holding the note my daughter had brought home. I was stunned and felt sick to my stomach. Barely a month into the semester, the district announced to the parents and community the necessity to investigate whether to close five public schools in the Desert School District (DSD)[1] in order to save district dollars in the economic financial crisis. Tears stung my eyes as I imagined my daughter's school doors locked forever. I believed this school was making a difference in the lives of its students and in my daughter's bilingual education. I shuddered thinking about the bright faces in her kindergarten classroom. Ten students were native Spanish speakers and my daughter was one of ten native English speakers. The children worked together to learn each other's language in this dual immersion school. They sang Spanish and English songs together, while literacy, social studies, science, and math were taught in both their

Envisioning Critical Race Praxis in K–12 Leadership Through Counter-Storytelling, pages 107–138
Copyright © 2016 by Information Age Publishing
107

native language and the second language. I volunteered weekly, and as both a school leader and teacher educator, I witnessed the culturally responsive techniques utilized in this bilingual school.

The teachers conduct home visits to learn about each of their students. One of the teachers at Mariposa Dual Language Elementary School shared,

> I learn more about my Native Spanish speaking students, how they live, and it surprises me that most of the parents are overly committed to their children's education. I wouldn't know this if I did not conduct home visits. I learn so much and it is shocking to me how different their lives are compared to mine and how I grew up.

She also explained having a high learning curve when she began teaching in this dual language school. Her professional development led by the previous principal, Dr. José Martínez, was invaluable. She learned the significance of culturally responsive teaching. Dr. Martínez held open dialogues in staff meetings about the "elephants" nobody wants to discuss. The topics of regular staff meetings examined the systemic and inequitable impacts of poverty, racism, language, and culture. Engaging his staff to inquire and learn beyond their individual notions of racism and class-based oppression, he asked his staff to conduct book studies reading authors including Paul Gorski, Lisa Delpit, Richard Valencia, Zeus Leonardo, Chris Knaus, Geneva Gay, Richard Valencia, and Gloria Ladson-Billings. He challenged his staff to interrupt *deficit perspectives* of their students, especially when they come from poverty. A deficit perspective "blames the victim" by believing students and parents are motivationally deficit rather than examining the institutional structures bound in politically, socially, and economically inequitable schooling arrangements (Valencia & Black, 2002). The principal had worked for five years with his staff to learn the context of the children's culture by honoring their language, culture, and socioeconomic background. He hired bilingual Spanish-speaking teachers and staff so the students would flourish in the achievement of their native Spanish language while learning English, their second language. Not only did he continually uphold the district motto, "Educate and meet every child's learning needs every day," but he continually encouraged his teachers and staff to uphold the highest expectations for every student to learn every day. He continually challenged the staff to discover the cultural assets and tools of the student's families and community to provide opportunities for students and teachers to redefine student engagement.

I had much respect for Dr. Martínez's leadership. In fact, my husband and I purposefully decided to exercise our school of choice options by choosing to place our first child into this school because we were so impressed with how he was leading Mariposa. However, Dr. Martínez had learned in the spring of 2013 that DSD may close some schools. Having been given indications that Mariposa may be one of the schools included in the school closure process, he decided he would seek employment elsewhere. Within a five-year time frame, he turned this failing school around, but his desire was to continue to work for positive change in a district that valued his leadership. As a Latino male native Spanish speaker, he not only related to the students, families, and community, but he guided his staff to meet annual yearly progress (AYP) for three consecutive years. He left the district before they announced Mariposa's possible closure.

The purpose of this chapter is to challenge institutional majoritarian stories of school closure processes by providing a counterstory that highlights the nexus between education and policy. As a Latina critical race theory (CRT) and LatCrit scholar, I wanted to examine the manner in which racism seemed to be entrenched in this school closure process. This chapter utilizes faction, both fiction and facts (Akintunde, 1999), to provide my counterstory based on my personal experience of advocating and participating in the stoppage of the closure of five schools in DSD. The purpose of this counterstory grounded in CRT framework directly centers my counternarrative voice as well as Dr. José Martínez's[2] in the school closure process. The story presented uses several email dialogues between Dr. José Martínez, a fictional muse, and myself. My inspiration for the usage of a muse is derived from the work of Derrick Bell (1987), who interweaves a fictional alter ego named Geneva Crenshaw in his foundational work in critical race theory. This fictional technique allows for exploring various aspects of racism affecting Latin@s[3] in this school closure process. Prior to presenting the email dialogues between the author and Dr. José Martínez, I will provide the theoretical framing and data sources used within the counterstory.

CRT & LATCRIT: THE FRAME AND METHOD OF THE COUNTERSTORY

Whiteness shapes educational norms, behaviors, policies, and practices in P–20 education in the United States (Leonardo, 2013; Yosso, 2006). As such, school closures are also influenced by Whiteness and are sociopolitically racialized acts (Aragon, 2014b). According to Solórzano and Yosso (2002), critical race theory focuses on race and racism as a form of systemic oppression. CRT challenges endemic dominant ideologies imbedded in educational theory and practice and evokes critical examinations and social justice action against traditional educational institutions practicing deficit notions of objectivity, colorblindness, and race neutrality (Yosso, 2005). Critical race scholars argue that these are rhetorical and camouflaged ideologies that operate in the self-interest, power, and privilege of dominant groups in U.S. society (Solórzano & Yosso, 2002).

LatCrit theory, a congruent outgrowth of CRT, elucidates Latin@s' multidimensional identities addressing the intersectionality of racism between and among gender, ethnicity, culture, language, and social class (Solórzano & Delgado Bernal, 2001; Villalpando, 2004; Yosso, 2006). The inquiry and analysis of intersectional oppressions allows for a more holistic approach outside of race/ethnicity, specific to the inequities of Latin@s (Solórzano & Delgado Bernal, 2001; Solórzano & Yosso, 2002; Villalpando, 2004; Yosso, 2005).

As a first generation Latina/Chicana scholar who grew up in a low-income, working class home where my parents spoke Spanish to us but asked for responses back to them in English so that we did not face discrimination based on an accent, I not only heard their counterstories, but also counterstories from many people in my large extended family. There is a rich oral tradition in Latin@ communities where their counterstories may display reflections of their lived experiences to raise critical consciousness about social and racial injustices (Yosso, 2006). CRT/LatCrit counterstorytelling is a method of recounting the experiences and perspectives of racially and socially marginalized people, challenging the majoritarian stories that omit and distort the histories and realities of oppressed people (Yosso, 2006).

I adopt CRT/LatCrit counterstorytelling methodology to demonstrate the institutionalized discrimination in the academic and social structure within the school closure process. My analysis to create this counterstory includes data from reflective conversations, experiences, emails, notes, analysis of public Desert School District (DSD) school board meetings, videos, letters, emails, documented minutes of meetings, personal voice recordings, academic literature, newspaper articles, and Facebook groups. In analyzing the data to write this counterstory, I read and reread over my personal journal narratives and notes including the written public speeches and letters I wrote to school board members; I watched video recordings of DSD school board meetings and read pertinent emails and autoethnographic collections of my actions as an activist-scholar in a grassroots campaign advocating to keep five schools open.

RACISM UNVEILED: ONLINE CORRESPONDENCE
WITH DR. JOSÉ MARTÍNEZ

It was fall and the sun shone brightly on this hot September day. I felt overwhelmed thinking about the DSD school board's information circulating on the district website related to the school closures. I kept thinking about how I was going to present information countering their majoritarian story. My mind was racing and I wanted to reach out to the former Mariposa principal because I believed he had a wealth of information to share to assist in keeping the schools open. As the serendipity of life happens, I had an appointment in my neighboring town. After the appointment, I stopped at Target to buy shoes for my daughter since her feet were growing an inch per week. I turned a corner and guess who I ran into? I was shocked when I saw his full white head of hair from behind and thought, I wonder if that is Dr. José Martínez. I knew he had just moved to River City to become an elementary principal. I felt like I was related to him when I spoke to him since he looked like my own grandpa. He also had a deep Spanish accent, and when he spoke you could feel kindness flowing from his soft eyes. Suddenly he turned around and he almost ran right into me.

"Antonette, what brings you to River City? You are almost an hour away from your desert town, aren't you?"

I smiled and let him know I had an appointment and we stood there for a bit exchanging niceties. I then let him know that I was doing research to advocate for Mariposa and would testify in front of the school board in a few days. I let him know I was part of the newly formed Coalition Against School Closure (CASC); I asked him if he would be willing to answer some of my questions. He looked sad, and his kind eyes watered. He said that he would be happy to assist, but his time was saturated in his new job and email would be the best mode of communication. He hugged my daughter and me, and we said goodbye.

I was sad as we left and couldn't help but feel deflated after seeing him. He was really kind-hearted, the sort of principal anyone would want for their child. I could see why the staff seemed to be in a state of mourning now that he had left their school. I wanted his voice to be heard in the school board meetings. I sent my first email to him and the following email dialogue occurred.

To: Dr. José Martínez <Jose.Martínez@cityschool.edu>

From: Antonette Aragon<culturallyrespond@smail.com>

Sent: Mon, September 20, 2013 2:47 pm

Subject: What insights might you provide about to keep Mariposa from closing

Dear Dr. José Martínez, How are you? It was so nice to see you at Target this weekend. I know you are adjusting to your new school, and I imagine there is much to learn in order to lead your staff to experience the kind of success you had here. I wonder if you have been thinking about Mariposa and the future of the students and staff. As a new parent in this school, I cannot stop thinking about this school's fate. I can only imagine how you must have felt to leave this school after a successful tenure of leadership. I feel the district is steam rolling their agenda to possibly close at least one of these five schools, if not all. As I stated to you in Target, I am working many angles with the social justice grassroots coalition. The assault to the Latino community is disgusting and it is part of covert discrimination that people do not even know they are part of. I want this school to remain open for my daughter but even more so for the community of learners that really need this school! I wish you were still our fearless leader. Your guidance is still felt in the classrooms of this school. Some teachers have let me know they miss you and the familial climate you created. They work so diligently hard with great care and love for their students. They are a top-notch group of teachers. I am wondering if you have any insights for me to investigate or report as I will testify in front of the school board tomorrow.

Thank you,
Antonette

He responded later that night.

To: Antonette Aragon<culturallyrespond@smail.com>
From: Dr. José Martínez <Jose.Martínez@cityschool.edu>
Sent: Mon, September 20, 2013 11:58 pm
Subject: What insights might you provide about to keep Mariposa from closing

Dearest Antonette: Upon learning of Mariposa's possible closure, I began to research the national trend of school closure. I began to ask, who will be excluded, if schools close in this district? My research provided insights about national school closure trends. Throughout the United States, every student should have the right to a high-quality education. Unfortunately, this educational right is not a reality for many students of color (Darling-Hammond, 2007; Delpit, 2012; Valencia, 2010). Nationally, public schools across the country close, disproportionately influencing students from communities of color and low income families (de la Torre & Gwynne, 2009; Kirshner, Gaertner, & Pozzoboni, 2010; NOLC, 2013). When schools close, students do not improve their academic performance when transferring to a different school (Kirshner & Pozzoboni, 2011). Consequently, closures also do not improve district financial shortfalls (Kirshner, Gaertner, & Pozobonni, 2010; National Opportunity to Learn Campaign, 2013; Sunderman & Payne, 2009).

Nationally, there have been hundreds of school closures in cities throughout the nation. The Chicago Teachers Union and parents held a massive three-day march protesting the nation's largest proposed school closures in one city. In spite of the united activism by parents, students, and the teacher's union, Chicago Public School Board voted in favor of closing 50 schools. Such school closings promoted a business model competitive corporate vision. Providing school choices through more charters, magnets, and specialized schools, parents may shop for schools that fit their child's needs. However, in reality the competition to get accepted into charters and magnet schools creates a more privatized system (Winslow, 2013) and neoliberal approaches to education (Giroux, 2013). Chicago's closures displaced 40,000 primarily low-income African American and Latin@ students of color to crowded schools that were no better performing than their closed school (Alter, 2013; Wisniewski, 2013).

Moreover, according to the National Opportunity to Learn Campaign (NOLC), this trend has been ongoing for years, and back in 2010–2011, the three cities with the largest numbers of school closures were found in Chicago (29 schools were closed), New York City (22 schools were closed), and Philadelphia (23 schools were closed). In all three of these cities, up to 94% of the students were again low income, and the majority were African American (up to 87%) and Latin@ (up to 41%). In these same cities, white students only constituted up to 4% of the populations undergoing school closure (NOLC, 2013). In other large school districts such as in Kansas City, Missouri 50% of their schools were closed (Volche, 2013). Detroit, Milwaukee, and Pittsburgh closed up to 20 schools detrimentally influencing the life opportunities of students of color (Samuels, 2011); and between 2001 with the inception of No Child Left Behind (NCLB) until 2005, 200 schools were closed within various California school districts (Globalet, 2005).

There is no arguing that some schools are not serving their students of color and perhaps closure may be an option. However, with the nationwide systemic closures happening in multiple school districts, there is not a method for school districts to have better performing schools for the displaced students of color to attend, creating understaffed and overpopulated classrooms (Winslow, 2013). Not to mention, students from closed schools are often sent to schools that do not practice culturally responsive techniques honoring the community cultural wealth, civic capacity, and funds of knowledge of students and parents (Aragon, 2014a; González, Moll, & Amanti, 2005; Kirshner & Pozzoboni, 2011; Kretchmar, 2014; Pérez Huber, 2009). Such closures have a dire influence on student achievement, attendance, and community involvement; incurred district financial strain; and a negative to neutral impact on the academic performance of students transferring from closed to new schools (Engberg, Gill, Zammaro, & Zimmer, 2012; Kirshner et al., 2010). Not only do closures influence students' lifetime social and cultural capital (Kretchmar, 2014; Zachary, 2011), but they disrupt whole communities, especially when school buildings house health clinics and preK programs, and operate to assist the community during non-school hours. In some communities, closed schools destroy the hub of community resources, investment in the public housing, and employment (NOLC, 2013).

Antonette, since you are going to speak to the school board, please mention these facts to them because school closures are directly negatively influencing the lives of students of color. If DSD doesn't stop this closure process, they will just be another statistic about students of color having education busted out from under them.

Dr. Martínez

The next day I responded to Dr. Martínez because I too had researched similar information to report to the school board that evening.

To: Dr. José Martínez Jose.Martínez@cityschool.edu

From: Antonette Aragon<culturallyrespond@smail.com>

Sent: Tuesday, September 21, 2013 1:00 pm

Subject: DSD's profile of schools closing

Dear Dr. Martínez: Thank you so much for providing the national school closure trends. I too found much of that information in my own research and will report on some of it tonight in the 3 minutes that the district allows in public testimony. As I am sure you are aware, the national trends also align to this local school closure process.

A friend of mine who lives in another state is also facing possible school closures. We compared our school profiles and here is the information that I sent to her about our school district's reasoning for choosing the five schools for possible closure.

Out of 52 schools in this majority White populated midsized suburb in our mountain range state, the DSD chose the schools with the largest enrollments of low income and Latin@ students. This is the national trend. However, I wanted to believe our district led with a propensity to serve and uphold all students, especially students of color. Nevertheless, I also recognize from my research that well-intentioned people follow the requirements of the law, such as NCLB, in the name of objectivity, progress, and policy. My daughter's school, Mariposa, has a 50% English language learners (ELL) population, and 70% of the students are Latin@, and 85.5% on free and reduced lunch (State Department of Education, 2013). Yet, the district claimed race, ethnicity, or socioeconomics had nothing to do with their decision to potentially close the five schools. Ironically though, one criterion that was not publicly displayed in the district literature promoting reasons for the five schools chosen was titled, "Underutilized Schools Criteria-Additional Supporting Data." Under this criterion the district determined the five schools according to their "Percentage of Free & Reduced" rank in the district. Additionally, this data displayed all five schools slated for potential closure as having the largest percentages of students on free and reduced lunch programs feeding into their respective "feeder" high schools. However, the school district focused their public rhetoric on the claims that all five schools had the lowest school building utilization in the district, without highlighting socioeconomic status as an overt reason for possible closure. School district criteria for underutilization was based on 65% building capacity usage or less (2005–2006 data), which is very outdated data; 40% choice out rate; 20% projected drop in enrollment (from 2005–2012); middle schools with fewer than 600 students or elementary schools with fewer than 325 students; or district monetary compensation of 3% or more due to low enrollment.

DSD superintendent and administrative officials commissioned DSD school board members to examine the required closure/consolidation plans from all five schools, listen to community input, weigh the pros and cons, and vote whether any or all of the schools should close. All of this information is district justification for possibly closing the five schools, and all five schools have the largest student of color and low income populations.

Take care,
Antonette

Days started to pass quickly. I began to wonder what other good information Dr. Martínez might provide, but I was so busy working what felt like two jobs—my regular tenure-track professor position as well as the major research I was pouring in to counter this closure. I began to notice that I was dedicating hours of time on research, meetings, and organizing against this closure. When Dr. Martínez responded, I had been so absorbed in my work, I hardly realized two weeks had passed.

To: Antonette Aragon<culturallyrespond@smail.com>
From: Dr. José Martínez <Jose.Martínez@cityschool.edu>
Sent: Monday, October 4, 2013 11:59 pm
Subject: How did the DSD School Board meeting go?

Dear Antonette: I never seem to be finished as a school principal. I work late, wake early, and still my work is never done. I've been wanting to respond to your last email but am just now barely getting to it. Your insights about how the DSD schools chosen for possible closure is no coincidence as I am sure you know. Primarily, the practice of school closure is warranted by the 2001 No Child Left Behind (NCLB) policy agenda. I wish the parents and the people in the community understood the magnitude of policy implications influencing schooling practices. When is the next school board meeting? As you are planning to speak; if so, will you please provide information about how NCLB is at the root of school closures?

Here's how I see it. The overarching NCLB Act was created by the Bush Administration to make it seem that it would assist with closing the racial and ethnic 'achievement gap' (Darling-Hammond, 2007). There were two main initiatives of the NCLB Act: to raise test scores and to provide parents with educational choice of schools for their children to attend. Unfortunately, NCLB evaluates students based upon overly simplistic measures, particularly standardized testing "criteria that has repeatedly been shown to be linguistically, culturally, racially, and economically biased" (Knaus & Rogers-Ard, 2012, p. 3). However, at the root, NCLB never was intended to address the inequitable schooling in the U.S. (Nieto & Bode, 2012; Valencia, 2010).

The general public does not understand how school funding is set up to create societal inequity. We live in a nation where inequitably funded schools exist where imbalanced high-spending and resourced schools outspend low-spending schools at least three to one in most states and produce the most inequitable education system in the industrialized world (Darling-Hammond, 2007). The root cause of such inequity is based on:

> An educational debt that has accumulated over centuries of denied access to education and employment, reinforced by deepening poverty and resource inequalities in schools. Until American society confronts the accumulated educational debt owed to these students and takes responsibility for the inferior resources they receive . . . children of color and of poverty will continue to be left behind. (Darling-Hammond, 2007, p. 2)

Also, the NCLB Act required schools to make annual benchmark improvements on standardized test scores in order to assist with higher graduation rates for racial and ethnic minority groups (Knaus, 2007). Yet the schools performing the worst on state measures leave the most children behind. Annual expected standardized tests set adequate yearly progress (AYP) measures determined by each state (Kim & Sunderman, 2005). However, NCLB required failing schools not making AYP for five consecutive years to restructure by possibly closing, turning around a school by firing teachers and administrators and replacing them, or coming up with an intervention plan. Schools not meeting AYP are seen as failing, and it provided justifications to families to opt out of those low performing schools and transfer into higher performing schools. When parents choose to leave lower performing schools for higher performing schools, it influences school enrollments. Now the current legislation created by the Obama administration's Blueprint for Reform, (BFR) reformed NCLB, and AYP is no longer mandated as part of Obama's BFR plan, yet many restructuring schools are still practicing AYP, the turnaround model, restart model, transformation model, or a closure model for intervention (Zavadsky, 2012). Unfortunately, there has been insignificant or no research conducted, meaning that all of these models are experimental and not solidly research based options (Berry & Herrington, 2011). The most vulnerable populations undergoing restructured measures as sanctioned by NCLB and BFR have been low-income students of color.

Antonette, please let me know how your work is progressing to push the district to look at their actions. I hope you provide insights for them to look closely at NCLB because I believe most board members do not know the policies that influence closure practices. I also really believe one of the only ways to stop the closure is through coalition building. How is your coalition work?

Dr. Martínez

After reading Dr. Martínez's email, I couldn't help but appreciate his knowledge about the NCLB implications, a policy that would influence all forthcoming educational practices. It was this type of policy rhetoric that closes schools and promises to create change on the backs of children of color. I started to reflect upon my own research of NCLB and nationwide school closures driving my coalition building momentum. I was seeking answers and couldn't do this work single handedly, as the school district decision to close schools appeared nonnegotiable. I had contacted the assistant superintendent to find more information and although he politely answered my questions, he ensured me that at least one, if not more of the five schools had to close in order to meet the district's financial demands.

My determination to stop the closure intensified. My commitment came every day as I walked into Mariposa, as a mother of a child at this school and as an educator recognizing children learning in a culturally relevant bilingual environment. I witnessed teachers and staff deeply engaged in building sound relationships with the students and parents. I also witnessed my own daughter's Spanish language increase. I had such respect and admiration for the staff because not only did the test scores show significant individual growth measures as well as meeting AYP requirements for all students, but students, families, teachers, and staff felt their school was a home away from home, welcoming the community. This school offered wrap-around programs meeting the needs of the families, students, and community. It housed the early childhood preschool program, and it offered after-school English and Spanish courses for families and after-school courses to teach families how to effectively work on homework, finances, parenting, and other skills that mattered to the community. In addition, the after-school programs were funded by a multimillion-dollar state grant providing students enrichment courses, such as Lego engineering, poet's pen club, the bicycling club, the chess club, taekwondo, art classes, reading clubs, and many other courses not otherwise offered to students in under-funded schools. After contacting the state grant officials, I discovered that the after-school programs would end if the school closed.

I have worked in many schools and I have seen dysfunctional staff members battle with one another; I have seen principals who are not committed and do not lead. Most importantly, I have witnessed multiple classrooms with disengaged students, with teachers not knowing how to spark their drive for learning. This was not the case at Mariposa. It was quite the opposite at this school. Moreover, the other four schools were also making a positive difference influencing the learning of their students. In fact, according to a state department assessment, our district was doing one of the best jobs in the state to increase Latin@ student achievement.

However, I felt the district made an attack against Latin@s, the largest population (18%) of students of color in our district. The additional hours I invested in keeping schools open was a result of my personal experience coming from a large extended Latin@ family, having observed too many of my own family members beaten down from a system of education that ultimately left them behind. I know school closures influenced my own family members who dropped out of school because their sense of place was torn away from them. For all of these reasons, I could not stand idle and watch these schools close. I had to do all I could to build a coalition.

To: Dr. José Martínez Jose.Martínez@cityschool.edu
From: Antonette Aragon<culturallyrespond@smail.com>
Sent: Tuesday, October 5, 2013 11:59 pm
Subject: Coalition building

Dear Dr. Martínez, tonight we had another school board meeting. To answer your question about the coalition work, we continue to make progress. I, along with a local grassroots community leader, Charli Custeau, created the Coalition Against School Closure (CASC). We have been collaboratively working with community members and parents through grassroots social justice efforts to keep these schools open. I know from history and research that social justice grassroots efforts may disrupt, expose, and unearth racist power arrangements set to marginalize students of color (Oakes & Rogers, 2006; Valencia, 2010). A democratic approach of reform where experts, community members, school employees, parents, students, and others involved in participatory social action through inquiry, information gathering, exchange, interpretation, and debate is at the core of educational reform (Oakes & Rogers, 2006). As I testify at the school board meeting, I present researched data, literature, and social justice support for and with the Spanish-speaking parents and students; my work on this coalition has created an additional 20–30 hours on top of my already 40 hour assistant professor position—taxing but necessary if we are to keep these schools from closing. Tonight, I presented persuasive evidence about the adverse repercussions of NCLB and how such closures are primarily negatively influencing low-income students, particularly students of color throughout the country. The other members of the coalition came together and also testified.

While our coalition started with 35 people attending meetings, there are now eight core decision makers who have the time to dedicate to the coalition campaign demands. There are four women (three White, and myself, Latina), and four men (three White, and one Latino) and all but one are parents of a child in one of the proposed schools of closure.

If you'll remember, Dr. Martínez, the DSD superintendent and officials unveiled their "Underutilized Schools Process" to the district community, city, schools, and parents in the middle of September 2013 and six weeks later, they are requiring the staffs at those schools slated for possible closure to present "closure, consolidation and efficiency plans." These plans are a way to make it seem that the schools are contributing and almost sharing in the idea of their own closure because they show they have a say in how they might propose to close. But we both know this tactic is like asking someone to participate in their own planned death. Yet this is all sanctioned by the NCLB policy through quick action so that the children can be shuffled to a new school regardless of whether it is a sound decision for parents, educators, and the community. In reality, it "demonstrates a lack of respect for the families, teachers, and school staff and they have no say in decisions that affect them. Their voices have been ignored…" (Lipman & Haines, 2007, p. 493). The board members reminded us at the board meeting tonight that they will examine the staff closure plans and eventually vote whether to close one or more schools by the end of January. Remember, the school board members are all White and there are only two women out of the seven members. This matters because six out of the seven desire to close the schools.

As a coalition we are meeting with each of the board members at least three times between now and mid-January. Each meeting with the board members averages two hours in length. In addition, our coalition justice building means that we are seeking support and advocacy to keep these schools open through informing a number of city, university, and community members about the social and economic implications of school closure to them and this community. We began having numerous meetings with the city officials, newspapers, neighboring university scholars, teachers, our local university professors, state representatives, principals, business associations and owners, staff, and other constituents. We are on the same page, Dr. Martínez, because I know our coalition has the potential to make a difference in this fight to keep the schools open.

Take care,

Antonette

I really valued Dr. Martínez's emails, but we were both busy and we kept in touch as time permitted. He continued to provide me with some fuel for the arguments I presented to the school board members.

To: Antonette Aragon<culturallyrespond@smail.com>

From: Dr. José Martínez <Jose.Martínez@cityschool.edu>

Sent: Monday, October 11, 2013 11:58 pm

Subject: Why keep Mariposa open?

Hi Antonette!

Your work on the coalition is a necessity. Communities throughout the country have opposition to closure but they may not have the momentum of strong coalitions, and if they do, they often times are going against district agendas with decisions to close schools without a due process of community involvement. Context matters, and one district's approach to school reform is dependent upon how district leaders interpret what they see fit for change (Zadvasky, 2012). I hope the DSD board will listen to the coalition and community members.

As I reflect on the fact that I am no longer a principal in DSD, please know that my reasons for leaving had nothing to do with the people at Mariposa. My best advice to you as you continue to speak to the DSD board of education is to let them know the strengths of Mariposa because it is a wonderful, high-achieving school meeting the educational and cultural needs of Latin@ students. My insights are based on my experiences at Mariposa, and if I were to speak to the DSD school board, I would have many key items to discuss. Below I provide reasons why I believe Mariposa must stay open.

First, the teachers are highly efficient, dedicated, and under my leadership they were learning how to be culturally caring and responsive educators. When working with my staff at Mariposa, I followed Villegas and Lucas' (2007) definition of cultural responsiveness.

a) It is vitally important to engage immigrant or native Spanish speakers and all students by believing they are capable learners. Furthermore, teachers must promote the salient qualities of successful teaching of students from immigrant and linguistically diverse backgrounds involving a mindset of understanding the role of culture and language in learning.

b) Teachers must understand how learners construct knowledge.

c) Teachers and staff need to know something about their students' family makeup, immigration history, favorite activities, concerns, and strengths. Teachers should also be aware of their students' perceptions of the value of school and prior knowledge and experience of subjects taught.

d) Teachers and staff must be aware of intersections between race,

ethnicity, gender and social class; "[t]o develop sociocultural consciousness, teachers need to look beyond individual students and
families to understand inequities in society" (Villegas & Lucas,
2007, p. 31)." Teachers need to be aware of the role that schools
play in both perpetuating and challenging those inequities.

e) Teachers and staff must see themselves as part of a community of
educators working to make schools more equitable for all students.
Teaching is an ethical activity, and teachers have an ethical obligation to help all students learn. To meet this obligation, teachers
need to serve as advocates for their students, especially those who
have been traditionally marginalized in schools.

When I was the principal at Mariposa, we worked as a family to understand the cultural and social contexts of our students. As you and I have
spoken before, I especially led my staff to provide equitable education involving the creation of possibilities for students to experience high levels of
academic success. I feel I had success by assisting my staff to understand the
complexities of our students' lives. However, it could not be learned by feeling sorry for our students and it couldn't be learned by believing our students
were deficient! Instead, we learned to listen to, involve, and bring forth the
families' cultural wealth (Yosso, 2006). The most important element was assisting the staff to view the realities of racism, sexism, linguicism, classism,
and the many other oppressions. The staff and teachers first have to learn
about their own White privilege, and people get turned off when they first
hear about it because we are trained in our life to believe that all students, all
people in this country have equality. But this is the majoritarian lie! We are
not born equally and this is something I asked my staff to engage in learning as we did trainings to examine the structural and systemic inequities in
society. People are taught to compartmentalize their understandings to the
individual level, which makes us only compare their lives to those of their
students, but I show my staffs how to examine the structures that are operating all around us at the institutional and societal levels causing individual
inequity. This inequity must be intelligently deconstructed so that teachers
understand their White privilege and the history of our society, which has
advantaged some at the expense of others. Such White privilege creates a
stratified society. But I found you can't tell teachers this without their resistance; they have to be educated, especially about the history of education in
this society—it takes time and they have to be willing to learn, which is why
we examined many books. But it is not easy since many educators have not
had this deep learning in their teacher education programs. I wish this was
better taught when they are working on their teacher licensure. But like any
learning, we as educators must start where our students are.

I know we have talked about all of this in our summer meetings when you
were trying to decide to send your daughter to this dual language school.

As I look at the school scores from last year, 2012–2013,; I am amazed at what that little school is doing not only for the students with the highest needs in Desert City but also for high-achieving students. Now that I am not the Mariposa principal, and I have no dog in the fight, I can tell you with confidence that I believe that Mariposa is one of the best schools in Desert City. I believe that your daughter is receiving a quality education at Mariposa Elementary. Not to mention, the kinder curriculum, Tools of the Mind, is one of the best in the country because it allows the students to construct knowledge in meaningful ways that connect to their culture. Through such age-appropriate curriculum it allows students to express what is happening in their daily lives, connecting to stories they read, and providing a foundation to literacy. The first grade teachers continue using this curriculum and it allows both English and Spanish speakers to thrive in their reading and writing skills. I believe it is this curriculum that establishes the foundation to their ability to do so well when they take the third grade NCLB state assessments. This assessment is not a holistic assessment of student learning, but instead it is only one measure that counts in how schools are measured in this profit for testing industry (Ravitch, 2013). If educational leaders provide evidence of passing these tests, then school districts need to listen and learn about the culturally responsive techniques used to guide their students to academic resiliency. I know the Mariposa students not only performed excellently on those tests, but they were also learning in other culturally relevant measures; the teachers have high expectations of their students and we had a school culture of believing all students can succeed, and this happens when children, their families, and the teachers are working together.

In addition, please remember that dual language schools provide the best instruction for our English language learners (ELLs). Starting in kindergarten at Mariposa, students learn to transition between English and Spanish as one week the core subjects (math, literacy, social studies, and science) are taught in Spanish, and the next in English. The students are grouped together in their native language with the same literacy teacher throughout the school year. This second language block of instruction increases annually until your daughter and the other students are ready to negotiate content in both languages. It is my belief that if we have culturally responsive schools meeting the language needs of students where they are immersed in their first language to become fluent in their second language, it provides a solid base in both languages as they learn to read, write, and speak. The Spanish speakers will be peer models to assist your daughter to learn Spanish and she will be a peer model to assist the Spanish speakers to learn English. It is a reciprocal learning opportunity, creating a real sense of community in the classroom. They are also very culturally proficient, which is a valuable 21st century skill.

As far as the district is concerned, they must adhere to School of Choice because they follow NCLB. Mariposa is a neighborhood school and we have many parents choosing to "choice in" their child to attend Mariposa. We have a 20% "choice in rate." This means that people like you and your husband have chosen Mariposa because it offers a specialized program of dual language. Your choice in Mariposa means that you are "choicing out" of your own neighborhood school that you reside near. It is this "choice out" data that the district is basing a major reason to close Mariposa and the other four schools they believe may need to close. However, the district is not showing the "choice in" data of the five schools, and this is how districts will provide only half-truths to prove their reasons for closure.

All five of the schools are serving their clientele, but knowing Mariposa firsthand, I believe it must stay open to continue to foster the wonderful learning occurring for the students, especially the Spanish speakers. I know that I have written a telephone book of information here and I have so much more to say, but it is late and I must get some rest to best figure out how to tackle the challenges in my new school. Let's keep in touch and I will be happy to provide more details to assist in keeping this school open.

Take care!!!!

Dr. Martínez

The next evening, in the DSD school board meeting, I presented data from my research as well as details from Dr. Martínez's emails. The madam chair of the school board asked that we not repeat the same information and she would give warning when we met the three-minute time limit of speaking. As a coalition we improved as presenters at the school board meetings, and we learned quickly that we needed to do a better job of organizing our information prior to the meeting. Yet I was learning that this opportunity for social justice advocacy meant learning organically in the moment how best to advocate for and with our community. I spoke about the positive aspects of Mariposa that Dr. Martínez had shared with me:

1. The meaning of culturally responsive education according to Villegas and Lucas (2007) began my three minutes as Dr. Martinez's examples were utilized to show the connection between the instruction of the teachers seeking to understand the students' lives. I touched upon language and curriculum.

2. Next, I spoke about Mariposa's positive three-year AYP assessment ratings. I rhetorically asked the board members why AYP was not examined. I provided academic literature to show that the school closures in this country were being based on schools not meeting AYP, yet Mariposa had met this national NCLB AYP requirement for the past three years.

3. Lastly, I briefly touched upon how my daughter along with 20% of the Mariposa student body had "choiced in" to this school. I ques-

tioned why the district was only focusing on a 40% "choice out" rate but it was not countered by the "choice in" rate. I asked the board if they would choose such a permanent solution of closure based on utilizing only half of the school of choice evidence, especially when NCLB demands that "choice in" be offered in districts.

My entire testimony represented a counterstory as I provided competing perspectives to keep schools open rather than closed. The majoritarian story here regarding "choicing out" is a double standard that was not addressed by the district. Yet the school district and the board believed their presentation of criteria for closure was objective and neutrally supported by solid evidence. Dr. Martinez brought up irrefutable evidence in a note he wrote after this board meeting.

To: Antonette Aragon<culturallyrespond@smail.com>
From: Dr. José Martínez <Jose.Martínez@cityschool.edu>
Sent: Friday, October 15, 2013, 7:58 pm
Subject: More important arguments

Dear Antonette,
    I watched the school board meeting on the district channel (did you know it airs several times throughout the week?). You and the CASC provided many counterstories, and many strong arguments will need to be stated to advocate to keep the schools open. However, if you are going to win this nasty dog fight, I want to stress to you more evidence to present in the counter arguments regarding AYP as it relates to the five schools in the Desert District. Only two out of the five DSD schools slated for possible closure had not made AYP for three consecutive years. This is significant because the school district criteria for school closure did not include academic performance as a reason for closure as you had spoken about. You did an excellent job of rhetorically asking the board members why they were not including these data, and it is an important question to keep asking. Desert's schools are in a high-performing suburban school district within the state. An external review committee commissioned by the State Department of Education in the spring semester of 2013, my last semester serving as principal, determined information related to AYP:

> The district enjoys a reputation of solid levels of performance on a number of achievement measures and innovations, and ranks within the top quartile of school districts in the state.... [And] over the last five years with a range in 2013 of 45% to 81% of the students performing at proficient or advanced levels with variations among grade levels and/or the content area assessed. (State Department District Report, 2013)

The state department's committee presented data about the district meeting most of the needs of their students, and compared to other schools in the state, their performance was average to above average when looking at individual academic growth (State Department of Education, 2010). This state department committee determined that English language learners had their learning needs met, particularly in specialized schools, such as the dual language programs. However, in my opinion, and I could be wrong about this, the district did not want to fund two dual language programs. In other words, the other well-established dual language school has been operating for almost twenty years, and I believe they only want one of these schools, instead of fostering the cost of running two of these specialized language schools.

Consequently, the district knew that if they used AYP as part of the reasons for closing schools, they would not have an argument since three out of the five schools have made AYP. The two schools not making AYP only missed it by one year and so they too are making strides in their academic achievements as they have restructured. Mariposa as you pointed out did make AYP for three years. Therefore, the district chose not to use NCLB's standards to warrant closing schools based on academic performance. Enrollment was supposedly a more salient reason for closure because all five schools struggled with higher numbers of enrollment according to how it was defined by the district. Mi amiga, be sure to check out the State Department of Education Report (www. StateDepartmentofEducation.Desert-District_2013Report) and check out the district overall strong academic performance. The information you find will show evidence compared to what the district is revealing in this school closure process. It is in what is not said that shows the fuller picture of this counterstory.

Dr. Martínez

I had much to read, research, and examine in the State Department of Education Report, and Dr. Martínez's points were easily found in the report. We were entering November, the coalition continued to testify at the board meetings, and we continued to seek support regarding the strong performance of these schools.

We also continued to meet with each of the school board members individually. Our meetings with school board members were held at either a local nondenominational church or a coffee shop. One individual meeting with a school board member, Sally Hughes, served to provide information and answers to the coalition's questions and main points. As we talked with Sally, we explained that the state standards for reading, writing, and math were mostly adequate or going beyond proficient levels in the five schools on the closure list. We brought up many points and I asked why was it necessary to pursue closing schools if the schools were mostly meeting academic proficiency with their students. The board member used a bait-and-switch argument and did not completely answer my question. Instead, she reverted to enrollment levels and how many parents viewed these schools as undesirable for their children to attend, forcing lower populations at these schools. I was getting frustrated that Sally switched the subject. I recognized the majoritarian story told throughout many school districts across the nation regarding enrollment levels of closing schools. Sally was not stating the part of the majoritarian story that was most obvious to me, which was that White parents were choosing different schools. However, schools with large populations of students of color were being left behind due to inequitable funding, untrained teachers, and rigid curriculums. The interest of the Desert School District focused on the camouflaged ideology that supported the behaviors of White parents maintaining the power and privilege without the disruption of closure on their schools.

Anna, another coalition member, followed up Sally's comment with a question: If parents deemed these schools undesirable, do you think racism is a primary reason? The temperature of the room was cold and I thought Sally looked at Anna with a shivering lip as her smooth words trailed out of her mouth stating that racism has no part in this district or in this school closure process. Sally's answer showed a colorblind perspective, which is how most people tread when discussing the politicized topic of racism. Anna sat at the end of the table and I swear I could see steam coming out of her head as she just about stood up in disgust. But she grunted heavily and stated sternly, "Sally, racism is at the core of this whole school closure process but it is an elephant nobody wants to discuss." She further explained that in our city, privilege, power, and oppression operate as they do in all cities because White racism is at the root of how things work. It distorts how people look at people of color and low-income students, and there is bias against Latin@s in this town as they are viewed as having deficits that need to be fixed in their schools. If Latin@s were viewed without deficits, we would not be debating whether the schools with the most low-income students, particularly Latin@s in our district, should have their schools closed. The deficit perspective of Latin@s occurs because people receive limited information about these schools and they may barely perform at the low end of proficiency in our district, but they are performing well in the state. Anna stated that racism is covert and people do not realize it is happening but those with resources, powerful voices, and schools that are working optimally according to the institutional system or district rules receive the advantages and they are not the schools placed on such lists for closure. I was proud of Anna for putting words to the counterstory I was thinking. Anna's arguments reminded me of Beverly Tatum's (1992) definition of racism as a system of advantages and privileges provided to the dominant group in power while marginalizing oppressed groups in society. Furthermore, I expressed a counter argument about the majority of White parents who are utterly concerned with test scores while learning minimal information about schools based on limiting test scores. If the public knew that Latin@s in this district were leading the state in achievement according to the State Department of Education Report, they might find better reasons to attend these schools. Charli, the coalition leader, stated that the school district does not advertise to support these particular schools. Other schools are supported, but these schools seem to be overlooked or ignored. Sally's school board authority seemed frozen as our intent eyes waited for her response. She was quiet and did not address the coalition member's concerns with racism other than to say that she believes parents make decisions to send their children to schools based on many different factors.

That night, I wrote Dr. Martinez and let him know about this meeting. He responded with profound insights, particularly about how critical race theory and LatCrit may operationalize the interaction with Sally.

To: Antonette Aragon<culturallyrespond@smail.com>

From: Dr. José Martínez <Jose.Martínez@cityschool.edu>

Sent: Fri, October 25, 2013 11:45 pm

Subject: The frigid discussion with Sally

Dear Antonette,

In your meeting with Sally, it is obvious to people like you and me who study racism to understand Anna's centralized arguments. Anna recognizes the necessity to discuss racism as central to the school closure process. I taught my staff at Mariposa to examine Solórzano and Yosso (2002) when they state: "Unacknowledged White privilege helps maintain racism's story" (p. 27). In your meeting tonight, Sally does not acknowledge racism. Instead, she is colorblind to the discussion and rests her defense back on low enrollments. White privilege is not only unacknowledged, but it is invisible because it is deemed the norm (Solórzano & Yosso, 2002). Furthermore, simply by the dismissal of the coalition member's comments about racism, as a board member in a position of power, Sally further substantiates Solórzano and Yosso (2002) when they assert: "The unspoken discourse is that White communities are 'good' communities that house 'good' schools, and these 'good' places do not experience such tragedies. 'Other' communities, 'colored' communities, or those 'bad' communities are the ones who experience such events" (p. 28). I believe you will continue to receive little response by the school board members or the district officials to such discussions about racism. Yet because racism is at the core of this struggle, it must be addressed. No district or institution wants to face their racist actions, and by pointing it out, you may be onto something. I urge you to continue your efforts by writing letters to the local newspaper, building advocacy with the city and all other parties you are meeting with, as well as countering privilege, power, and oppression during school board meetings. In addition, ask the Latin@ community to speak at the upcoming school board meetings. I know you have had a good handful speaking, but get a large group in that board room. Such counterstories need to be stated.

Dr. Martínez

I took Dr. Martínez's advice to heart. When our coalition met, we decided to do all we could to invite the Spanish-speaking members in the community to speak at the school board meetings. We held our coalition meeting at the local Spanish-speaking church so more of the community could participate in our meetings. Some coalition members went door to door in the neighborhood inviting the Latin@ families to speak, and some of the teachers who attended the coalition meetings urged their students in the schools to speak at the board meetings.

We also encouraged them to come in large numbers during press conferences. In December, we had a press conference where the majority of the people in the audience were Latin@s. We wanted the school board to listen to the people who had the most to lose if closure prevailed.

I felt the Latin@ voices were strong and necessary to counter school closure. Yet not everyone in a meeting with many Spanish speakers would feel comfortable. In fact, one of the coalition members came to me after overhearing the school board president state in the bathroom that she was scared of having so many Spanish speakers in this meeting. I initially felt shocked by this White woman's fear and wondered why she was scared of a packed boardroom of Spanish speakers. I reflectively wondered if she anticipated no participation from the Latin@ community. Oftentimes, community members meet school closures with little resistance, since closures are completed with alacrity and little invitation is extended to the community to participate in such decisions. I spoke to Charli, the coalition leader about why she thought the board president was scared, and she let me know it made perfect sense to her since the board president had never been in a room with this many Spanish speakers. I agreed and felt the board president was insulated in a White world of existence where she does not have to think of people of color if she so chooses. Unfortunately, the board did not provide Spanish translators at this meeting or some of the other meetings, and they did not understand the words presented by the many Latin@ speakers.

In writing to Dr. Martínez after this incident, he reminded me that Charli and I were right.

To: Antonette Aragon<culturallyrespond@smail.com>
From: Dr. José Martínez <Jose.Martínez@cityschool.edu>
Sent: Tuesday, December 14, 2010 9:30 pm

Subject: The board president doesn't have to ever interact with Spanish
        speaking people if she doesn't want to . . .

Dear Antonette,

Remember, if White people choose to live in White neighborhoods, send their kids to White schools, and associate and have their primary relationships with Whites, they may easily do so without ever being in the presence of this many people of color (Bonilla-Silva, 2006; Johnson, 2006). They exude this afforded privilege. This too is why the majoritarian story about school closures exists. Most people in power making decisions about the fate of people of color in these school closure events have never been around to learn about people of color's social existence. In fact, my staff and teachers were shocked to learn that we live in a very segregated society today. Nieto and Bode (2012) state:

> At the same time that diversity in schools around the country is growing, racial and ethnic segregation has been on the rise. That is, students in U.S. schools are now more likely to be segregated from students of other races and backgrounds than at any time in the recent past. . . . Latinos are now the most segregated of all ethnic groups in terms of race, ethnicity, and poverty. Despite this trend, there is growing evidence that schools with diverse student populations are good for students of all backgrounds. (p. 29)

And at the same time of this racial segregation, the majority of this nation's teachers are white (82%, NCTE, 2013). But just like the experience tonight, there is a disconnect because White teachers, White board members, White principals, White district administrators have not taken the time to learn about the people of color in this country, let alone their own neighborhoods, districts, or classrooms.

Dr. Martínez

I responded immediately to his email. His points were critical to understanding the way White people never have to think, live, feel, understand a single element of people of color's lives. Yet White people are the majority who operate all facets of schooling and the disconnect between them and students of color is beyond the distance between the earth to the sun and back.

To: Dr. José Martínez Jose.Martínez@cityschool.edu
From: Antonette Aragon<culturallyrespond@smail.com>
Sent: Tuesday, December 14, 2013 9:45 pm
Subject: The board president doesn't have to ever interact with Spanish
        speaking people if she doesn't want to . . .

Dear Dr. Martínez,
    Tonight after the meeting, I sat and wrote this counter poem. I responded to this packed school board meeting overwhelmed by the distance between the White school board members, White district officials, White community that did not know, understand, or value the Spanish-speaking audience. I wrote:

"Ignored by the Board" (December 14, 2013)

Spanish is spoken, English is heard,
People are labeled, Spanish is blurred,
Spanish is heard; but the board ignored,
Spanish is spoken, English is heard,
Dismissing the marred,
Whose opportunities?
Whose doors open?
Who's visible?
Who's ignored?

Our interchange continued, as Dr. Martínez wrote immediately back to me.

To: Antonette Aragon<culturallyrespond@smail.com>
From: Dr. José Martínez <Jose.Martínez@cityschool.edu>
Sent: Tuesday, December 14, 2013 10:14 pm
Subject: The board president doesn't have to ever interact with Spanish speaking people if she doesn't want to . . .

Dear Antonette,
    Your counter poem is similar to Solórzano and Yosso (2002) when they explain that we must "challenge the perceived wisdom of those at society's center by providing a context to understand and transform established belief systems" (p. 36). Such commentary serves to provide insight about this school closure process. You display your participation and observation of a moment of time when the voices of Spanish speakers are distanced and ignored in a White racist boardroom where their words were not understood, absorbed, listened to, or acted upon because they speak a different language. The Spanish-speaking students, parents, and community members requested that their schools stay open but their requests fell on deaf ears without the use of translators. Yet you had reporters there for the press conference and this kind of spotlighting of a district is exactly what they don't want. This is the history of so many other school districts as they ignore the people they think they are most helping. Your poem reflects an analytical intuition based on bearing witness to a school board meeting where Latin@s were not acknowledged by the people claiming to help the most. Yet, continue to

squawk because the louder you become, and the more you insist on being heard, the more the district will listen; this is how coalition activism works. You have done much in this struggle to promote analysis and examination to counter the board and this district's stance against students of color. You and the coalition are doing outstanding work to present the centering of the Latin@ voices in this fight to stop closure.

I swiftly responded back to him because I felt on fire about our coalition work.

To: Dr. José Martínez Jose.Martinez@cityschool.edu

From: Antonette Aragon<culturallyrespond@smail.com>

Sent: Tuesday, December 14, 2013, 10:40 pm

Subject: The board president doesn't have to ever interact with Spanish speaking people if she doesn't want to . . .

Dear Dr. Martínez,

As a Latina scholar, I promote analysis and evaluation examining the ideology of White privilege in operation, and this is how critical race scholars operate. But tonight my heart is heavy as I felt our people's words lay on deaf ears. The voices of the Latin@s held strong in affirmation and empowerment in countering the ignorance of the board, yet there was no effort by the district to provide translation and the people who most needed to hear the message of our gente (people) did not choose to do everything they could to understand. This makes me so angry and mad that the disconnect is beyond an ocean wide.

Dialogue is the lifeblood of democracy. Democracy without genuine dialogue is artificial and hollow (Friere, 1976). The critical resistance spoken by the Latin@ community is necessary to halt such school closure processes. But first, the board members must ensure translation services in order to understand this dialogical process.

We only have a month before this journey ends, and I hope tonight made some kind of impact on the people in power who will vote on the fate of the Latin@ community. However, I feel discouraged and angry that racist action is prevailing at the heart of this fight.

Antonette

Dr. Martínez offered a final email in this fervent email exchange. He so eloquently captured the essence of systemic racism as illuminated by the theory of CRT/LatCrit and practiced in this systemic school closure processs.

To: Antonette Aragon<culturallyrespond@smail.com>

From: Dr. José Martínez <Jose.Martínez@cityschool.edu>

Sent: Tuesday, December 14, 2010 11:45 pm

Subject: The board president doesn't have to ever interact with Spanish
speaking people if she doesn't want to . . .

Dear Antonette,

As we both know, race and racism are at the systemic core of this country,
our neighborhoods, and our schools. It is in the ideologies, epistemologies,
laws, and power dynamics of actions and educational practices. I read a
Facebook post by the Latino author who writes about matters of racism,
Eduardo Bonilla-Silva (2015), and I agree with his stance:

> The maintenance of white supremacy via the defense of white space
> is a collective [systemic] white project . . . . The defense of white turf in
> stores, neighborhoods, parks, churches, jobs, etc. involves ALL whites.
> After all, no social system based /rooted in domination can be repro-
> duced by the actions of the few. Thus, neither the Klan nor the police
> are the reason why our racial order remains in place. Our post-racial
> racist system exists through the behavior, cognitions, and practices of
> nice, good whites. It is them who patrol borders, enforce white norms,
> and discipline folks of color most of the time. It is them who in jobs
> keep us in "our place." . . . It is time to let whites who walk around as
> self-proclaimed saints know that racism exists not because of the Klan
> or the police, but because of THEM. They are responsible for the pro-
> duction and reproduction of white privilege. Period.

And that "ick" anger you feel is precisely why you do the work you do! This
is the way our society operates in white racism. What the school board members and leaders of the DSD school district don't understand is the complexity of how such a closure will displace the students in schools that are not
set up to culturally respond to them. They surely showed a lack of respect
for their language tonight because they didn't have a means to understand
their words. Such lack of respect comes easy when they believe they can
close schools and then send the native Spanish speakers to schools that are
producing stronger AYP measures, but they are not equipped with Spanish
speaking teachers to assist Spanish speaking achievement. You might ask
me, what must be changed? Schools and districts must understand the vital
cultural life force of their students to meet their social, cultural, and language needs. The five schools slated for closure are meeting the social, cultural, and language needs of their students, but the grass is always greener
elsewhere especially when districts across the country are on fire to close
schools according to laws such as NCLB, promising to provide a trend that
seems to be an answer. But closed schools will only mean the failure of

students of color and their neglected achievement. School districts are closing schools; districts do not create school climates that meet the needs of incoming displaced students from closed schools because they don't truly care to know their students most influenced by closure, which is a vicious cycle leaving children behind.

Keep strong! Stay encouraged and continue on! You have time to make the impact to stop closure.

Dr. Martínez

FINALE: ENDING SCHOOL CLOSURE

This school closure process was supported by the majoritarian story in the United States under NCLB legislation to close failing schools. Yet the Latin@ community, the coalition members of CASC, and constituents contending to keep these schools open, deplored the ramifications of another school closing and contributed to the propensity of integrating the values of social justice against closing achieving schools. On January 25, the last Desert School District board meeting debating school closure ended as the coalition, Latin@ community, and constituents victoriously succeeded in keeping the five schools open (Aragon, 2014b). Focusing on the inquiry of normative arguments found in the NCLB policy, reform, and practice, I worked as a social justice activist scholar with our coalition and the Latin@ community to argue, present, create, and develop ways to highlight the dialectical reasoning to keep these schools open to serve their primarily large populations of low-income Latin@ students.

CRT and LatCrit call upon educational leaders deeply bound to the politics of negative policy implications, such as school closure sanctioned through NCLB, to commit to the liberation and praxis of compassion for their students and staff, guiding them with an ethic of care through culturally responsive and transformative techniques. In this counterstory, Dr. José Martínez surfaces as my alter ego to reveal the ways school principals may engage in learning with their staffs about systemic racism and other oppressions affecting their lives and their students. Dr. Martínez reflexively displays high expectations of Latin@ students, while affirming their Spanish language through dual language instruction. He recognizes his educational leadership must abate the odds of his students' personal failure in the milieu of the collective disregard in the system of racist education, responding through culturally transformative education and emancipation of his students. He challenges the majoritarian status quo notions of racism that his students of color fail and produces results through elevated levels of academic achievement, utilizing culturally responsive techniques that honor and nurture the language, ethnicity, and cultural wealth and assets of his students, families, and community.

In reality, Dr. José Martínez partially represents an educational leader who left the summer prior to learning about the possible closure of Mariposa. Leading for five years, he promoted academic achievement in the nexus of transformative cultural responsive techniques. His ardor for his students, staff, and community and thriving leadership became irrevocably lost when closure supervened. Yet neutral policy practices of school closures may avert the leaders who imbibe and live in the communities of their students and families, understanding the intersectional implications of race on achievement, and the role of social class in shaping opportunity, knowing how to structure and operate.

I document in this counterstory my journey showing my action clarified through CRT and LatCrit dedicated to social justice. My journey began with the examination and analysis of a set of concepts, ideas, and experiences deconstructing and denunciating the layers of systemic neutral, natural, and normative racist practices set in motion to detrimentally castigate Latin@ students from lower socioeconomics if closure succeeded.

CRT and LatCrit reveal the moniker of present day closures shaped by NCLB policy producing failing schooling systems in our purported post-racial society. Such educational normative policies as NCLB regulate what, how, and by whom educational decisions and practices are determined (Basile & Lopez, 2015). School boards may close schools under NCLB legislative mandates utilizing deficit cultural beliefs and assumptions while utilizing technical arguments such as *objective* enrollment data without fully listening or debating the ramifications relegating further racial disparities within a district. Such *objective* enrollment data becomes a technical approach to proposed equity, but schools end up closing and children are left further behind because White privilege is an endemic ideology of the educational system.

Efforts to redress policies and strategies of White privilege often encounter powerful practices that sustain exclusion. When school boards open their doors to listen to all community members yet lack translation services to understand the Spanish speakers, it presents the type of insular methods producing and reproducing White privilege. The context of the DSD school closure process had a strong Latin@ community network working toward transformational resistance to keep these schools open. Furthermore, the White board members' inability to understand the message of the Spanish-speaking resistors promoted persistent vocal presence and community commitment at the board meetings. The human agency and resistance is empowered through the activism of the Spanish-speaking community and is evident in the final vote to keep the schools open. Such action interrupted the ramifications of another school closing in this nation adding to the already thousands upon thousands of displaced low-income students of color in crowded schools that are not prepared to take them (de la Torre & Gwynne, 2009; Kirshner et al., 2010; NOLC, 2013); closure translates into disastrous academic, social, and economic outcomes for students of color (Kirshner & Pozzoboni, 2011). CRT and LatCrit display the importance of Latin@s to transformationally resist at the intersection of language and cultural rights (Solórzano & Delgado Bernal, 2001). CRT and LatCrit operationalize our knowledge-generated conceptions specific for the purpose of addressing and ameliorating conditions of systemic oppression, poverty, and inequitable education.

NOTES

1. All names (including names of the district, schools, people, and the coalition) have been changed to maintain confidentiality.
2. Please note that José Martínez's character is based on a principal that the author knew and worked with; however, the muse in the counterstory is fictionalized.
3. Latin@ is a constructed ethnically descriptive term and is used in this chapter to include women and men who are Hispanic, Mexican, Spanish speaking, or who have immigrated from Latin American countries (Espino, Leal, & Meier, 2008).

REFERENCES

Akintunde, O. (1999). White racism, White privilege, and the social construction of race: Moving from a modernist to postmodernist multicultural education. *Multicultural Perspectives, 1*(4), 2–8.

Alter, T. (2013). "It felt like community": Social movement unionism and the Chicago Teachers Union strike of 2012. Chicago Teacher's Union strike! *Labor: Studies in Working-Class History of the Americas, 10*(3), 11–25. DOI 10.1215/15476715-2149461

Aragon, A. (2014a). *Chicana feminist epistemology: Reclamation of our schools, disrupting school closure.* Manuscript in revision.

Aragon, A. (2014b). *Keeping schools open: Critical race inquiries by a Chicana activist.* Manuscript in revision.

Basile, V. & Lopez, E. (2015). And still I see no changes: Enduring views of Students of Color in science and mathematics education policy reports. *Science Education, 99*(3), 519–548.

Bell, D. (1987). *And we are not saved: The elusive quest for racial justice.* New York, NY: Basic Books.

Berry, K. S., & Herrington, C. D. (2011). States and their struggles with NCLB: Does the Obama Blueprint get it right? *Peabody Journal of Education 86,* 272–290. doi: 10.1080/0161956X.2011.578982

Bonilla-Silva, E. (2006). *Racism without racists: color-blind racism and the persistence of racial inequality in the United States.* 2nd ed. Lanham, MD: Rowman & Littlefield.

Bonilla-Silva, E. [Eduardo]. (2015, June 9). What's new, if anything, in the McKinney, TX, incident? It is not police brutality and misbehavior. And it is certainly not the police role in maintaining racial control. [Facebook status update]. Retrieved from https://www.facebook.com/eduardo.bonillasilva.7/posts/10153442381994668

Darling-Hammond, L. (2007). Evaluating 'No Child Left Behind.' *The Nation, 284*(20), 11–18. Retrieved from http://www.thenation.com/doc/20070521/darling-hammond/print?rel=nof

de la Torre, M., & Gwynne, J. (2009). *When schools close: Effects on displaced students in Chicago public schools.* Consortium on Chicago School Research, University of Chicago. (ERIC Document Reproduction Service No. ED 506 954). Retrieved from http://ccsr.uchicago.edu/

DeLeon, A. P. (2010). How do I begin to tell a story that has not been told? Anarchism, autoethnography, and the middle ground. *Equity & Excellence in Education, 43*(4), 398–413. doi: 10.1080/10665684.2010.512828

Delpit, L. D. (2012). *Multiplication is for white people: Raising expectations for other people's children.* New York, NY: New Press. Retrieved from http://www.CSU.eblib.com/EBLWeb/patron/?target=patron&extendedid=P_844470_0

Engberg, J., Gill, B., Zammaro, G., & Zimmer, R. (2012). Closing schools in a shrinking district: Do student outcomes depend on which schools are closed? *Urban Economics, 71,* 189–203.

Espino, R., Leal, D. L., & Meier, K. J. (Eds.) (2008). *Latino politics: Identity, mobilization, and representation.* Charlottesville, VA: University of Virginia Press.

Freire, P. (1976). *Education: The practice of freedom.* London, UK: Writers and Readers Publishing Cooperative.

Giroux, H. (2013). *America's education deficit and the war on youth: Reform beyond electoral politics.* New York, NY: Monthly Review Press.

Globalet, J. (2005). *The school closure crisis: A challenge for demographers.* Retrieved from www.demographers.com/SchoolClosureCrisis/pdf

González, N., Moll, L. C., & Amanti, C. (2005). *Funds of knowledge: Theorizing practices in households, communities, and classrooms.* Mahwah, NJ: Erlbaum.

Johnson, A. G. (2006). *Privilege, power, and difference.* New York, NY: McGraw-Hill.

Kim, J. S., & Sunderman, G. L. (2007). Measuring academic proficiency under the No Child Left Behind Act: Implications for educational equity. *Educational Researcher, 34*(8), 3–13. doi: 10.3102/0013189X034008003

Knaus, C. B. (2007). Still segregated, still unequal: Analyzing the impact of No Child Left Behind on African American students. *State of Black America 2007: Portraits of a Black Male,* 105–121. Washington, DC: National Urban League.

Knaus, C. B., & Rogers-Ard, R. (2012). Educational genocide: Examining the impact of national education policy on African American communities. *ECI Interdisciplinary Journal for Legal and Social Policy, 2*(1). Retrieved from http://ecipublications.org/ijlsp/vol2/iss1/1

Kirshner, B., Gaertner, M., & Pozobonni, K. (2010). Tracing Transitions: The effect of high school closure on displaced students. *Educational Evaluation and Policy Analysis 32*(3), 407–429. doi: 10.3102/0162373710376823

Kirshner, B., & Pozzoboni, K. M. (2011). Student interpretations of a school closure: Implications for student voice in equity-based school reform. *Teachers College Record, 113*(8), 1633–1667.

Kim, J. S., & Sunderman, G. L. (2005). Measuring academic proficiency under the No Child Left Behind Act: Implications for educational equity. *Educational Researcher, 34*(8), 3–13. doi: 10.3102/0013189X034008003

Kretchmar, K. (2014). Democracy (In)Action: A critical policy analysis of New York City public school closings by teachers, students, administrators, and community members. *Education and Urban Society, 46*(1), 3–29.

Leonardo, Z. (2013). *Race frameworks: A multidimensional theory of racism and education.* New York, NY: Teachers College Press.

Lipman, P., & Haines, N. (2007). From accountability to privatization and African American exclusion: Chicago's "Renaissance 2010." *Educational Policy, 21*(3), 471–502.

National Opportunity to Learn Campaign (NOLC). (2013). Debunking the myths of school closures. Retrieved from http://www.otlcampaign.org/blog/2013/04/05/color-school-closures

NCTE, (2013). Complete reference information not provided to maintain confidentiality.

Nieto, S., & Bode, P. (2012). *Affirming diversity: The sociopolitical context of multicultural education* (6th ed.). Boston, MA: Pearson.

Oakes, J., & Rogers, J. (2006). *Learning power: Organizing for education and justice.* New York, NY: Teachers College Press.

Pérez Huber, L. (2009). Challenging racist nativist framing: Acknowledging the community cultural wealth of undocumented Chicana college students to reframe the immigration debate. *Harvard Educational Review, 79*(4), 704–729.

Ravitch, D. (2013). *Reign of error: The hoax of the privatization movement and the danger to America's public schools.* New York, NY: Alfred A. Knopf.

Samuels, C. A. (2011). School closings no fiscal savior, study cautions. *Education Week, 31*(10), 1–13.

School District Website. (2010). Complete reference information not provided to maintain confidentiality.

Solórzano, D. G., & Delgado Bernal, D. (2001). Examining transformational resistance through a Critical Race and LatCrit Theory framework: Chicana and Chicano students in an urban context. *Urban Education, 36*(3), 308–342.

Solórzano, D. G., & Yosso, T. J. (2002). Critical race methodology: Counter-storytelling as an analytical framework for education research. *Qualitative Inquiry, 8*(1), 23–44.

Sunderman, G. L., & Payne, A. (2009, December). *Does closing schools cause educational harm? A review of the research.* Bethesda, MD: Mid-Atlantic Equity Center.

State Department of Education. (2013). Complete reference information not provided to maintain confidentiality.

Tatum, B. D. (1992). Talking about race, learning about racism: The application of racial identity development theory. *Harvard Educational Review, 62*(1), 1.

Valencia, R. R. (2010). *Dismantling contemporary deficit thinking.* New York, NY: Routledge.

Valencia, R. R., & Black, M. S. (2002). "Mexican Americans don't value education!"—On the basis of the myth, mythmaking, and debunking. *Journal of Latinos & Education, 1*(2), 81–103.

Villegas, A., & Lucas, T. (2007). The culturally responsive teacher. *Educational Leadership, 64*(6), 28–33.

Villalpando, O. (2004). Practical consideration of critical race theory and Latino critical theory for Latino college students. *New Directions for Student Services, 105,* 41–50.

Volche, D. (2013). Over-represented and under-served: Mitigating the impact of school closures on English language learners (ELLs). Retrieved from http://afterbloomberg.commons.gc.cuny.edu/files/2013/04/Voloch.pdf

Winslow, S. (2013). In Chicago and Philadelphia, closing schools and funding charters. *Labor News.* Retrieved from http://www.labornotes.org/2013/09/chicago-and-philadelphia-closing-schools-and-funding-charters

Wisniewski, M. (2013, May 22). Chicago board approves largest school closing. *Chicago Tribune.* Retrieved from http://articles.chicagotribune.com/2013-05-22/news/sns-rt-us-usa-education-chicago-votebre94l15p-20130522_1_karen-lewis-elementary-schools-chicago-board

Yosso, T. (2005). Whose culture has capital? A critical race theory discussion of community cultural wealth. *Race Ethnicity and Education 8*(1), 69–91.

Yosso, T. J. (2006). *Critical race counterstories along the Chicana/Chicano educational pipeline.* New York, NY: Routledge.

Zavadsky, H. (2012). *School turnarounds: The essential role of districts.* Cambridge, MA: Harvard Education Press.

Zachary, E. (2011). *Young people speak out on the impact of closing schools.* Providence, RI: Brown University, Annenburg Institute for School Reform.

PART III

TEACHING AND LEADING

PART III

CHAPTER 7

TRANSFORMATIVE LEADERSHIP AND CREATING CONDITIONS TO EMPOWER STUDENTS MARGINALIZED BY LOW ACADEMIC EXPECTATIONS

Daniel D. Liou
Arizona State University

René Antrop-González
Dalton State College

"You won't be able to go to college. You are dreaming too big," and "Your destiny is the military" are comments that were told to us by our high school guidance counselors as we approached our final years of high school. For the first author, it was already a journey to be the first in his family to ever graduate from high school, but his mother continued to stress college as the best way for his family to climb out of poverty. Growing up in a single parent household and the experience of taking care of his younger brothers

Envisioning Critical Race Praxis in K–12 Leadership Through Counter-Storytelling, pages 141–162
Copyright © 2016 by Information Age Publishing
141

reinforced the importance of continuing his education beyond high school. As his counselor told him college was out of his reach, he also pondered the reasons for the first author's aspirations to go to college and asked him, "Have you taken your A–F requirements?" referring to the courses required to matriculate into the University of California system. Like many low-income first-generation and immigrant students, it was the first time he realized that high school graduation does not automatically make him eligible for college admission. After spending three years in the vocational track in high school, he suddenly found himself rushing to take courses that would make him college eligible. Like the time his father left his family, there was a feeling of being abandoned and without an advocate at his school.

Even though our respective conversations with our guidance counselors would linger with us to this present day, we finally have the chance to reflect upon these moments and the ways they have shaped our identities as faculty members at the university. We realized that our guidance counselors had very different academic expectations about what we were capable of in high school, so we lingered in lower-tracked classrooms without being aware of its consequences. For Daniel, this meant a two-year placement in a class called "retail merchandise" where he was taught to use the cash register and sell sporting goods. Daniel had no idea that the lower-track classroom was a dead end to his dreams of going to college. On the other hand, the advanced level classes were always being discussed as a place only for the so-called "smart kids," not someone like him whose everyday reality was far from those of White upper-middle-class kids from the hills.

We also realized how endemic and destructive low academic expectations have been to others, especially for students who come from low income and immigrant backgrounds who attended school where they are expected to learn very little. This included Daniel's African American classmates in the lower-track classrooms, where the boys are repeatedly being written up for referrals and suspensions. Daniel remembers how his Spanish teacher, a light skin Chicano, used to shout, "Escuchen!" at students who failed miserably every time when he needed their attention. In fact, the level of classroom disruption usually escalated the more the teacher raised his voice. He also remembers how his history teacher, an African American man who has taught in the district for 35 years, showed movies every day as he sat and read the newspaper. That year, he also served as the department chair, and who would ask for his removal since the class got to watch all sorts of movies without doing any work? It was obvious that he did not care if anyone was paying attention to the film, as long they remained quiet. Daniel also remembers the English teacher who would spend more time writing referrals to send African American students out of her classroom than to find ways to keep them on task and interested in the curriculum." Don't be like the other ones," she told him. Then she suggested that good behavior would qualify as passing for her class. The perception of Daniel as a model minority in a lower-track classroom was already an oxymoron, but it was also this contradiction that rendered his needs invisible. Daniel also remembers the chemistry teacher who insisted on giving him an "F" grade for not understanding the course materials due to his difficulties with the English language. The chemistry teacher believed he was going to learn how to become more accountable for the class by giving an F instead of letting him know where he could access help on the homework assignments. The issue was never about a lack of will to do the work but a matter of understanding the materials in order to reach mastery.

René vividly remembers his geometry teacher never teaching, but spending much time flirting with the popular young women in class. In our two decades of observing life in urban classrooms, the struggle to understand has been the case for many students who have fallen behind. For us, it was already difficult to make it through the day, so it was troubling to know that we had to navigate high school without anyone caring if we graduated or dropped out of the educational system. When students face these learning conditions with regularity, their interactions with teachers are often a sign of widespread ineffectiveness at the systemic level.

Once we became K–12 practitioners, we began to understand how problems associated with low academic expectation are far worse than imagined. We wanted to be advocates for those who were cast in the shadows of low expectations without a voice but in need of being heard. Low expectations often suggest to students in overt and subtle ways that failure is inevitable and students' needs are beyond what anyone at the school can do to help. In turn, students are taught to pull their bootstraps to meet higher expectations or let failure to define who they are. Many of our former teachers would declare that they had high expectations for their students, but the way it was often communicated came across fundamentally different from its intent.

For example, many of our high school teachers would simply yell at students, suggesting they would end up in jail if they did not pay attention in class. These hypothetical threats did little to let students know that they were being respected and cared for. It was only when we entered college that we began to interrogate these messages and realize how our first-hand experiences with low expectations in classrooms informed our ways of thinking about the inequitable distribution of educational opportunities. We find it ironic that our respective meeting with our high school counselors would lead us to closely examine this issue, but epistemologically it makes sense since our experiences with schooling have been completely different from those who benefited from it.

The purpose of this chapter is to highlight some of the problems of school expectations for students' academic success and examples of leadership practices that contribute to meaningful school reform. First and foremost, it is imperative for school leaders to have theoretical groundings in their professional commitments. We say this in the context where some students in principal preparation programs do not see the practicality of critical theories. One day, Daniel received an email from a student suggesting that he would "spit on the next reading assignment that talks about theory."

In this chapter, we intend to provide leadership examples grounded in theories to show how we have engaged in school reform that enables young people who have experienced low academic expectations in the classroom to critique and act upon them. We employ a race lens due to years of witnessing how race, ethnicity, and language are central in high school students' understanding of schooling in the U.S. context. We apply these frameworks to describe the extent to which we had to negotiate the realities of race, ethnicity, and language in order to effectively serve students in the school. This standpoint allows for the examination of teacher expectations as the mechanisms that shape one's self-concept as citizen and place in school and society.

GUIDING QUESTIONS

By definition, teacher expectations refer to the use of personal and formal assessments of students as predictors of their future probability of academic success (Liou & Rotheram-Fuller, 2016; Milner, 2012a). This work is important because there is concrete evidence that teachers' low expectations for students can induce poor academic performance (Cooper & Tom, 1983). It is clear that teachers' expectations for students have tremendous power in influencing the classroom environment and relationships with students (Cooper & Tom, 1983). However, over the years, we have also seen students who refused to succumb to these expectations and were able to navigate the school system to accomplish their aspirations and dreams. It would be a mistake to not account for students' abilities to navigate the educational system, and therefore, it is imperative that we have discussions about how to effectively serve students who have been socialized by low expectations in their classroom. In this chapter, we begin with the following guiding questions to initiate a conversation with school leaders about effective schools from the perspectives of expectations at the systemic level:

1. What are the frameworks that are helpful to prepare school leaders to address the problems of low academic expectations in the classroom?
2. How can these frameworks be put into action to initiate the change process to transform schools?
3. How can the change process inform school leaders to further theorize the problem of low academic expectations from the perspective of school reform?

REVIEW OF RELEVANT LITERATURE

Research clearly suggests that students of color, regardless of social and economic status, continue to face widespread problems of low teacher expectations (Conchas & Clark, 2002; Diamond, 2004; Stuart Wells & Crain, 1997). The issue exacerbates the condition that already exists in struggling schools that relate to teacher and resource shortages in the urban context (Howard, 2003). As a form of intervention, the No Child Left Behind Act (NCLB) was put into place to ensure accountability of high expectations in every classroom. However, more than a decade later, the goal remains unrealized while teachers' expectations of students continue to vary across student populations based on race and social class (Liou & Rotheram-Fuller, 2016; Milner, 2012b). Some have argued that NCLB was undermined by the lack of funding mechanisms reserved to assist students to meet new standards (Welner & Weitzman, 2005). However, as a nation we have not yet come to terms with the destructive nature of low expectations, the belief of who is likely to be a good student, and how to address this deep-seated problem through school leadership. Although NCLB has brought wider attention to the problems of low expectations, school leaders have yet to engage this body of research to inform their leadership practices and reform efforts.

The literature on teacher expectations has convincingly documented the inseparable relationships between teacher quality, expectations of students, and achievement outcomes (Brophy & Good, 1974). While there has been progress made in determining the attributes of a highly qualified teacher and defining student achievement, a deeper conversation about teacher quality and their impact on low-income students of color are sorely missing in our policy debate about school reform. This body of research has been robust over the years, but recent inquiries have been sparse with limited analysis at the organizational level. As one of the most important but also deeply neglected research areas of our times, the literature has pointed to the impact teacher expectations have on pedagogy (Becker, 1952) and styles of communication in the classroom (Woolfolk & Brooks, 1983). Regardless of teachers' racial and ethnic backgrounds, researchers have pointed to both conscious and unconscious beliefs that teachers often subscribe to in middle class White students' academic superiority and the disbelief in the educability of low-income students of color (Foster, 1997; Lipman, 1993; Noguera, 2003). While federal provisions have been put into place to hire better teachers, low-income students of color are still disproportionally impacted by under-qualified teachers in struggling schools (Darling-Hammond, 1996a; 1996b; Darling-Hammond & Sykes, 2003; Howard, 2003).

Furthermore, Howard Becker (1952) found that teachers in urban schools have lower expectations and a less demanding pedagogy than their counterparts in White suburban schools. Subsequent studies confirm that teacher expectations of students are a major factor in differential student achievement (Rist, 1970; Rosenthal & Jacobson, 1968), and these differences have been consistently linked to students' race, class, and gender at all levels of education (Ambady, Shih, Kim, & Pittinsky, 2001; Rist, 1970; Solorzano & Solorzano, 1995; Steele, 1997; Steele & Aronson, 1995). As a result, students' ability to receive resources and opportunities to learn are implicated by teachers' expectations and assessments of their progress and educability (Oakes, 1985; Rosenthal & Jacobson, 1968; Solorzano & Ornelas, 2002). In effect, teachers' expectations for students are influenced by the following visual markers: students' previous grades and track record of behavior, the teacher's previous encounter with the student's older siblings or those who act remarkably similar, other colleagues' accounts of interactions with the student, initial impressions from meeting with the student and family members, and personal attitudes toward people who look, speak, and dress differently from them (Rist, 1970). Although much of the literature has discussed the salience of teacher expectations in teacher–student interactions, recent studies have increasingly shown patterns where teacher expectations have influenced student access to course placement and resources that have direct impacts on their future social and economic mobility (Oakes, 1985; Rosenthal, 1974; Solorzano & Ornelas, 2004).

The problem with these patterns is the fact that academic performance can have influence when students internalize the expectations of their teachers (Merton, 1968). Thomas' theorem (1928) suggests that a person's definition of her or his situation has a profound impact on his or her experiences in what is perceived as reality. Applying this idea to the school context, there is no greater impact on a student's perception of reality in the classroom and the conditions that exist to shape how they relate with the teacher, peers, the subject matter, and a sense of collective purpose in the classroom. To date, it is still unclear about how the problem of low expectations for students can be addressed through school leadership. Invariably, an examination at the systemic level through leadership praxis is warranted. Moreover, an examination of the salience of race and ethnicity at the organizational level is necessary when it comes to how students interpret norms and expectations that define acceptable behaviors and academic engagement. Despite its flaws, the design of NCLB to tackle "soft bigotry" shows that racism is a reality and is central to the problem of low expectations in classrooms.

THEORETICAL FRAMEWORKS

This work is grounded in two theoretical frameworks: critical race theory and transformative leadership. Although the study of school expectations is a severely under-researched area, it can nonetheless extend school leaders' understandings of its challenges from a systemic perspective. David Stovall (2004) argues that the examination of racism that reduces it to individual behaviors is insufficient without recognizing the structural conditions that justify the social meanings of race. To this end, Rhona Weinstein (2002) argues for a school-wide analysis of expectations so it can effectively tackle school leaders' shared thinking about the educability of students. From a reform standpoint, the role of school leaders to create conditions to support the praxis of high expectations is critical to how students learn in every classroom. Just as important, it is imperative for school leaders to counteract learning conditions that reinforce the racial ideologies of academic achievement that perceive race and class as predictive typologies for learning outcomes. This includes both conscious and unconscious behaviors that reinforce the hierarchies of race, intelligence, and the imagined educability of students.

To underscore the importance of leadership driven by a set of purpose to transform school and society, Michael Dantley (2003) stated the role of school leadership consists of providing the capacity and technical skills to fight for social justice, critique hegemonic school structures, and participate in the work of social transformation. Carolyn Shields (2009; 2010) pointed to the different levels of leadership engagements in the school context: transactional leadership, transformational leadership, and transformative leadership. In order for school leaders to pursue justice, they must take into account the social justice context of students, and actively address the inequitable conditions within and outside of the classroom to assist students towards a higher level of achievement (Shields, 2010). In this chapter, transformative leaders are those who are working beyond higher test scores and normative measures of achievement, but they ask questions about how can student learning be informed by, and contribute to the social justice context of the community? There is an urgent need for school leadership to go beyond "business as usual" that makes low expectations for students a normal part of the school day. Rounaq Jahan (1999) observed,

> The disenfranchised are no longer willing to put up with such "business as usual" politics. They are looking for a very different kind of politics and governance. And they want a very different type of leadership. A discussion on transformative leadership and transformative politics is, thus, very timely at this critical moment in our history. (p. 2)

In retrospect, we need school leaders to have a sense of urgency in responding to our students' aspirations instead of treating them as another number in their caseload. To this day, many schools have not changed their attitudes of complacency to meet the needs of children. Some may contemplate this as a case of not having the resources. However, what is more important is whether school leaders have the political will to respond to the call for educational equity and assume attitudinal, pedagogical, and technical responsibilities for student learning. For example, one of the critical elements within the school that does not require additional resources is the issue of governance. As Jahan (1999) noted, school systems need the kind of leadership that will bring forward the kind of politics that will put students and their needs at the center of governance. Hence, the social justice dimension in this work exists in the literature and is fundamentally different from NCLB that has since produced a testing culture that has failed to address the legacy and sustainability of presumed educability across race and other observable markers.

To engage in this social justice work, the role of school leadership in tackling the bigotry of low expectations is paramount and an enduring challenge. David Stovall (2004) observed,

> At this moment, it's fair to say that social justice agendas in schools are a hard sell. It's considerably easier to do what you're told. Going "against the grain" is not received with accolades of achievement. In sum, school administrators with social justice agendas find themselves immersed in the balancing act of meeting the needs of students, while resisting mandated "drill and kill" policies that only measure how well a student takes a test. (p. 8)

Stovall's observations put school leaders at a crossroad where bureaucracy and the pressure to raise test scores conflict with efforts to level the playing field. Applying Derrick Bell's (2004) theory of interest convergence, school leaders must recognize that school policies and procedures are not neutral but embedded in a belief system that guides its articulations and implementations. The premise for this presumed conflict of interests puts a limit to equity-related reform efforts to only function within and to the benefits of the existing belief system that perpetuates differences in expectations and outcomes. This is especially true when the transformation of inequitable conditions necessitates the alterations of benefits and privileges afforded to those that have always historically benefitted from a discriminatory system of practice. Meaningful reform becomes fundamentally difficult for school leaders in the change process, but equally important is the change in the belief system that functions to resist and maintain its ideology and relations of power.

Reform initiatives that solely target student behaviors without changing school leaders' belief systems are examples of interest convergence that do not radically change that structure that differentiates expectations for students. Therefore, educators should perceive the call for leadership as a task of social justice. Colleen Larson and Khaula Murtadha (2005, p. 135) asked, "If administrators or teachers do not believe that promoting equity and justice through the policies and practices they enforce in schools is their job, whose job is it?" We posit that combating the racial ideology of academic achievement is one of the critical social justice issues in education. Therefore, it is imperative for school leaders to come together to collectively reflect, theorize, and envision a plan of action to counteract against raced, classed, and gender-based expectations for students (Jean-Marie & Normore, 2008).

CRITICAL RACE THEORY AS LEADERSHIP PRAXIS

Despite the robust teacher expectations literature, the topic remains under-theorized from the standpoint of race and the racial ideology of superiority in academic achievement. School leaders must be reminded of the legacy of the eugenics movement, which had a large influence in educational policy and school leaders' attitudes towards students (Shelden, 1999). Shelden's work also points to the large extent that biology played a large part in how people viewed intelligence and abilities during that historical period and the extent to which social policies steered towards giving advantages to those deemed as biologically superior.

Critical race theory (CRT) in education plays a critical role in shaping this new body of scholarship in educational leadership. Educational researchers have pointed to the origins of critical race theory in legal scholarship (Ladson-Billings & Tate, 1995; Parker & Villalpando, 2007), which uncovers the ways in which racial inequities based upon property rights, citizenship, and presumed colorblindness in the law are also part and parcel of education policy and practice. Although some scholars have extended this analysis into education from a structural and symbolic analysis of Whiteness and property, the application of this work in the school context still needs to expand further into the examination of racial attitudes and academic expectations for students. Connecting this work to the topic of school reform, Seymour Sarason (1990) argues that change initiatives are doomed to fail if they do not tackle inequitable systems from the perspective of school culture. To this end, leadership praxis must be perceived as the work of culture to reject the normalization of student failure from biological and cultural explanatory lenses (see Solorzano & Solorzano, 1995).

The evolution of this work has been interdisciplinary, with contributions by scholars who look at race from critical perspectives. The earlier thinking of Gloria Anzaldúa (see Solorzano & Yosso, 2002), Frederick Douglass (see Ladson-Billings & Tate, 1995), W. E. B. Du Bois (1908), Paulo Freire (1970), Karl Marx (see Tucker, 1978), Linda Tuhiwai Smith (2012), and scholars from a variety of other disciplines have contributed to or been used in conjunction with critical race theory in education (Yosso, 2005). Since its inception, CRT has been framed as a social movement (Stovall, 2004) and used as an analytical tool that has resulted in the emergence of new frameworks to examine race and the educational context (DeCuir & Dixson, 2004).

Although this body of scholarship has begun to generate a broader reach in the last decade, scholars primarily agreed on a set of tenets that inform their approach to social science inquiry. To name a few, these tenets are designed to critically examine dominant ideologies that render deficit views of people of color; to shed light on the deep seeded problems of racism, colorblindness and power; and to create a space for the public to learn from the voices of those whose lives have been impacted by the intersections of race and other forms of identity in oppression (Solorzano & Yosso, 2002). Over time, many of these frameworks have expanded into education in ways that are no longer confined to understanding the legal vernacular of race. In areas where inquiry has taken the inductive approach to generate theory through the experiential knowledge of marginalized peoples, CRT has taken on various directions through empirical evidence and new methodologies to advance the interdisciplinary nature of this work. The specific frameworks that will be discussed in this chapter are (1) racial formation (Omi & Winant, 1994), (2) community cultural wealth (Yosso, 2005), and (3) interest convergence dilemma (Bell, 2004). We find these frameworks useful as an analytic tool to evaluate inequitable conditions that exist within a school that have been normalized over time and to inform leadership praxis to remove structural barriers and effectively meet the needs of students. Just as important, we see the importance of these analytic frameworks in helping to inform the larger purpose of school leadership and school reform.

One of the methods that critical race theorists employ is the use of narratives and storytelling to counter prevailing deficit discourse on immigrants, students of color, and those of low-income backgrounds (Solorzano & Yosso, 2002). A school principal used to say that "I cannot advocate for students" as his leadership framework that focuses on colorblindness, neutrality, and objectivity. Even though the school principal may want to strive for a level of fairness at his school, these leadership decisions can carry great consequences for students across race and other important social categories. For a long time, Daniel's voice as a bilingual administrator was dismissed and not valued because his commitment to educational equity and social justice focused on the needs of the individual with attention paid to ways society and social institutions impacted students by race, class, gender, sexuality, and language. Thus, critical race methodology sees the necessity of recentering epistemologies and experiences of the marginalized through storytelling. Whereas stories of contestation and resistance often go unaccounted for, critical race methodology creates a space for us to critically reflect upon our leadership practices as knowledge that can benefit our social justice colleagues in the field.

Racial Formations

Michael Omi and Howard Winant's (1994) theory of racial formation argues that race has sociohistorical meanings where categories are created, inhabited, contested, transformed, destroyed, and then coopted again. They argue that race has social meanings, as it has been used to biologically justify control and dominance as methods for policymaking and organizing a society. According to Omi and Winant (1994), the two distinct processes of racial formation take part in historically situated projects in which "human bodies and social structures are represented and organized" (p. 56). The second process is the relationship between racial formation and the evolution of the hegemony that changes over time to rearticulate the meaning of race and social order. In the U.S., there is a strong relationship between race and language in one's account of identity, citizenship, and access to institutional resources.

When Daniel was an administrator at a high school in California, his responsibilities were to work closely with students, parents, teachers, and administrators to ensure a "fair" education for students of bilingual and immigrant backgrounds. The bilingual position he filled was created when predominantly Latina/o parents in the school district became dissatisfied with the large number of their children being wrongfully placed into what was formerly known as the English as a second language program. Hence, he was recruited to fill this position when his predecessor left to pursue his doctorate in education. Some of his daily responsibilities included student assessment, course placement, community partnerships, parent advisory, and coordinating a network of support for students that had missed school for an extended amount of time. There was a wide range of diversity that existed among the students. This was a school of 3,000 students and 200 staff where students speak more than 56 different languages from all over the world.

For a decade at this school, student populations had held steady with African Americans at 32%, Asian Americans 10%, Latina/os 14%, mixed race 10%, and Caucasians 34%. The city is known for its liberal politics and racially integrated schools. There is only one high school in the city, and it is known as a bimodal school that sends its White affluent students to Ivy League universities versus low-income students of color who experienced an 80% D and F rate on their report cards. To address the racial opportunity gap, reform efforts were put into place but met with resistance by affluent parents who wanted to maintain their advantages at the school and by pro-tracking teachers who saw higher professional status in teaching White students as they subscribed to a racialized ideology of academic achievement.

Students of immigrant backgrounds come to school with diverse range of English proficiency, academic skills, and life experiences. Two major aspirations most students shared with their English-speaking peers were doing well in school and attending college. The first author held this position for six years and it was clear that by observation and conversations with parents and students, college was a top priority. Even though he had repeatedly brought the community's aspirations and concerns to teachers' attention, there were disagreements on how to respond to the needs of immigrant students. Much of the disagreement came from colleagues who did not believe "everyone should go to college."

His first plan of action was to bring the idea of a college-going curriculum to both teachers and counselors. The purpose of this strategy was to help identify individuals and allies who shared the same views and were willing to act in the interest of his students. His second purpose was to get his colleagues to discuss these issues with each other to generate a buzz, so that he was not alone in advocating for students' college-going needs.

To begin this process, he brought specific cases of students who had expressed their desire to attend college to individual teachers and counselors. The context of these meetings often involved methods of creating a system of support to assist students' academic success. The results of these meetings were often frustrating, as one teacher said, "I don't think the 'Hispanic' culture is interested in sending their students to college." Several counselors said, "These students shouldn't go to college because they are not ready." One school administrator said, "These students should learn basic skills, so they can look for work after high school." Another school administrator suggested that these students' later generations would eventually be ready for college once they assimilated into the American culture. Another teacher said, "These students shouldn't expect me to help them if their parents can't come to school to attend a meeting." Several support staff also informed him that there was even one teacher who openly suggested to students that college "isn't for everyone. You are setting them up to fail."

What boggles us in these conversations is that not once did anyone raise the question: How can this school work to ensure that immigrants are prepared for college like their White counterparts? And, if college is not for everyone, then why was that message not conveyed to White, affluent students as a part of the school norm? Our advocacy operates with a different paradigm that centers on students' interests and aspirations. Even if by chance a student decides not to pursue college, the decision is made independently from issues around eligibility, ability, or self-doubt. Based on our conversations with teachers, counselors, and administrators, there were biological, cultural, linguistic, and economic explanations given as reasons that college should not be one of the primary focuses of immigrants' education. These discrepant expectations were rendering schooling inequitable as many immigrant students were placed into classrooms that did not provide college preparatory credits.

Despite the discrepant expectations, all of our colleagues' children were either in college or had college degrees. Additionally, the message that "college is not for everyone" did not apply to the ways in which teachers viewed White, middle-class students and their needs to become college-ready. This raised the challenge for us to identify the rationalizing ideology that differentiates teachers' expectations for English-speaking students versus those of immigrant backgrounds. Coupled with this norm was the fact that immigrant students were rarely included in educational opportunities that were afforded to English-speaking students. Opportunities such as yearbook, debate team, and honors courses did not reach out to or enroll any immigrant students. Instead, many immigrant students were sociologically and academically bound in a particular area of the school that was isolated from the rest of the teacher and student population.

To unpack the underlying ideological assumptions that teachers have about immigrant students, we have to first engage with the idea that language classes are historically viewed in deficits terms that lack the same rigor and status as those that enroll English-speaking students. Additionally, there are also widely held perceptions that immigrant populations come to the U.S. undereducated, even though all recent statistics suggest otherwise (Suarez-Orozco, 2014). Either real or imagined, this deficit view comes with the understanding that language classes are assimilationist projects that center on the definitions that good citizens must learn to speak "standard" English (Lippi-Green, 1997) and understand the Eurocentric way of life. The assimilationist paradigm has proven to be an ineffective method of instruction for the ahistorical approach to building knowledge that dismisses the rich experiences that immigrant students bring to school (see Valenzuela, 1999). To contextualize the creation of "language minorities" as an educational category, we need to be reminded of the Supreme Court decision of Lau v. Nichols where race, language, and schooling were contested by civil rights leaders to transform the experiences of immigrants in school. As a result, the Lau v. Nichols (1974) Supreme Court decision stated the following to enforce the idea that school districts have the responsibility to fix the language deficiency in the children, which in turn, the race-based framework in the Fourteenth amendment became the equal protection clause that cemented these students' minoritized status in schools:

> Where inability to speak and understand the English language excludes national origin minority group children from effective participation in the educational program offered by a school district, the district must take affirmative steps to rectify the language deficiency in order to open its instructional program to these students. (Gonzalez, 2008, p. 519)

Thus, the equal protection clause becomes the condition in which immigrant students' educational rights were articulated. However, immigrant students' rights to equal protection were not based upon inequitable learning opportunities at the school, but rather, students' "language deficiency" that schools needed to address. Even though schools were required to be integrated, the way the decision was framed subjugates immigrant students to subordinated status that keeps them academically and politically isolated within the school context.

In effect, at the school level, language classes around the country often do not provide students with college credits, so these classes often are perceived to remediate instead of providing the equivalent rigor and grade level content. The problem relegates immigrant students to extended stays in language classes as teachers face the dilemma as to whether students are "ready" for mainstream instruction and teachers who may not have the sensibility to the needs of these students. By default, students' presumed "language deficiencies" are coupled with their lack of educational opportunities to further reinforce their subordinated status that results in racial and linguistic stigma at the school. To this day, there are many students who are U.S. born, but due to their last name or home language they were placed into language classes until high school graduation.

Even though the Supreme Court also stated in the *Lau* decision that tracking and ability groupings of immigrant students should not be permanent (Gonzalez, 2008), the way that educational opportunities are structured within the school requires their permanent stays. ESL programs often had to keep students in their classes in order to maintain funding sources. Additionally, mainstream teachers are either not interested or do not have the proper preparation to ensure their transition from ESL programs. The extended stay renders a fixed status for English language learners, and as such, their presumed accent and intelligence becomes stigmatized and racialized to justify that these students are "not ready for college" or less deserving of educational opportunities than their English-speaking counterparts (see Wiley & Lukes, 1996).

Community Cultural Wealth

The discussions we had with our high school colleagues were reminiscent of the disbelief we had experienced with our guidance counselors. Rather than going along with school norms, we began to employ several strategies to counteract against the deficit views that teachers had about immigrant students. Much of the reform process was guided by the needs of students, the aspirations of their parents, and the University of California's criteria for admissions. These guides then were translated into a set of praxis to assist students to reach a higher level of academic success.

To tackle the problems of low expectations at the structural level, Daniel allied with a vice principal at the school and began to push for more ESL and content courses to receive college preparatory credits. He then worked directly with officials at the University of California to obtain college credits for intermediate and advanced level language and sheltered courses. Daniel then began to counsel students to develop their navigational skills to complete the ESL program requirements, the requirements for high school graduation, and the University of California admissions requirement. He also strategically chose the University of California requirements so that students were likely to also qualify for other college and universities around the country. He would bring students' individual academic plans in home visits and discuss with parents the step-by-step plans on how their child can graduate from high school and have the opportunity to apply to college, and what they can do to contribute to this process at home and at the school. Since many ESL students were behind credits for graduation and college admission, he frequently encouraged students to take classes in the evenings and during summer at the local community colleges. These courses were free to high school students at the time, so many ESL students were able to take additional classes to make up credits, gain new skills, and get a glimpse of what college is about without resulting in additional economic hardship. By doing this, students got the chance to be exposed to higher forms of classroom expectations that eventually had an impact on their self-concept as high achievers.

Daniel also made use of school assemblies to hold college orientations specifically for immigrant students so teachers, students, and parents were able to learn about the admissions process and the numerous ways their students could qualify for college. He also invited admissions officers and alumni of the ESL program to come back to talk to the immigrant community about their experiences transitioning from high school to college. In these efforts, he worked closely with the high school college counselor to ensure that she was aware of and responsive to the needs of immigrant students. As a result of building relationships with allies across the school, Daniel participated on the school's scholarship and other decision-making committees to ensure there was advocacy at that level.

In responding to voter-approved Proposition 209, a law that banned affirmative action in California's public universities, Daniel responded by creating a number of clubs and activities after school so ESL students could participate in extracurricular activities to add to their accomplishments as scholars. He also collaborated with a number of ESL teachers to establish the school's first award-winning ESL speech and debate team. ESL students wrote and recited poetry and speeches that were relevant to their lives as immigrants, and they got the chance to meet other immigrant students from the Bay Area. Since many of these competitions were held at local colleges and universities, such as the University of San Francisco, Holy Names College, and Cal State East Bay, Daniel also took advantage of the opportunity for students to tour these schools and learn how each school may further their academic aspirations and career goals. At times, he would invite community activists and parents to accompany students on these trips, and they often came away with new perspectives about how to further support their children towards higher goals.

During those six years, Daniel managed to visit hundreds of families at school and in their homes. The parents were primarily interested in understanding how their child was doing in the classroom and what they could do to reach college. Of all the parent advisory committee meetings that he had planned, the ones that had the highest attendance were the ones included discussions on students' report cards, opportunity to meet a teacher, and college and scholarships on the agenda. He used these topics as "interest convergence" to bring parents to school but also to have them to take on participatory roles in the ESL program's decision-making process. Similar to Pedro Nava's (2012) work, the question that he frequently encountered was, "How is my child doing?" While many teachers often associate these types of questions with student behavior, it was actually a cultural cue that asked teachers to share the academic progress of their child. College readiness, then, became a framework to which Daniel engaged parents on their expectations when they read their child's report cards, engaged with teachers, and participated in advisory situations. He also made sure that parents had direct access to the school's bilingual staff, White teacher allies, church leaders, and nonprofit organizations as a way to identify and integrate social services into the school culture to address the needs of the immigrant community.

Therefore, one important lesson we have learned is the importance of using college-going opportunities as an anchor to engage parents in an ongoing needs assessment. In doing so, we are able to increase our understanding about immigrant parents' aspirations and life challenges. We can then bring this information back to the school to share with teachers, so they can buy into the role they play in the web of networks that is being designed to serve a particular student. Often, these conversations with teachers can be very challenging, as some colleagues are not always understanding or cooperative, but these methods of engagement should be framed in the context of increasing student attendance, improving behaviors in the classroom, and increasing the opportunity to graduate from high school.

As we continued this work, we realize that we must do something to create a pipeline of effective multilingual teachers of color into the teaching profession to add another layer to the existing reform strategy. To cultivate these interests, Daniel reached out to a local university to recruit 80 classroom mentors per year and matched them with the students who needed the most help. These mentors were mostly first-generation undergraduate students of immigrant backgrounds who wanted to explore the teaching profession and opportunities of working with young people. He developed partnerships with ethnic studies, social welfare, and the school of education so that mentors could receive field study units that counted towards graduation. The purpose of the program was to prepare immigrant students to become academically successful and ready for college. The program was called After School Academic Program (ASAP), and Daniel's collaboration with undergraduate students allowed him to apply for funding at the college and high school to hire people to recruit, train, and coordinate undergraduate mentors. He would provide continuous preparation by teaching a class at the local university once a week, and the rest of the time the undergraduate mentors were placed into the classroom to tutor ESL students and to mentor them after school. This is where he began to take a systems approach by designing a program that added to the school's capacity to help immigrant students to succeed in the classroom. Years later, Daniel ran into one of his students, Rita, on the streets of San Francisco, and she talked about her aspirations in high school and how they differ now. She said,

> Back in Mexico, I have always wanted to be a farmer. That was because that was what people were doing for a living in the town where I grew up. However, coming to the U.S. my perspectives have changed because of economic necessity but also because of the wide range of careers to choose from. I realized how important it is to have a college education, and I wished my high school teachers had encouraged me to pursue a bachelor's degree.

Many of these leadership lessons stem from the theory of community cultural wealth (Liou, Antrop-Gonzalez, & Cooper, 2009), where school leaders view students and parents as assets and draw upon their aspiration, navigational, linguistic, and familial capitals to create the capacity and network of support as critical components of school culture and as extension of the classroom. Pedagogically, we also want to make sure that students are connected to adults who care about them, who care to see schooling from their students' perspectives, and believe in their future as contributors to our multiracial democracy. From a leadership, capacity-building, and pedagogical standpoint, there were many political barriers that were placed in front of this work. However, the strategies to build coalitions with White ally teachers, teachers of color in other academic departments, and community groups enable us to push for several important changes in school culture. One of the changes was the organization of educational opportunity for immigrant students that went beyond the limits of state compliance and Lau v. Nichols (1974).

IMPLICATIONS

Obviously, there are limitations to this work that are worthy of criticism. Many administrators operate at a time where the school principal's philosophy for leadership is one of neutrality and the belief that educators should not have a role in advocating for students. Ideas of fairness applied to school policy often entail the belief that everyone can be educated in the same manner without having any perspective on the structural inequities and racial attitudes that perpetuate low classroom expectations. The pro-tracking views of teachers at schools also take on this leadership approach as a method to maintain tracking and the hierarchy of academic achievement by race and social class. To couple such a school culture that is power-blind by nature with those who have strong disbelief in immigrant students' intellectual capacities to become ready for college complicates the political terrain for any social justice educator. Our ability to negotiate the structure and culture of schools has to constantly make sure that we do not threaten the status of Whites who benefit from the system. Furthermore, the only way that racist teachers will listen to any advocacy is by serving to their needs in the classroom, which in effect enables them to attend to the needs of those who they believe ought to go to college and keep the racist academic apparatus intact. Even though the self-determined approach to create conditions of equity within the ESL program has its limitations, our experiences also demonstrate that the mission and purpose of inclusion and integration will require some rethinking about its aims and unexpected consequences.

A major part of this consequence is that the programs that Daniel developed operated on soft money and were never a threat to changing the status of programs that were established to serve the affluent students. However, the high school had every interest in these projects, because they kept the school in compliance with the state's bilingual mandates and added to the city's liberal reputation and values of equality. In the end, the praxis that challenged the racial hierarchy of academic apparatus functioned only to the extent that it positively impacted immigrant students. This movement also enabled Daniel's network of allies to fight against other forms of oppression, such as tracking and providing instructional leadership with the development of ethnic studies courses.

In all, it was a liberatory space created at a specific political moment. However, the rigidity of low teachers' expectations outlasted Daniel's time at the high school and the network of allies that were positioned to serve immigrants and other students of color. School leaders who aspire to adopt some of these reform strategies should keep in mind that leadership, good teaching, parental engagement, and community partnerships matter. Efforts of reform have to engage all levels in order to build the counterhegemonic culture that one attempts to establish.

So where does this conversation leave school leaders in the broader dialogue about critical praxis? First, from the perspective of school reform, we must engage in the quest for equity and social justice from the following questions: What are the belief systems that guide school leaders in creating a culture of equity and social justice in the school? How can school leaders sustain this mission by creating conditions to support high expectations for all students? Can schools ever achieve equity if affluent English-speaking parents and students are able to maintain their educational advantages in the school? Finally, what is the fight that school leaders must take on in order to continue improvement for racially and linguistically diverse populations? We believe every school leader must seriously consider these reform questions by critically examining the widespread problems of low expectations in the classroom.

These questions can best be addressed when school leaders and teachers begin a process of critical self-reflection. This process can be facilitated by moving to create reading and discussion groups that serve to raise sociopolitical consciousness around race/ethnicity, class, gender, and immigration matters. White allies and politically conscious people of color must consistently structure school cultures that call out inequitable learning conditions for their students and their communities. Moreover, high expectations through culturally and linguistically relevant pedagogies and conducting research with youth of color have the potential to open and sustain spaces of speaking up, reading, and writing in college ready ways.

As practitioners, we operate knowing that middle-class White parents will never give up the advantages their children have. We know this from the perspective that having immigrant students enrolled in advanced level classes will be perceived as threat to their children's educational opportunities and pursuit of meritocracy. There is actually no secret about the unparalleled power affluent parents have to advocate and maintain their racial advantages. However, we often hear school administrators who operate out of fear because "I have a family to feed," and that they would risk losing their jobs if middle-class White parents were to protest and thwart efforts towards equity. Given this reality, it is much more comfortable for school leaders to think along the lines of equality and equal treatment. Derrick Bell's (2004) work suggests that the reality of equal treatment will keep the gridlock of power intact for the advantaged to continue to exploit the public school system that is historically designed to be the "Great Equalizer" (Mann, 1848). In so doing, school leaders inadvertently surrender their power to counteract against these forces that seek to maintain unequal footing and hierarchical educational status across race, class, gender, language, and other visual markers. Conversely, the presence of power and the culture that there must be winners and losers also create the conditions of stereotype threat for those who are sensitized by the racial ideology of academic achievement (Steele & Aronson, 1995).

Without the ability to achieve real equity, it is fundamentally impossible to engage with the problems of low expectations in the classroom because the change in power and status become unattainable in spite of school reform. Therefore, school leaders who want results must be politically courageous and critical of the power apparatus to ensure that all parents and students have a fair chance of academic success. Critical educational leadership, then, should embody the use of critical race, class, and gender theories to navigate and counteract forces that seek to make schooling undemocratic and unjust. It is both a charge and purpose that school leaders have a clear sense of self in terms of personal biases, privileges, strengths, and limitations to commit to the work of equity and social justice. In doing so, leaders will be able to have a critique of hegemony and urgency to change society through critical praxis that impacts the ideology of race and academic achievement.

Finally, we would not be able to accomplish some of these goals without building coalitions with parents, teachers of color, and White allies who are critical of the system and are committed to improving it. By creating a diverse social justice network, school leaders can collectively take on responsibilities to promote educational opportunities for those most in need of our support and attention.

REFERENCES

Ambady, N., Shih, M., Kim, A., & Pittinsky, T. L. (2001). Stereotype susceptibility in children: Effects of identity activation on quantitative performance. *Psychological Science, 12*(5), 385–390.

Becker, H. S. (1952). Social-class variations in the teacher-pupil relationship. *The Journal of Educational Sociology,* 451–465.

Bell, D. (2004). *Silent covenants: Brown v. Board of Education and the unfulfilled hopes for racial reform.* New York, NY: Oxford University Press.

Brophy, J. E., & Good, T. L. (1974). *Teacher-student relationships: Causes and consequences.* Austin, TX: Holt, Rinehart & Winston.

Conchas, G. Q., & Clark, P. A. (2002). Career academies and urban minority schooling: Forging optimism despite limited opportunity. *Journal of Education for Students Placed at Risk, 7*(3), 287–311.

Cooper, H. M., & Tom, D. Y. (1984). Teacher expectation research: A review with implications for classroom instruction. *The Elementary School Journal,* 77–89.

Dantley, M. E. (2003). Purpose–Driven Leadership The Spiritual Imperative to Guiding Schools Beyond High–Stakes Testing and Minimum Proficiency. *Education and Urban Society, 35*(3), 273–291.

Darling-Hammond, L. (1996). What matters most: A competent teacher for every child. *Phi Delta Kappan, 78*(3), 193.

Darling-Hammond, L., & Sykes, G. (2003). Wanted, A national teacher supply policy for education: The right way to meet the" highly qualified teacher" challenge. *Education Policy Analysis Archives, 11,* 33.

DeCuir, J. T., & Dixson, A. D. (2004). "So When It Comes Out, They Aren't That Surprised That It Is There": Using Critical Race Theory as a Tool of Analysis of Race and Racism in Education. *Educational researcher,* 26–31.

Diamond, J. B., Randolph, A., & Spillane, J. P. (2004). Teachers' expectations and sense of responsibility for student learning: The importance of race, class, and organizational habitus. *Anthropology & Education Quarterly, 35*(1), 75–98.

Du Bois, W. E. B. (1903). *The souls of black folk.* New York, NY: Oxford University Press.

Foster, M. (1998). *Black teachers on teaching.* New York, NY: The New Press.

Freire, P. (1970). Cultural action for freedom. *Harvard educational review. 68*(4), 476–522.

González, J. M. (Ed.). (2008). *Encyclopedia of bilingual education.* Thousand Oaks, CA: Sage Publications.

Howard, T. C. (2003). Culturally relevant pedagogy: Ingredients for critical teacher reflection. *Theory into Practice, 42*(3), 195–202.

Jahan, R. (2000, March). Transformative leadership in the 21st century. In *Asia–Pacific Women Parliamentarians' Conference on Transformative Leadership for Good Governance in the 21st Century* (pp. 24–25).

Ladson-Billings, G., & Tate IV, W. (1995). Toward a critical race theory of education. *The Teachers College Record, 97*(1), 47–68.

Larson, C. L., & Murtadha, K. (2002). *Leadership for social justice. Yearbook of the National Society for the Study of Education.* Hoboken, NJ: Wiley Publisher.

Liou, D. D., Antrop-González, R., & Cooper, R. (2009). Unveiling the promise of community cultural wealth to sustaining Latina/o students' college–going information networks. *Educational Studies, 45*(6), 534–555.

Liou, D. D., & Rotheram-Fuller, E. (2016). Where Is the Real Reform? African American Students and Their School's Expectations for Academic Performance. *Urban Education.* DOI: 0042085915623340.

Lipman, P. (1993). *The influence of restructuring on teachers' beliefs about and practices with African American students (Vol. 3).* University of Wisconsin–Madison.

Lippi-Green, R. (1997). *English with an accent: Language, ideology, and discrimination in the United States.* New York, NY: Taylor & Francis Group.

Mann, H. (1848). Twelfth annual report to the Massachusetts Board of Education. *The republic and the school: Horace Mann and the education of free men.* New York, NY: Teachers College Press.

Merton, R. K. (1968). *Social theory and social structure.* New York, NY: Simon and Schuster.

Milner, H. R., IV. (2012a). Challenges in teacher education for urban education. *Urban Education, 47,* 700–705.

Milner, H. R. (2012b). Beyond a test score: Explaining opportunity gaps in educational practice. *Journal of Black Studies.* 0021934712442539.

Nava, P. E. (2012). *Sin Sacrificio No Hay Recompensa: Apoyo as (Im) migrant Parental Engagement in Farmworking Families of the California Central Valley.* University of California, Los Angeles.

Noguera, P. (2003). *City schools and the American dream: Reclaiming the promise of public education (Vol. 17).* New York, NY: Teachers College Press.

Normore, A. H., & Jean-Marie, G. (2008). Female secondary school leaders: At the helm of social justice, democratic schooling and equity. *Leadership & Organization Development Journal, 29*(2), 182–205.

Oakes, J. (1985). *Keeping track.* New Haven, CT: Yale University Press.

Omi, M., & Winant, H. (1994). *Racial Formation in the 1960s to the 1990s.* New York, NY: Routledge.

Ornelas, A., & Solorzano, D. G. (2004). A critical race analysis of Latina/o and AfricanAmerican advanced placement enrollment in public high schools. *The High School Journal, 87*(3), 15–26.

Parker, L., & Villalpando, O. (2007). A race (cialized) perspective on education leadership: Critical race theory in educational administration. *Educational Administration Quarterly, 43*(5), 519–524.

Rist, R. (1970). Student social class and teacher expectations: The self–fulfilling prophecy in ghetto education. *Harvard Educational Review, 40*(3), 411–451.

Rosenthal, R., & Jacobson, L. (1968). *Pygmalion in the Classroom: Teacher Expectation and Pupils' Intellectual Development.* Austin, TX: Holt Rinehart and Winston.

Sarason, S. B. (1990). *The predictable failure of school reform*. San Francisco, CA: Jossey–Bass, Inc.

Selden, S. (1999). *Inheriting shame: The story of eugenics and racism in America*. New York, NY: Teachers College Press.

Shields, C. M. (2009). Transformative leadership: A call for difficult dialogue and courageous action in racialised contexts. *International Studies in Educational Administration, 37*(3), 53–68.

Shields, C. M. (2010). Transformative leadership: Working for equity in diverse contexts. *Educational Administration Quarterly, 46*(4), 558–589.

Smith, L. T. (1999). *Decolonizing methodologies: Research and indigenous peoples*. London, UK: Zed books.

Solorzano, D. G., & Ornelas, A. (2002). A critical race analysis of advanced placement classes: A case of educational inequality. *Journal of Latinos and Education, 1*(4), 215–229.

Solorzano, D. G., & Solorzano, R. W. (1995). The Chicano educational experience: A framework for effective schools in Chicano communities. *Educational Policy, 9*(3), 293–314.

Solorzano, D. G., & Yosso, T. J. (2002). Critical race methodology: Counter–storytelling as an analytical framework for education research. *Qualitative Inquiry, 8*(1), 23–44.

Steele, C. M. (1997). A threat in the air: how stereotypes shape intellectual identity and performance. *American psychologist, 52*(6), 613.

Steele, C. M., & Aronson, J. (1995). Stereotype threat and the intellectual test performance of African Americans. *Journal of personality and social psychology, 69*(5), 797.

Stovall, D. (2004). School Leader as Negotiator: Critical Race Theory, Praxis, and the Creation of Productive Space. *Multicultural Education, 12*(2), 8–12.

Suarez–Orozco, M. M. (2014). Everything you ever wanted to know about assimilation but were afraid to ask. *The New Immigrant in American Society: Interdisciplinary Perspectives on the New Immigration, 51*.

Thomas, W. I., & Thomas, D. S. (1928). *The Child in America*. New York, NY: Alfred A. Knopf, Inc.

Tucker, R. C. (Ed.). (1978). *The Marx–Engels Reader*. New York, NY: W. W. Norton & Company

Valenzuela, A. (1999). *Subtractive schooling: Issues of caring in education of US–Mexican youth*. Albany, NY: State University of New York Press.

Weinstein, R. S. (2002). *Reaching higher*. Cambridge, MA: Harvard University Press.

Wells, A. S., & Crain, R. L. (1997). *Stepping over the color line*. New Haven, CT: Yale University Press.

Welner, K. G., & Weitzman, D. Q. (2005). The soft bigotry of low expenditures. *Equity & Excellence in Education, 38*(3), 242–248.

Wiley, T. G., & Lukes, M. (1996). English–only and standard English ideologies in the US. *Tesol Quarterly*, 511–535.

Woolfolk, A. E., & Brooks, D. M. (1983). Nonverbal communication in teaching. *Review of research in education*, 103–149.

Yosso, T. J. (2005). Whose culture has capital? A critical race theory discussion of community cultural wealth. *Race ethnicity and education, 8*(1), 69–91.

CHAPTER 8

PREPARING TEACHERS TO WORK IN DISENFRANCHISED COMMUNITIES

Deconstructing Latina/o Historical Trauma and Internalized Racism

Marcos Pizarro
San José State University

Our Latino children were in pain: had seen, heard, witnessed so much in their every-day lives, yet they had no sacred spaces to be held and heard, to share what mattered to them. What part of their humanity was wounded, unseen and invisible to their families, their friends, their teachers, the society that was raising them?
—Alicia Garcia[1]

LIFE LESSONS FOR TEACHER PREPARATION

When I took my first teaching job, as an elementary school teacher in inner-city Los Angeles, I knew I was unprepared. But I had no idea how unprepared I was. As a new teacher on an emergency credential with no teacher preparation classes under my belt, I thought the lack of courses on content

Envisioning Critical Race Praxis in K–12 Leadership Through Counter-Storytelling, pages 163–182
Copyright © 2016 by Information Age Publishing
All rights of reproduction in any form reserved.

delivery and pedagogy would be my downfall. Now, over 20 years later, having watched teacher preparation closely as a teacher educator, I know that I was unprepared in the same ways that even those who attend top-notch credential programs often are.

Teachers who work in urban, working-class communities, if they were enrolled in a well-designed teacher preparation program, took one or two courses that are intended to introduce them to the complexities of teaching in diverse contexts (but even this is rare).[2] These courses often address the benefits of acknowledging and understanding the cultural backgrounds of non-White students. They may also consider the history of racism that has shaped the experiences and schooling of communities of color. These are critical steps in teacher preparation, and yet this training does not begin to prepare teachers for being effective in classrooms with students of color in working-class communities. The coursework may provide future teachers some understanding of the history and cultural background of students, but it does little to help them recognize how these histories shape the lives of youth in these communities, and in particular, the identities that their students learn to embody in the classroom.

What I found over the course of that first year in the classroom was that I needed something that I did not have: something that teacher preparation programs were not teaching their students and that most of my fellow teachers did not know to concern themselves with. I needed tools for understanding myself in the context of teaching in a Black and Brown working-class community. I needed ways of understanding how my students manifested the pain and trauma that they and their families had experienced for generations. I needed a means for helping them recognize their brilliance in the midst of all this, for nurturing that brilliance, and for pursuing meaningful goals that acknowledged their challenges. I needed a process for understanding and addressing the collective pain that was so much a part of our everyday experience in the classroom. I needed exactly what Alicia Garcia (quoted above, personal communication, September 17, 2011) realized she needed, teaching in a different part of the city, years later.

Having worked in the Bay Area for the last 15 years supporting raza[3] teachers in communities very similar to the one where I started teaching, I have found that these are the most pressing needs for our teachers who are committed to social justice in communities of color. In communities from inner-city Oakland to Richmond to east San José, and from Dixon to Salinas to rural Castroville, we have consistently seen our young people overwhelmed by the pain they experience and have felt at a loss for resources to help us as we work with them. As a result, a collective of raza teachers and community workers—MAESTR@S—came together to develop a model for dealing with these realities as we work for social justice with young people.[4] This chapter explains the applied theoretical work we developed to help us understand our experiences as raza students and teachers. The next chapter in this volume explains an evolving model of walking social justice: a holistic framework and daily practice for pursuing racial and educational justice in educational communities. Both chapters offer a challenge to how we prepare future teachers for their work in the classroom and how leaders create environments in which teachers can engage in that work in transformative ways. In the next chapter, these lessons are shared from our work in two unique contexts: (1) the group itself (because this aspect of the project provides an understanding of how the model was created among a collective of teachers and youth workers); and (2) our applications in classrooms (because this allows teachers to consider how they can adapt the model to their own work in classrooms). Both chapters also include insights for school leaders to begin the process of applying this work to their efforts to pursue racial justice in schools. In this first chapter, we will consider where the current research on the Latina/o educational crisis leaves us, a theoretical framework for deconstructing racial injustice in the schools, followed by background on the MAESTR@S group and our methods for using applied theory.

FRAMING THE LATINA/O EDUCATIONAL CRISIS

The most recent body of research demonstrates that across multiple social factors, Latina/o youth in the United States are in dire jeopardy (Covarrubias, 2011; Gandara & Contreras, 2009; Murrillo, Villenas, Galván, Muñoz, Martínez, & Machado-Casas, 2010; Torres & Fergus, 2012; Valencia, 2011). The data on Latinas/os in the schools reveal that 44% of Chicanas/os in the United States are not graduating from high school (Covarrubias, 2011). Just as powerful is the fact that another 29% of Chicanas/os graduate from high school but do not enter college (Covarrubias, 2011). This may be attributable to the fact that, although they are graduating from high school, Latina/o students are not prepared for college by their secondary schooling. In my own community of Santa Clara county, only 26% of the Latina/o students *who graduate high school* have completed the requirements necessary to enroll in the state universities, compared to 55% of Whites and 71% of Asians (Kids in Common, 2009). The suspension rate for students in the largest high school serving the Latina/o community on the east side of San José is .64 for each student, while the rate for both high schools in a district serving a White community only a few miles away is .04 for each student (Kids in Common, 2009). The latter district spends $11,264 per student annually, while the east side district spends $8,966 per student (Kids in Common, 2009).[5] I highlight these few data points to emphasize the severity of the issues facing raza youth in our schools.

There have been countless studies that have mapped out different facets of the Latina/o education crisis. Gandara and Contreras (2009), whose book is titled *The Latino Education Crisis,* expose the multifaceted inequities Latinas/os experience in the schools, including a lack of preschool opportunities, inadequate school facilities, a technological divide, tracking and limited access to higher-level curriculum, a lack of quality teachers and strong school leaders, segregated schooling, a paucity of safe schools and extracurricular activities, and, perhaps the most powerful force underlying the persistence of these issues: stereotypes and self-fulfilling prophecies. Valencia (2011), now in his third edition of *Chicano School Failure and Success,* adds to this overview by including the powerful negative effects of assessment and high-stakes testing, special education, school finance, and the role of language suppression and cultural exclusion. Murrillo et al. (2010) compile another major overview of raza schooling in the *Handbook of Latinos and Education,* covering history and policy in greater depth to provide a more complex understanding of the issues underlying raza school performance, as well as highlighting resources to help those working to confront these issues. Although these compilations have provided significant advances in the understanding of raza schooling, two authors in particular have been essential to framing the core issues affecting the daily lives of raza students in United States schools: Valenzuela (1999) and Yosso (2005). Valenzuela (1999) breaks down the powerful forces underlying the issues covered in these three volumes, as she explains the ways in which United States schools engage in forms of subtractive schooling with raza youth, ignoring and even taking away the strengths Latinas/os bring into the school, and leaving them poorly prepared for post-secondary life. These forces are even more clearly understood through the lens of Yosso's (2005) analysis, whereby she explains the ways in which deficit models have led to schools ignoring the "community cultural wealth" in raza neighborhoods. Yosso highlights the insidious ways by which racism, often in the form of racial microaggressions, serves to shape and limit the schooling of raza students at every level of education. Together, these authors help us understand the ways in which race and racism today have a dramatic impact on the daily lives of raza youth. Despite the growing body of research that seeks to explain, and even challenge these realities, as Alicia Garcia demonstrates in the opening quote, teachers working in disenfranchised Latina/o communities struggle to find ways to support their students who face the issues so powerfully deconstructed by Valenzuela (1999) and Yosso (2005).

MAESTR@S: LEARNING TO "MAKE SENSE" OF RAZA SCHOOL EXPERIENCES

Recognizing this reality, in 2000, I convened a gathering of Bay Area educators who were committed to addressing the issues faced by raza youth and their families in the local schools. This session led to the formation of a group that was intended to provide immediate support for teachers and community workers looking for tools to help them in their work. Our own training in schools of education had not prepared us for what we were living in our classrooms. As we met that first day, participants described the challenges they saw their youth facing. We were seeing Latina/o youth struggle with school at every imaginable level, dealing with irrelevant and unengaging curricula; hostile peer groups; and teachers, administrators, and on-campus police with low or no expectations for them. We were seeing them struggle in their homes: trying to find ways to negotiate between the experiences and culture of their parents and the dominant culture, and between the world their parents hoped they would be able to live in and the one they actually had to face on a daily basis. We were seeing them struggle in their communities: trying to find a place that they fit and could still survive. We were seeing them struggle with the media and what it tells them they are, can be, and even what they should desire. We were seeing them struggle with themselves: working to create a sense of self that fully incorporates all of who they are as Latinas/os, as young men and women, as working class. We were seeing them struggle to envision and move toward a future they really want and feel they can attain. These are the issues that shape the lives of our students and have perhaps the greatest impact on our work in the classroom. MAESTR@S came together to develop collective ways of supporting our students as they faced these struggles.

Even after leaving our credential and graduate programs, we had read countless articles and books that considered the experiences of Latina/o youth in the schools (including many listed in the previous section), but we still found that we did not have the tools that we needed.[6] We had also attended local, state, and national conferences in education, sociology, bilingual education, social science, and Chicana/o and Latina/o Studies to seek support. We left these conferences knowing that the specific tools we sought were not provided, nor was there a clear understanding of the concrete issues we faced with youth in our communities. In short, we sought a deeper analysis than that included in most education research and conferences. We needed an analysis and classroom tools that considered the realities we were witnessing: criminalizing schools, police harassment, extreme violence, dramatic suicide rates, severe poverty rates, lack of access to healthcare and to other critical community resources—the severity of growing up in disenfranchised communities.

MAESTR@S, therefore, began its efforts by identifying people who were doing innovative work that was engaging raza youth in schooling or education (Pizarro & Montoya, 2002). We traveled to different communities and presented participatory workshops designed to give teachers and youth workers specific tools that they could immediately use in their classrooms and communities. Over the course of five years, we organized countless *encuentros* for teachers, students, and communities, leading to the development of a model that will be described later. The first thing we recognized through our work, however, was that we needed a clear, shared analysis of what was happening to us and to our youth through the schooling process. We needed that analysis to speak of and to our students, who were currently struggling. We needed a way of "making sense" of what we and our students were experiencing on a daily basis so that we could take thoughtful steps toward addressing these realities. We sought insights that spoke to the students' and our emotional and spiritual realities.[7]

A PERSONAL NOTE ON NEEDING TO "MAKE SENSE OF ALL THIS"

When I began my work with MAESTR@S, I was tired. I was tired of reading works that provided a powerful critique of the school system and identified all of the major changes needed in that system but left me with no help for working with a group of students immediately. I was tired of attending conferences where similar critiques were made by prominent scholars who received ovations but left me wondering what we could actually do with the vast number of raza youth being broken by the schools at that very moment. I was tired of walking into classrooms driven by testing and standards that left no room for students' and teachers' humanity to be affirmed in any meaningful way. I was tired of feeling like so many of us were going through the motions without recognizing what was truly going on and how it had been going on for generations. I needed a way of dealing with the pain I saw in the eyes and spirits of the raza youth I met and worked with in countless classrooms. I needed a way to understand that pain, where it came from, and how it played itself out in raza students' lives and in our classrooms. MAESTR@S became a space for me to voice this, and our collective became a place for us to do lived theory work that we could use immediately in our classrooms and communities. The rest of this chapter explains that lived theory work.

THEORY-BUILDING FOR DECONSTRUCTING RACIAL INJUSTICE IN THE SCHOOLS[8]

One of the most significant challenges researchers have struggled with in approaching the Chicana/o community over the years is the complexity of the social forces at work in shaping the multiple manifestations of the Latina/o educational crisis. Focusing on any one of the aspects of this reality (as we typically do in writing for publication) makes our research manageable and possible, but it also leaves us only addressing one facet of the issues involved and possibly not developing comprehensive strategies to meet the real needs of youth. This was the problem that MAESTR@S faced early on in our work. We knew we needed to confront this challenge and spent a couple of years analyzing our own experiences to help us do the work we knew our students needed. In this section, as a means of building a holistic foundation for addressing these realities, I outline a theoretical framework for addressing the complexity through an analysis of deficit models, historical trauma, the normalization of racial inequality in schools, the individualization of Latina/o school failure, and the internalization of racism among students.[9] This is an extension of the work we did in MAESTR@S. We began by analyzing the historical forces that we saw at work in our lives and classrooms and then sought to explain how these forces manifested themselves in our students' experiences. The contemporary applications we made left us on our own since there is very little research that has approached these issues. My own work with raza students at all levels of the K–20 pipeline has shown me the relevance of these approaches to framing their experiences and their power in helping students make meaning of those experiences and pursue their life goals with clarity and confidence. I end this chapter with consideration of how students apply these insights to their own experiences and also how teachers and school leaders might learn from this to assist in their work for racial justice.

Deficit Models

How are all of these issues connected? The answer to that question is complicated, but one way of answering it that allows for some clarity is simply through historical reflection. There is a strong body of research that has demonstrated the way in which deficit models define the institutional experiences (including schooling) of people of color, particularly in the early 20th century in the United States (San Miguel & Donato [2010] provide an overview of early Latina/o schooling, while Valencia [2010] exposes the sway these models had as well as their blatant inaccuracy). Deficit models were used to explain the failure of people of color to achieve in the United States compared to the success of White communities. Prominent White scholars in a number of fields during this time explained these differential outcomes by way of the alleged genetic, cultural, religious, social, and/or moral inferiority and deficiencies of the different communities of color that were being analyzed (Menchaca & Valencia, 1990; Valencia & Solorzano, 1997). In fact, the eugenics movement of the early 20th century that included scientists, psychologists, education scholars, and others reflected the desire of prominent White scholars to prove the inherent genetic superiority of White people. These models have long since been debunked (Valencia, 2010), but it is critical to recognize that they dominated the social and educational landscape of the United States during the time in which schools and other social institutions in the U.S. were being shaped into what they are today. Furthermore, these popular understandings became embedded in the genetic blueprint of schooling as an institution, leaving an impact that lasts to this day, as explained in the subsequent section on normalization.

Historical Trauma

Critical research has challenged the deficit models for a number of years (Valencia & Solorzano, 1997)[10] and so this is not a theme that will be explored here. Still, there has been very little analysis of the cumulative effects of these models on communities of color today. A few Indigenous, Chicana/o, Pacific Islander, and African American thinkers and researchers have suggested that many of the issues we see facing disenfranchised communities of color (including cyclical poverty, dissociative behaviors, substance abuse, and violence) reflect the ongoing and unaddressed impacts of historical trauma. Scholars investigating the contemporary effects of these historical legacies on people of color agree that the violent acts of slavery and conquest impacted entire communities in ways that have shaped the lives of each future generation.[11] These scholars explain that acts of cultural genocide created a soul wound in the survivors because their entire understanding of who they were as a people (their educational systems, philosophies, religions, and life ways) was deemed both inferior and amoral. This left these communities with nothing to hold onto, creating a psychological, emotional, and spiritual wound that, because it never healed, was passed on to each subsequent generation. As Sousan Abadian explains in reflecting on this process, "Defeating a people has as much to do with destroying their sense of purpose—their confidence in their world-view and meaning system—as it does with physical conquest" (Lambert, 2008, p. 42). Abadian's analysis demonstrates how the processes of conquest and colonization had impacts on communities of color that were felt long after these specific events. The devaluing and attempted replacement of their worldview was intellectually and socially debilitating for many. Susan Yellow Horse and Maria Yellow Horse Brave Heart (2005) provide a specific definition: "Historical Trauma is cumulative emotional and psychological wounding, over the lifespan and across generations, emanating from massive group trauma experiences" (p. 39). They go on to describe the impact of this trauma on individuals that "includes depression, self-destructive behavior, suicidal thoughts and gestures, anxiety, low self-esteem, anger, and difficulty recognizing and expressing emotions" (p. 39). Yellow Horse and Brave Heart explain how the processes of conquest and colonization, and the destroyed sense of purpose that Abadian describes, have a host of cultural impacts that affect the psyches and behaviors of those who experience these attacks on their lifeways and knowledge systems. Eduardo Duran (2006) links these processes directly to internalized oppression through his research, explaining that "the pain and learned helplessness of internalized oppression continue to plague our relatives despite massive amounts of interventions that have been provided to treat the *symptoms* of individuals. Eventually, what is needed is a preventive intervention that addresses these issues at the source" (p. 23, my emphasis). Duran points us to the key problem that we see with teaching and other services in many disenfranchised communities: interventions designed to "help" these communities do not deal with the core issues but instead focus on their surface level manifestations.

In considering the era of the deficit model, this analysis is particularly important because these deficit models are directly connected to the underlying logic used to rationalize slavery, conquest, and other acts of cultural genocide. The thinking that shaped the research conducted by White scholars in the early 20th century was the direct descendant of the reprehensible religious rationalization used to conquer peoples of color in the Americas, Africa, and Asia. And while these acts are commonly understood as atrocities today, their ongoing impact on communities of color and public schooling in the United States is little understood. Gonzales (2006) provides one example when she explains that, "our antepasados [ancestors] believed that our heart was the seat of intelligence" (n.p.). The construct of historical trauma suggests that when a central way of life is extricated from a people and replaced with its antithesis, the impact on that community is continually felt. Current research that analyzes the challenges Latina/o students face in U.S. schools, such as Valenzuela's (1999) analysis of *educación*,[12] affirm the connection between conquest and the struggles raza students experience in schools today, as she demonstrates that Mexican students still center their approach to schooling on their hearts, emphasizing the necessity of caring in their learning environments, while schools often work to subtract this lifeway from their students. A careful analysis of racism in schools today (such as Valenzuela, 1999) helps us understand these connections. Furthermore, the ongoing reliance on deficit models in framing the schooling opportunities for raza students has dramatic effects on these students as they experience a retraumatization through these processes of denying both their strengths and the possibilities for success.[13] Not only do the effects of historical trauma impact raza youth through their intergenerational aspects, but the youth actually share similar experiences with their ancestors as they face contemporary deficit approaches to their schooling that are the offspring of the racist thinking at the time of conquest and colonization.

The research on historical trauma provides a direct connection between the impacts of early conquest/colonization and deficit models and, in our own theorizing in MAESTR@S, led us to identify the fact that current manifestations of deficit models often result in the retraumatization of raza students in the schools. We were able to connect these historical and evolving processes with the disengagement raza students exhibited in the classroom.[14]

Normalization of Latina/o School Failure

This analysis of historical trauma suggests that the many "problems" Latina/o youth face, which were outlined in the opening, are also connected to historical processes that are embedded in evolving ideologies of Latina/o inferiority imprinted on school life in the United States today. Focusing on just one issue here will demonstrate this reality. As stated in the introduction, in the county in which I work and live, only 26% percent of the Latina/o students who *graduate* from the high schools have also completed the necessary coursework to attend a public university in California. Many working in schools have standard and commonly accepted explanations of the different factors involved in this reality: student disengagement, lack of interest in and preparation for college preparatory classes, limited English abilities, lack of familial social capital, and many others. As the introduction suggests, we can also come up with a list of school-related influences, including disciplinary practices, limited resources, low expectations, and underprepared teachers. The focus of my analysis, however, is on the public reaction to the reality of persistent and dramatic inequality such as that reflected in the highlighted data. For the most part, there is no reaction. If we found similar numbers for White students in our county, where three of four White students graduated high school unable to attend a four-year state university, there would be an uproar. In contrast, we have grown comfortable with the reality of the majority of Latina/o youth. It does not surprise us, and even those of us who find it morally objectionable also learn that this is the way things are and will be. In short, we have a societal expectation of Latina/o student failure that is deeply embedded in our subconscious as a function of the historical processes described above (Pizarro, 2014, details this process).

Racial inequality is so deeply ingrained in our everyday existence that we organize our understanding of these inequities around the racist ideologies that have been used to rationalize them for hundreds of years. All of our social institutions, including schools, were founded on the understanding that people of color were/are inferior to Whites. The explanation for the basis of this inferiority has changed over the years, but the underlying belief in the inferiority has not. This is what allows us to justify the dramatic educational inequality described in the previous section and exposed in generations of research on the Latina/o community. It allows us to maintain fundamentally unequal opportunities for people of color in the United States (through policy and practice) and to rationalize their existence. This reality reflects the fact that we have *normalized* both racial inequality and racism to the extent that dramatic inequalities and injustices are accepted on a societal and community level. The goal of this analysis is not to convince the reader of the reality of inequality and racism. The extant body of research on racism in the United States and in schools specifically does this more than convincingly. Rather, the objective here is to pinpoint the normalization of inequality, injustice, and racism as intrinsic to the organization of schooling in the United States today and to consider this as fundamental to the reality that our youth face in schools so that we can consider the impact that this has on our youth.

Latina/o youth who grow up in working-class communities and attend public schools learn to expect their own failure.[15] Even if they aspire for educational success, they still learn that there is a societal expectation that, as a community, they will not be successful in school. Raza youth are not immune to the fact that there are dramatic inequalities in United States education, and despite their dreams of success, they know that the schools they attend do not expect them to succeed. I intentionally describe the force behind this expectation as *the school*, because for the majority of their time in school, most Latina/o students do not hear this message directly from a teacher or administrator, but they feel this expectation hanging in the air and experience it through disciplinary procedures, the organization of the curriculum, and the lack of energy and resources put into their learning by the institution as an entity.[16] What is most important is that raza youth experience a culture of expected failure (or at best mediocrity) over years and years in schools. By the time they enter high school, many working-class raza youth have experienced almost a decade of low expectations. It has become normalized and expected for them.

Individualization of Latina/o School Failure

This normalization of inequality and racism is connected to the individualization process that Latina/o students experience as part of how they learn to "make sense" of inequality. The message students often hear out loud in schools from teachers and administrators is that they want these youth to be successful. They are told that they should aspire to attend college, even though there is a rarely spoken, underlying assumption that most will not. Because of the subtlety of these processes, and because the youth rarely, if ever, have the chance to talk about any of it (as a result of the unspoken, normalization of failure), raza students blame themselves for their failure or struggles in school and do not talk about this with others. A Latina student, for example, who does poorly in math classes over the years, will hear multiple messages from teachers on the importance of school success and going to college (often despite not being provided the tools for this success), and so when she struggles, she learns to believe that she does not have the skills to be successful in math and does not have what it takes to thrive in school. Latina/o students most often lay exclusive blame on themselves and their families for their struggles. Ironically, in so many cases, these students are sitting in classrooms where large numbers of their peers are going through the same process.[17] This is ironic simply because, going back to the example of the affluent White community, if a majority of students were struggling to be successful in a class in that community, without question the community would not blame individual students for the failure, but would point the finger at the teacher or school. The public message raza students hear from their schools is one that espouses their need for success. Most of these schools, however, do not exhibit a belief in the actual possibility of success for most of these students, but rather simply make vocal their belief that the students should strive for success. Simultaneously, schools make sure that students understand that if they are not successful, it is because of their own individual lack of effort and commitment. Thus, schools shield themselves from culpability in the normalization of the failure of raza students, and most students then individualize their own failure. The process whereby, as part of normalizing racism, raza youth also individualize their failure solidifies the effect of that racism on their school lives, not just as individuals but as a community.

Internalized Racism

Over the course of their schooling, many Latina/o youth learn to internalize the racism that shapes the organization of school. This is a byproduct of the normalization and the individualization of inequality and racism because, as a result of these processes, there is usually not a conversation in schools about the causes of the inequality. There is, instead, simply an acceptance of that inequality, which is manifested in the low expectations that schools create based on historical trends in academic performance in given communities. Due to the normalization, students need to create a different explanation for their lack of success in school that does not implicate the school system at large, which is understood to be doing its best with communities that, in most cases, have too many challenges for them to overcome. Most Latina/o students, like all students, begin school aspiring for success. However, many soon learn that to achieve success, it will require extraordinary effort, along with a strong dose of luck. They know that very few of the students who preceded them in their classrooms were successful in school. They know how few actually graduate from high school, and that even fewer go on to college, and that most of those attend a nearby community college for a few years but never transfer to a four-year university. They know the jobs that these former students, who live in their neighborhoods, end up working. Because of all this, they begin to doubt that they will be one of the very few who are successful in school. For example, through their schooling, many raza youth learn that they do not have the requisite language skills to be successful. They learn that having Spanish as a first language, for example, is a handicap that will follow them for the rest of their lives. Further, they learn that they are not expected to write well nor to be engaged by reading. This is just one aspect of Latina/o students' lives through which they begin to understand that their racial identities limit the possibilities for them to become successful students. Schools teach them that their racial identities are incongruent with strong academic identities (Pizarro, 2005). This is the internalization of racism, which is insidious because, as a byproduct of the normalization of inequality, it is typically unseen by the students due to the covert ways in which it manifests itself in their lives (individualization). Although it was much more prevalent in previous generations, it is far less common for raza youth to hear anyone explicitly tell them, "Mexican kids can't do well in school because they are inferior." And yet most learn that very idea through the subtle organization of their school lives and the mundane, persistent, covert messages that students from these communities, as a collective of individuals, are not expected to do well. As a result, many raza youth learn to apply this shared societal understanding to themselves as individuals.

The normalization of inequality and racism—working-class Latina/o students grow up from their earliest days knowing that the inequality they live is just the way it is and should be expected—leads most to anticipate their own failure. They internalize the racism that normalizes the inequality so that they blame themselves as Latinas/os for their failure in school.[18] This internalization process itself demands the individualization of inequality so that these students learn that it is their fault on an individual level. This prevents them from connecting their struggles with those of their peers and engaging in a critique of these processes. At the same time, they also learn that being Latina/o makes their failure much more likely.[19]

This is the racialized context into which teachers insert themselves, typically without any space to explore what these realities mean to their students and to their own efforts to help students achieve school success. These processes are propelled by the historical and institutional inertia behind our understanding of the relationship between race and school performance in the United States. The manifestations of racism have changed dramatically over the past fifty years, but as this analysis explains, the impact of that racism in shaping inequality has not. Well-intending teachers, wanting to make a difference and to help raza youth, work in these communities, but without an understanding of these processes or the tools to confront them, they can do little more than hope for the best. As the data on raza school performance demonstrate, their best is often not enough.[20]

APPLICATIONS IN THE CLASSROOM:
THE POWER OF APPLIED THEORY

The analysis developed in MAESTR@S was based on our own experiences as students and teachers but also on our ongoing work with students to provide them tools they could use in their efforts to negotiate school and life. As we engaged students, we took the emerging insights from the classroom and used those experiences to strengthen the model and our analysis. As a collective, we found this to be the most affirming and important work we had done as educators. We developed this evolving analysis of our work with students through engaging the youth and saw that the students experienced a sense of relief, clarity, and renewed commitment to their goals by engaging in this work with us. Our latest example provides some insights into the benefits of using these insights in our work with youth.

In the 2012–2013 school year, I worked with an 11th grade English teacher in the development and teaching of a Latina/o literature course. In our work with three periods of this class, we applied all of the concepts covered in this chapter into our approach and also shared them with the students. Introducing, analyzing, and applying deficit models, historical trauma, normalized and individualized Latina/o school failure, and internalized racism was helpful to the students. As they explained throughout the school year, these concepts became tools in their lives. They were able to reflect on past experiences and explain what had happened and why it had happened, often alleviating their feelings of guilt and self-blame. Each of the constructs came up at different times during the year when students were exploring issues (both personal and related to class work). For example, students had many experiences with low expectations from teachers. Using these constructs, students were able to identify when teachers, counselors, and administrators systematically imposed low expectations and limited opportunities on their Latina/o students, and many of the students stopped blaming themselves for their teachers' limited expectations. The high expectations we set for them helped them recognize their abilities and begin to counter the profiles that many school personnel reduced them to.[21]

This analysis and understanding was framed in the context of students seeking success in school and life, and so students were asked to think about what they could do about these issues as individuals and as a group. Students chose many different paths after they began to adopt the analyses they found helpful: some challenged the realities they had experienced simply through retelling stories using the constructs that they found applicable, while others challenged the school itself to confront the issues. Most importantly, the students began to see their own power, no longer feeling resigned to the fate that their schools seemed to have already determined for them. By the end of the year, students were engaged in projects analyzing the issues they had determined were important and considering what these projects meant for them and the school. During one class period, one of the groups was discussing the possibility of presenting their work on Latina/o student motivation to teachers. I asked what they would share with teachers about the causes of a lack of student motivation. One student, who had been struggling in her classes and had also faced discipline issues at the school during the semester, took the lead and said that she felt like it was all tied into the normalization of Latino student failure and then explained how that translates into low teacher expectations and behaviors toward students and how those messages and actions influence student attitudes and behaviors related to failure. Being able to provide a complex analysis of issues she had always seen gave her the confidence to begin to engage her teachers in discussions and advocate for herself rather than only lashing out in class, leading to greater success in all of her classes that final semester of her junior year. This one example reflects the ways in which the students in our classes were able to take our applied theoretical work and translate it into their lives in ways that they found powerful and immediately applicable.

SCHOOL LEADERSHIP FOR RACIAL JUSTICE

The objective of this chapter was to expose the forces at work in shaping Latina/o schooling. Specifically, the goal was to demonstrate the importance of addressing the most complex issues at work in schools serving disenfranchised Latina/o communities. The focus was on developing a historical, theoretical analysis that can be used to frame the dominant approaches to schooling in these communities today.

The challenge for school leaders is to create spaces and mechanisms whereby teachers can engage in an analysis of these kinds of explorations and reflect on their own experiences and understandings. Teachers and school personnel need to be able to confront their own racial-ideological upbringing and the way that is manifested in their classroom practices.

Unfortunately, with all the demands placed on schools, administrators, and teachers, this is rarely part of the dialog in schools related to meeting their objectives. MAESTR@S began this work with an understanding that it must be. We saw that the focus on testing, standards, and other policies and procedures ignored what was most profoundly affecting our youth and their families and communities. This is the work that leaders need to address in their schools. The results of our work in the high school doing exactly that paid off in all the ways that district officials push school leaders: greater student interest and engagement in school, better school attendance, and higher grades and test scores.[22] The following chapter demonstrates specifically how leaders can create counterspaces for engaging raza students in schools and the ways those spaces impact students and lead to greater individual and school success.

NOTES

1. Alicia wrote this in a reflection on teaching third grade in East Los Angeles and the challenges she faced in helping students deal with their pain (personal communication, September 17, 2011).
2. This statement is supported by a quick review of the fall 2012 course requirements of the private university and both tiers of the public university single-subject credential programs that serve the San José area, all of which are well attended and known to produce large numbers of teachers in local schools. The public university programs both require a course on language acquisition for nonnative English speakers and a course that covers educational foundations and applies aspects of that content to issues of teaching in a diverse society through historical and contemporary topics. The private university requires a course on language acquisition and one course that covers "Teaching Nonconventional Youth."
3. I use a variety of ethnic labels in this paper. Latina/o is used to refer to all Latin American descent peoples. Chicana/o is commonly used among organizers in our communities because it refers to Mexican descent Latinas/os (the vast majority of Latinas/os in many parts of California) and also because it implies a radical political analysis that many in these communities adopt, including some non-Mexican Latinas/os. I also use raza because it is an umbrella term and it is often used in communities. Chicano and Latino are used specifically to refer to males, and Chicana and Latina for females. I use these ethnic labels interchangeably because that is how they are used in our schools and communities.
4. MAESTR@S is a Bay Area-based collective of teachers and educational justice workers dedicated to addressing the needs of Latina/o communities and students. I will describe the group in more detail as the analysis evolves.
5. This is a modest difference in per pupil spending. An analysis of the annual reports released by school districts shows majority Latina/o schools in close

proximity to majority White schools have as little as 1/3 the per pupil spending as their nearby counterparts.

6. As some of us looked back at history to understand these issues more deeply, we became even more frustrated, recognizing that many of the issue we saw in the schools had been identified in research 70 or more years earlier (Manuel, 1930; Sanchez, 1939).

7. We had learned that the emotional state our students and we experienced was the most dominant and powerful force at work in the classroom. Related to this, we were feeling that the spirits of our youth, as well as our own, had been assaulted and that we all needed support to be able to develop a positive way of living and being in the classroom.

8. This analysis has been greatly informed by my teaching of these topics over the years. Some of these concepts came into much sharper focus through my work with graduate students who integrated them into their own research, building on the insights we were covering in class. Alicia Casas, Yanira Madrigal-Garcia, and Robert Unzueta are former graduate students whose work helped me develop my own understanding of the issues discussed here, particularly normalization and internalization. I am grateful to them for their hard work, complex research methods, and sharp insights.

9. As a reminder, the focus of this chapter is on working with Latinas/os in disenfranchised communities, and so this theoretical analysis is based on issues and experiences that students face in those communities. This analysis is the product of our extensive work with raza students in disenfranchised communities and demonstrates one outcome of the first phase of our model, which will be described in the next chapter.

10. Even so, every few years a new study comes out that attempts to validate deficit analyses of communities of color. Herrnstein's and Murray's *Bell Curve* of 1994 resurrected these beliefs in academic research in ways that many thought would not happen in the post-Civil Rights era. Scholarly work like this can often dominate thinking in educational institutions for years to come, especially in those contexts uninterested in more complex analyses of issues like the "achievement gap." In 2013, the power of these deficit models in academia were highlighted when excerpts from Jason Richwine's (2009) doctoral dissertation from Harvard University were reported in the media. Richwine asserts that the differences in IQ between ethnic groups are genetically caused and permanent.

11. In addition to the scholars cited in this paragraph who have analyzed the impacts of historical trauma on indigenous communities in the Americas, others have found similar effects among African Americans (DeGruy, 2010), Hawaiians (Laenui, 2000), and Australian aboriginal people (Raphael, Swan, & Martinek, 1998).

12. Valenzuela (1999) describes *educación* as "a foundational cultural construct that provides instructions on how one should live in the world " (p. 21) and as "the family's role of inculcating in children a sense of moral, social, and personal responsibility [that] serves as the foundation for all other learning" (p. 23).

13. Duran (2006), Torres (2003), and others highlight the importance of intergenerational trauma as they explain that the impact of these traumas are passed on between generations.

14. Pizarro (2014) explains these processes in greater depth through the lens of ideology, the evolution of racism, and the dominance of racial microaggressions in the school experiences of so many Latina/o youth.

15. My own extensive research with high school, community college, and university students in East Los Angles and rural Washington demonstrated this clearly. Pizarro (2005) provides countless examples and stories describing the realities outlined in this section, as well as a theoretical framework for explaining the impact they have on student identities and school performance.

16. Gregory, Nygreen, and Moran (2006) provide a critical analysis of the way in which one high school rationalizes discriminatory, disciplinary practices due to the fact that the failure of African American students has been normalized in that school. They found that, "Whether we were talking about the achievement gap or the discipline gap, the disparities among groups have become so commonplace that they are taken for granted" (p. 142).

17. This was powerfully demonstrated to me through my individual conversations with dozens of Chicana/o students in my work to understand these processes and their impacts on youth (Pizarro, 2005).

18. See Huber, Johnson, and Kohli (2006) for an overview of the internalization of racism in US schools, including an historical overview of research on this subject.

19. It is critical to distinguish these processes and their impact on raza communities from the logic used to validate the deficit models. The student failure described here is not the product of student deficits. The power of the ideological forces analyzed above is overwhelming for most, so that in order to maintain their psychological well-being, as shaky as it might be for some, Latinas/os are typically compelled to adapt the popular discourse that explains their educational and life outcomes, and so they do individualize and internalize their own failure.

20. This analysis clearly leaves no room for raza students to fail because of their own lack of effort, for example. This is a definite possibility. This intentional omission is designed to force us to look at the systemic effects of the historical and contemporary manifestations of deficit models on raza students. Furthermore, it is informed by our own experiences working with these youth and finding that those who put forth little effort, when exposed to our model and support, often begin to demonstrate significant effort, as discussed below and in the subsequent chapter.

21. We also introduced the students to the concept of community cultural wealth (Yosso, 2005) as a means of countering the negative impacts of the forces we analyzed. This was linked to our own emphasis on their unique intellectual strengths.

22. The school compared students in Latina/o literature to those in other 11th grade English classes and found that the Latina/o literature students had significantly better attendance and GPAs, greater improvements in test scores, and increased levels of engagement and interest as reflected in responses to surveys.

REFERENCES

Covarrubias, A. (2011). Quantitative intersectionality: A critical race analysis of the Chicana/o educational pipeline. *Journal of Latinos and Education, 10,* 86–105.

DeGruy, J. A. (2010). Post-slavery syndrome: A multigenerational look at African American injury, healing, and resilience. In A. Kalayhian & D. Eugene (Eds.), *Mass trauma and emotional healing around the world: Rituals and practices for resilience and meaning-making, Vol 2: Human-made disasters* (pp. 227–250). Santa Barbara, CA: Praeger.

Duran, E. (2006). *Healing the soul wound: Counseling with American Indians and other native peoples.* New York, NY: Teachers College Press

Gandara, P., & Contreras, F. (2009). *The Latino education crisis: The consequences of failed social policies.* Cambridge, MA: Harvard University Press.

Gonzales, P. (2006, February 11). Patzin: Yolpahtli—Heart medicine. Column of the Americas. Retrieved from http://aztlannet-news-blog.blogspot.com/2007/02/lunes-febrero-12-2007-aztlan-news.html

Gregory, A., Nygreen, K., & Morgan, D. (2006). The discipline gap and the normalization of failure. In P. A. Noguera & J. Y. Wong (Eds.), *Unfinished business: Closing the racial achievement gap in our schools* (pp. 121–150). San Francisco, CA: Jossey-Bass.

Herrnstein, R. J., & Murray, C. (1994). *The bell curve: Intelligence and class structure in American life.* New York, NY: Free Press.

Huber, L. P., Johnson, R. N., & Kohli, R. (2006). Naming racism: A conceptual look at internalized racism in U.S. Schools. *Chicana/o-Latina/o Law Review, 26,* 183-206.

Kids in Common. (2009, December). *Issue brief: Santa Clara county children's agenda* (vol. 2, no. 6). San Jose, CA: Author.

Laenui, P. (2000). Processes of decolonization. In M. Battiste (Ed.), *Reclaiming indigenous voice and vision* (pp. 150–160). Vancouver, Canada: UBC Press.

Lambert, C. (2008, March-April). Trails of tears, and hope. *Harvard Magazine, 110,* 39–43, 85–87.

Manuel, H. T. (1930). *The education of Mexican and Spanish-speaking children in Texas.* Austin, TX: The Fund for Research in the Social Sciences, the University of Texas.

Menchaca, M., & Valencia, R. R. (1990). Anglo-Saxon ideologies in the 1920s–1930s: Their impact on the segregation of Mexican students in California. *Anthropology & Education Quarterly, 21,* 222–249.

Murrillo, E. G., Villenas, S. A., Galván, R. T., Muñoz, J. S., Martínez, C., & Machado-Casas, M. (Eds.). (2010). *Handbook of Latinos and education: Theory, research and practice.* New York, NY: Routledge.

Pizarro, M. (2005). *Chicanas and Chicanos in school: Racial profiling, identity battles, and empowerment.* Austin, TX: University of Texas Press.

Pizarro, M. (2014). The twists and turns of ethnic prejudice and discrimination: 21st century manifestations of historically entrenched racial ideologies. In M. Urbina (Ed.), *Latinas y Latinos in the United States: 21st century dynamics of multiculturalism* (pp. 153–170). Springfield, IL: Charles C. Thomas Publisher.

Pizarro, M., & Montoya, M. (2002). Seeking educational self-determination: Raza studies for revolution. *Equity & Excellence in Education, 35,* 276–292.

Raphael, B., Swan, P., & Martinek, N. (1998). Intergenerational aspects of trauma for Australian aboriginal people. In Y. Danieli (Ed.), *International handbook of multigenerational legacies of trauma* (pp. 327–339). New York, NY: Plenum Press

Richwine, J. (2009). IQ and immigration policy (Doctoral dissertation). Retrieved from ProQuest Dissertations and Theses (Accession Order No. AAT 3365409).

Sanchez, G. I. (1939). *The equalization of educational opportunity—some issues and problems.* Albuquerque, NM: University of New Mexico Press.

San Miguel, Jr., G., & Donato, R. (2010). Latino education in twentieth century America: A brief history. In E. G. Murrillo, S. A. Villenas, R. T. Galván, J. S. Muñoz, C. Martínez, & M. Machado-Casas (Eds.), *Handbook of Latinos and education: Theory, research and practice* (pp. 27–62). New York, NY: Routledge.

Torres, E. E. (2003). *Chicana without apology: The new Chicana cultural studies.* New York, NY: Routledge.

Torres, M., & Fergus, E. (2012). Social mobility and the complex status of Latino males: Education, employment, and incarceration patterns from 2000–2009. In P. Noguera, A. Hurtado, & E. Fergus (Eds.), *Invisible no more: Understanding the disenfranchisement of Latino men and boys* (pp. 19–40). New York, NY: Routledge.

Valencia, R. R. (2010). *Dismantling contemporary deficit thinking: Educational thought and practice.* New York, NY: Routledge

Valencia, R. R. (Ed.). (2011). *Chicano school failure and success: Past, present, and future* (3rd ed.). New York, NY: Routledge.

Valencia, R. R., & Solorzano, D. G. (1997). Contemporary deficit thinking. In R. R. Valencia (Ed.), *The evolution of deficit thinking: Educational thought and practice* (pp. 160–210). Washington, DC: The Falmer Press.

Valenzuela, A. (1999). *Subtractive schooling: US–Mexican youth and the politics of caring.* Tucson, AZ: University of Arizona Press.

Yellow Horse, S. & Brave Heart, M. Y. H. (2005). Healing the Wakanheja: Evidence based, promising, and culturally appropriate practices for American Indian/Alaska Native children with mental health needs. *Wellbriety: White Bison's Online Magazine, 6*(6), 35–43.

Yosso, T. (2005). *Critical race counterstories along the Chicana/Chicano educational pipeline.* New York, NY: Routledge.

CHAPTER 9

RACIAL JUSTICE LEADERSHIP IN DISENFRANCHISED LATINA/O COMMUNITIES

A Model for Walking Social Justice in Schools

Marcos Pizarro
San José State University

with Jaime,[1] Rosalva Gaytan, Martha Naranjo, Carlos Navarrete, and the MAESTR@S Collective

Perhaps the greatest challenge faced by school leaders who strive to engage in transformative racial justice work in their schools is the lack of models available. Because of the often impenetrable dominance of conventional learning models within United States schooling, even school reform is defined by these conventions, so that "innovation" is superficial, leaving racial inequality intact. The members of MAESTR@S[2] came together out of a desire to create new models. We had grown tired of failed efforts to rethink the

Envisioning Critical Race Praxis in K–12 Leadership Through Counter-Storytelling, pages 183–209
Copyright © 2016 by Information Age Publishing

work being done to address racial inequality in schools. Our recurring disappointment with school reform inspired us to look for a different way. We saw that top-down approaches simply led to the reproduction of dominant methods of confronting long-standing problems. We sought real methods of daily practice that addressed raza[3] students' deepest and most immediate needs.

The focus of this chapter is to demonstrate how school leaders and teachers can approach social and racial justice work with their school communities. The real lessons for leaders are in *how* we engage in this work, much more than what we cover when we do the work. By analyzing the processes MAESTR@S developed, we highlight the ways in which teachers and school leaders can walk social justice with their school communities.

THE EVOLUTION OF MAESTR@S: LEARNING TO WALK SOCIAL JUSTICE

In MAESTR@S, as we found clarity in understanding the complexity of raza youth realities through our work with them, we realized that even our own focus on developing innovative classroom strategies for engaging the youth over our first five years was not addressing their deepest needs (those outlined in the previous chapter). Perhaps the biggest lesson we learned as we shifted our focus to directly meeting these needs was the importance of moving beyond our own talk about them. In our ongoing workshops, we had talked about strategies for helping our youth, but we realized that we had to develop those strategies by actually engaging in them ourselves, focusing on what *we* need given that we have lived these same experiences, albeit in our own ways. What we learned from this was that we, ourselves, had been there—confronting the pain of living with historical trauma, having to constantly fight against the normalization of inequality and racism, working to counter the individualization of school failure that so many of our peers and students and we, ourselves, are quick to adopt, and the often-overwhelming internalization of racism, both within ourselves and among our students. We found that we each carried that pain with us. As we moved into this new phase of our work, looking back at our own lives, we saw that we had unconsciously developed strategies to avoid dealing with this pain. For example, through our process, we exposed how we had often masked our pain with anger, even rage, because it was an easier emotion to express. We also realized that we hid from our own fears by distracting ourselves, staying hyper-busy, again because that was easier than dealing with the pain and subsequent fear we had experienced and continued to face. As we processed these and other survival tactics, we could see the struggles of our students and knew that the lessons we were learning in this process were essential to our work with youth. If we were struggling to consciously and effectively deal with these realities, we recognized, then we could not expect our youth to take on the same issues on their own.

The process helped us see that we were a reflection of our students as they were of us. This meant that we were not creating a model for students, but that we were building a model for all of us. This was essential. We were not just helping students or imparting knowledge to them, but rather we were embarking on a process that we needed just as much as they did, and we were learning together and from each other along the way. The development of this unique approach, therefore, includes two interwoven phases. First, we went through the process of challenging ourselves to build a model by experiencing it ourselves. Next, we began to adopt this model in our respective jobs and community work, bringing it directly to youth, families, and communities and having them help us deepen the model. The critical lesson here is that all of us, regardless of race and class, have been deeply shaped by racial ideology (see the framework from the previous chapter), and if we do not explore that consciously and collectively, it is all but impossible to understand how it manifests itself in our lives and how we can counter it in our work and schooling.

As this project evolved, we developed steps that helped us on our path of social justice work, but even more importantly, we found that it was the emerging ethics informing our approach that were most essential because, despite the different ways in which we might implement one of these steps, it was the underlying principles upon which we based our work that made it so effective. These ethics defined our approach and included: (1) seeing ourselves in others and others seeing themselves in us (the Mayan concept of *in lak ech* and the Mexica concept of *nehuan ti nehuan*), (2) deep honesty grounded in familial love, and, (3) community accountability to and nurturing of each individual. We understand these ethics as, collectively, manifesting justice in every action. Every step we take in our process (in our work together and in our work with youth) has to be a holistic embodiment of principles of justice. This is why we had to take ourselves through the model before we did any work with youth. As these ethics helped us create the model, we found that the project was really about relationship- and community-building as justice work, because we needed to do this work in community in order for us to sustain ourselves and walk social justice for the rest of our lives. This is the lesson that we, as educators and as school leaders, embodied to amplify our effectiveness in addressing racial justice issues.

A NOTE ON METHODS: WALKING SOCIAL JUSTICE AS RESEARCH

In MAESTR@S, from early on, we knew that research was essential to our work. Research, however, was not a distinct aspect of our process. We saw each step of our process as part of a larger whole, walking social justice, which was most deeply shaped by the ethics that guided this collaborative work (as discussed in the previous section).

When we eventually began to talk about the research component of our work, it was inseparable from the process. We were the researchers and the researched. We saw that we each had to play a role in every facet of the process: the development of the model itself, the testing of the model through our experiences, the revising of the model based on these applications, and the analysis of its overall impact on our lives. The research aspect of our work was, therefore, an unconscious part of the model from its inception. Like the larger process, the research was organic and evolving, as we constantly revisited each facet of the model and integrated the experiences and insights of every person involved in the group.[4]

Conventional research methods are typically shaped by the centrality of validity of all aspects of the research process. The goal of the researcher is to obtain data that can objectively answer specific questions, which is often understood as possible only by the separation of the researcher from the researched. Our approach represented a challenge to that understanding. Our experiences working with youth suggested that we needed to live in their worlds to be able to effectively work with and support them. This meant that we needed to experience the model in community with them. It also meant that we had to construct the meaning from this work collaboratively. Our approach to this process as researchers was grounded in our pursuit of *ethical validity*. Our ethics required that we not take any part of the research process out of the hands of those who have to live in the realities we sought to understand and help them address. Furthermore, we were not concerned with data or publishing our work and instead were focused on developing a model for engaging youth and communities that actually met their/our needs for understanding their/our lives, identifying and pursuing their/our individual goals, and supporting the pursuit of equity and justice within their/our communities.

Still, there are parallels between our process and more conventional research methods. Together, we defined the research questions of the project: identifying the issues that needed to be "studied." We collectively designed the data collection instruments: through our gatherings, we discussed, introduced, and developed ways of confronting the issues that we were seeking to address. Each person played the role of researcher/interviewer: facilitating the different activities, asking questions of those who were participating and providing "data," and reflecting back what they heard participants sharing. Each person also played the role of research subject/interviewee: being asked to participate in activities, being a focal subject at given times, answering questions, and sharing stories related to the research questions. The group collectively conducted the "data analysis": responding to stories shared (both individual stories and the larger collective story) and explaining the meanings of those stories from the perspective of the researcher and of the researched. The collective also engaged in the writing of the findings: using group gatherings to write about our process, the most personally relevant insights, and the deeper meanings taken from different facets of the work (through stories), as they related to the evolving model that we were developing. Our "research" reflected the larger project as it was grounded in our ethics, demonstrating the importance of racial justice work always being based on principles in every aspect of the work.

This approach to the research components of our project was then mirrored in its next application, as we gradually took the model and brought it into our work with youth and communities. At the same time, we used our gatherings to develop the model based on the lessons from these applications.

The following sections integrate the lessons from both the process of developing the model in MAESTR@S and implementing it in the classroom. The MAESTR@S collective includes fifteen core members, two-thirds of whom are women, ranging in age from mid-twenties to fifties, almost all of whom had grown up in and continue to work with disenfranchised communities (most often in schools). The group meets about every six weeks throughout the year and also hosts an annual weekend retreat. The excerpts from our work that are discussed in this chapter come from the newest direction of the group, after the first five years, and reflect insights that the collective feels are a strong representation of the model and its strengths.

The applications of our model shared here comes from my [Pizarro's] own efforts to adapt our work to the college classroom. As the coordinator of MAESTR@S and the one with the most freedom to test our model and assess its impact in the classroom,[5] my applications of the model may be the most extensive. I focused these efforts on a college special topics course in Chicana/o studies intended to help train students who want to work for social justice in disenfranchised communities. The premise of the approach was that students needed to go through the process they hoped to offer youth. This class was taught in the fall semester of 2010 and 2011. The classes consisted of 22 and 19 students, two-thirds of both consisting of women, almost all in their twenties, most of them the first in their families to go to college, and many having grown up in disenfranchised communities themselves. The examples chosen from the classes were among those that the students identified as the most powerful lessons they took from our process together.

As explained, the MAESTR@S process was developed to meet the needs of students, teachers, and community members. It was not planned consciously as research, but rather as social justice work and community building. Even this new direction of the project has been years in the making, and throughout, our focus was always on how best to meet the needs of the participants. Therefore, it has been extremely difficult to simplify this work for a book chapter and to select examples that reflect the complexity and organic nature of the process. Whenever possible, we use the participants' own writing about the process in the sections that follow. In all cases, I shared this work with the members of MAESTR@S and the students in our classes and consulted them both individually and collectively at least three times before finalizing the writing. The work that follows represents this process and reflects just one of the ways in which we walk social justice as a collective.[6] While this is explicitly written as a note on research methods, as with all sections of this chapter, it is intended as a model of school leadership as well, demonstrating the possibilities of creating engaged communities of social justice, where participants (e.g., teachers) are centered and given the opportunity to explore their own experiences and needs earnestly.

BUILDING A MODEL FOR CONFRONTING INTERNALIZED RACISM AND HISTORICAL TRAUMA[7]

In plotting our work, a model for walking social justice, MAESTR@S designed a process that we went through first and then began to integrate into our individual work with youth and communities. Because of the complexity of this process, we will first share the critical steps that serve as the foundation of the approach and then provide examples in the subsequent section.

We envision our work as the evolving creation of a *LifeMap*. As suggested above, addressing the needs of disenfranchised raza youth requires that we engage in a process of understanding ourselves and our communities in the larger context of our society. This work on the LifeMap consists of three phases and several layers that are interwoven and ongoing.

The process begins with phase one, *developing a shared understanding of our communities and society*.[8] This first step entails spending the time to carefully observe the context in which we find ourselves (at a community level, as well as a societal level), explain why and how things are the way they are, and identify the most critical issues we face that need to be addressed. It is an empowering and often transformative experience, since the work being done to explain our lives happens through stories and unpacking their collective meanings as we discuss, debate, and work to develop a useable theory for explaining what we have lived and seen. This process helps individuals and the collective begin to deeply understand the issues we face in holistic ways, while also building community. This can take time and may involve arguments and obstacles, so it is our commitment to addressing the issues we live that allows us to keep working through the tough discussions and analyses to arrive at this shared understanding. Through this work, we also learn that our understanding is always evolving and in contention, because each of us embodies it in our own way. In our model, we describe phase one as *knowing and owning our lives and identities* because it is through this process that we begin to understand our deep personal and historical relationship to the forces shaping life in the United States today and how that impacts our daily experiences.

Phase two involves *understanding how the world we have to deal with has shaped and affected us* and how it continues to do so every day. The most effective way we met this challenge was through the development of the first layer of the *LifeMap*,[9] in which we created a visual map of the traumas/pain we have experienced: the *TraumaMap*.[10] Too many of us who grew up, work, or have lived in disenfranchised communities have no opportunity to process our feelings about what we have been forced to live with as part of daily life in these communities. The goal of the *TraumaMap* is to move beyond generic discussions of inequality and opportunity gaps, and to look deeply at our own experiences to begin to understand the relationship between those experiences and the larger social forces that we want to confront. This reflective process leads us to focus on how pain affects us in our lives, and we begin that analysis through the second layer of the *LifeMap*, an *EmotionMap* of how our trauma and pain impact us on a daily basis by way of the multiple emotions we experience as a result. Through this process, we push each other to explore the full range of emotions that have been shaped by our experiences with injustice, trauma, and pain. This can include anger, sadness, and a wide array of emotions that we often struggle to hide or ignore. As we begin to understand the terrain of our emotions, as well as the mechanisms we develop to deal with those emotions, we often recognize that the entirety of these processes can result in deeply embedded fears, which we typically do not confront. For this reason, the next layer of the *LifeMap*, the *FearMap*, involves deciphering and confronting the fears that we experience throughout our lives. What we soon learned is that, even in a group of strong and committed social justice workers, for example, fear can be a significant obstacle to our envisioning how we can live our lives in the best way possible in our work for social justice. We discovered how these limits, our fears, also shape our actions, hindering us and the effectiveness of our work. By providing a safe space to collectively look deeply at our fears, where they come from, and how they limit us, we can begin to more honestly understand ourselves and our needs as we strive to engage in our social justice work.

Throughout the second phase, group members are strengthened by the collective process that allows us to see that these realities do not belong to any one of us as individuals but happen to us as a community (including our families and home communities). This evolving realization helps us connect our work on the *LifeMap* back to our shared understanding about the social forces at work in shaping the inequality experienced in disenfranchised raza communities at large (phase one). This is a critical step because it allows us to realistically connect our daily lives, experiences, and challenges to a larger understanding of what is happening in our communities, to link our experiences with those of everyone else in these communities, and to use that as the foundation of our daily work. We also describe all of this work in phase two as *developing voice and a language of understanding and transformation* because it is through this process that we begin to really understand ourselves, opening the possibility for what we want to change in our lives and communities.

Having a clear vision of this relationship between social forces, our personal challenges and traumas, and the impact they have on us emotionally and through internalized fears (for example) logically moves us to the next step of the *LifeMap* process, phase three, *envisioning* what we want to change and how we can do that, at the individual, group, and community level. The challenge of this phase is to develop mechanisms that allow us to not just imagine the ideals we are seeking, but to create concrete and realistic steps that we can take to confront these issues in our everyday actions. This work returns us to the *LifeMap* as we develop the final layer, a map of our prayers. Using "prayer" as part of this model is a challenge. We envision prayer not as a specifically religious practice, but as a holistic and spiritual act. We recognize the need for a daily practice that informs every action we take. The previous phases of this process have shown how the daily forces that we are fighting against are constantly on the assault, often working at a subconscious level that hurts, creates emotional disequilibrium, and plants seeds of fear. This daily practice involves developing individual and connected, collective visions that are both short-term and long-term, and that include detailed roadmaps and check-ins with other group members. Through this process, we create personal and collective plans for the work that we want to do and how we can be whole people (emotionally, physically, intellectually, and spiritually intact and healthy) in the pursuit of our goals. We recognize that we have to integrate our spirits into this work, because spirit is where our most profound desires come from. Reflecting back on the earlier phases in the model, we also understand that it is our spirits that are most deeply affected by the pain, anger, and fear we face in our lives as raza living in the United States. We use the concept of prayer simply as a means of making this work a daily practice that involves how we approach everything we do, which is why we frame the overall model as walking social justice. We know that our work for social justice is a life journey and one that we need to pace ourselves for so that we can develop healthy ways of engaging in this process that are manifested in everything we do each day of our lives. We see this *LifeMap* work—creating a shared understanding of our experiences and incorporating the *TraumaMap, EmotionalMap, FearMap,* and finally the *PrayerMap*—as the development of methods of *living social justice*. This process incorporates the creation of a collective vision for our work: committing to that vision with discipline and daily action that brings it to life.

This process, reflected in the visual model in Figure 9.1, involves months of work and a number of different steps. It is one that the MAESTR@S

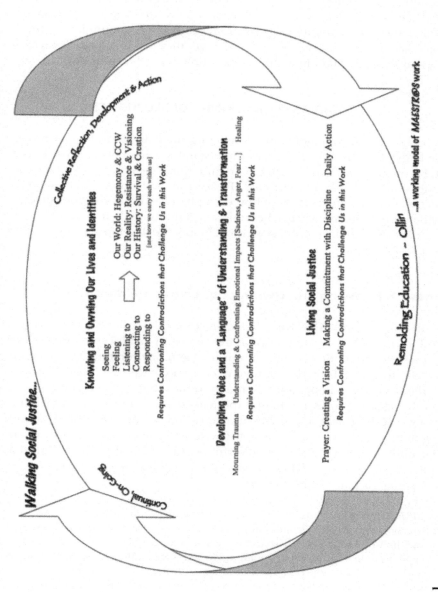

Collective Reflection, Development & Action

Knowing and Owning Our Lives and Identities

Seeing	Our World: Hegemony & CCW
Feeling	Our Reality: Resistance & Visioning
Listening to	Our History: Survival & Creation
Connecting to	
Responding to	[and how we carry each within us]

Requires Confronting Contradictions that Challenge Us in this Work

Developing Voice and a "Language" of Understanding & Transformation

Mourning Trauma   Understanding & Confronting Emotional Impacts [Sadness, Anger, Fear....]   Healing

Requires Confronting Contradictions that Challenge Us in this Work

Living Social Justice

Prayer: Creating a Vision   Making a Commitment with Discipline   Daily Action

Requires Confronting Contradictions that Challenge Us in this Work

Walking Social Justice...

Continual, On-Going

Remolding Education — Ollin

...a working model of MAESTR@S work

Figure 9.1

community is still engaged in, as we recognize that it does not end and that it requires continual development and interaction between the different phases, and ongoing effort to understand how we have experienced and internalized the complicated issues that we confront over the course of our lives.[11] Still, it is a process that, as we share it with youth and communities, is providing spaces for raza to confront the challenges they face in United States society and in their communities in complex, holistic, and realistic ways.

EXAMPLES OF WALKING SOCIAL JUSTICE

From our own involvement both developing and going through this model, we know that it is difficult to fully understand without having experienced it. For many of us, truly "getting it" requires approaching a given phase in at least a couple of different ways. To assist in explaining the model, this section includes an example of how each phase works through our process of developing it amongst teachers and a second example from implementing the model in the college classroom.[12] Later, we develop applications for K–12 schooling.

Phase 1: Knowing and Owning our Lives and Identities

In our work in MAESTR@S, phase one came naturally for us because we had worked together as a group for five years and had focused on developing a collective understanding of our lives and our communities since we initially formed. Through a number of exercises in which we shared our experiences in the schools as teachers and former students, and also brought youth together to discuss their experiences, we constructed an evolving analysis of those experiences in our schools and communities. After exploring these realities, we spent one day developing a manifesto that expressed our understandings. This was powerful because we had to strive toward a collective process of making meaning out of realities that were often overwhelming. As that manifesto explains,

> *MAESTR@S* is an educational movement founded on a politicized, anti-oppression analysis of the condition of raza and the powerful role of hegemony: racism/white supremacy, patriarchy/sexism, homophobia/heterosexism and capitalism, in shaping that condition. We attack institutional, interpersonal, and internalized oppression/colonization with a specific focus on dealing with how we as individuals experience oppression, which is internalized by way of both the media and schools. We engage in collective spiritual development with daily applications so that we can Walk Social Justice in our communities and with our youth.

This manifesto reflects our ongoing conversations through which we sought to understand our experiences and the challenges we faced. Beginning by developing this shared understanding allowed us as a community to create a foundational analysis to build upon as we moved forward. This phase of the work is best seen in the "theory-building" of the previous chapter, and readers should review that work for a clearer understanding of the power and complexity of this step in the process.

After we had carefully developed our model over a number of years, I [Pizarro] began applying this model to my work in a specific college class that is designed to walk students through a process of learning how to work for social justice in disenfranchised communities. We[13] took on this first phase of the model by telling our stories. Students were assigned an autobiography in which they had to explain their own identities and their experiences in their communities, families, and schools that shaped who they are. The critical piece of this assignment was the process of sharing stories in community. By telling their stories to a partner and then discussing this conversation with the class and sharing a key section of their autobiographies with everyone, the students began to understand more deeply their lives as they connected their experiences to others in the group. The students later recounted that this process not only helped them build community but allowed them to see that their lives are only truly understood in relation to the experiences of others who share similarities, but also exhibit significant differences. [14] Jaime[15] reflected on this exercise at the end of the class:

> One of the things I got out of this class was the opportunity to know myself on another level. Writing an autobiography was a great way to remind myself of how beautiful and powerful my life stories are. Before, I felt bad about some of the things that happened to me, but now I see it in a different way. All my stories are gifts and reminders of my experience of life. Even though some of the memories are sad, they have made me a stronger person.

In the case of Jaime, early on in the class he shared his own struggles dealing with his father's addiction, and the emotion that he exhibited during this process, of sadness and forgiveness/relief, resonated deeply with the community and created an opening for others (males in particular) to be introspective and vulnerable with the group.[16] Many people noted this as a turning point in the class. It was also a turning point for Jaime because his autobiography then melded into his father's biography (a follow-up assignment asked students to do a biography of an elder in their family). As he explained at the end of the semester:

> I am personally thankful for this class because it helped me get closer to my dad. I always had problems communicating with my dad because he put my family through rough times. I interviewed my dad for my second assignment

and I had the courage to ask my dad why he did the things he did. After having that conversation with my dad, I found out so many stories about him and commonalities. As Boyle [2010] said in his book, "We can never judge a book by its cover, nor can we judge a book by its first chapters." It took my dad many years to change but he did and for that I am grateful. Taking this class helped me understand that, as a people, we can offer so many great things, but we are not perfect, and sometimes being wrong or making the wrong decision is acceptable. To be able to help others, we need to first understand and help ourselves.

Jaime showed the class his process of beginning to make sense of his own experiences, connecting our work as a class to this understanding, and moving toward specific strategies of confronting complex personal, familial, and community issues in ways that mattered to him. The students were able to push their own understandings of their experiences in ways that reflected where they had been, where they are, and where they wanted to be. This process initiated the students' work to both know and own their lives and identities, and through it we were able to counter the individualization so many of us had learned through the normalization of the inequalities and injustices we had lived, so that we could unpack and contest the internalization of racism that we were beginning to clearly see in our own lives.

Phase 2: Developing Voice and a Language of Understanding and Transformation

The exploration of past traumas, their emotional impact on us, and the ways in which they can manifest themselves in our fears is truly challenging. Many of us find it much easier to talk about issues of inequality and oppression theoretically or in terms of how they affect others (our students and communities at large, for example), rather than how they affect us personally and emotionally.

The work on the *TraumaMap*, for example, can be difficult for some to conceptualize initially, but as we, in MAESTR@S, asked about the greatest obstacles we had to overcome, the most profound hurt we had to face, and the specific traumatic incidents we had to deal with, it became clear that these had been pivotal in shaping not only who we are, but also what we still need to confront to be able to live and do social justice work effectively. In MAESTR@S, one of the ways in which we approached the *TraumaMap* was to simply ask about a trauma we may have faced and then to leave everyone alone to journal for 30 minutes. Having established trust as a collective and then building this work on the foundation of our evolving understanding of the issues happening in our communities (phase 1), most of us found it easy to let this simple prompt carry us through our individual histories. The first time we did this, one of our members, who is our eldest core member, reflected on her own experiences with abuse in childhood. The power of her story deeply affected each of us, and this was the lesson: We learned the ways in which we all were reflected in and part of her story and then, as others began to share their reactions, she saw how she was part of and reflected in each of us. This gave us the opportunity to really begin to understand ourselves in the context of the social issues we wanted to confront and to recognize how those issues are embodied in us, even when they may not have affected us directly. This process strengthened our connections as well as our understandings of ourselves and our work for social justice.

In our class, we asked the students to actually draw their *LifeMaps*,[17] focusing on the experiences or forces that most deeply shaped them. We gave them a class session to reflect, draw, think out loud, and deeply focus on making sense of their own lives in community. This task can be a challenge to some of us because of the baggage we learn (often in school) about not being artistic, but with careful reframing of the concept of artistic expression and the provision of support, most of the students jumped into this work and pushed themselves to make sense of their lives.[18] Again, the most powerful part of this process was the sharing. Over the course of the rest of the semester, students explained their *LifeMaps*, and almost always, the student who shared did so at a time that fit with the work we were doing as a class. With each *LifeMap* shared, the students were making connections across their experiences, more deeply understanding the ways that, even through their greatest differences, they were connected. In addition, we found that, because of the internalization we have gone through, we often do not have a clear picture of ourselves, so it is through the understandings and connections that our community creates as we tell our stories and they reflect them back to us in the meanings they make that we finally begin to see ourselves completely in our beauty and strength. One example that resonated deeply with the class was shared by Rosalva Gaytan, whose LifeMap was a drawing of a snail. Her work inspired Pizarro to write about what happened through her sharing.

> On the spiral shell of the snail, Rosa wrote the multiple challenges she faced as a working class Chicana living in inner-city Oakland, and yet even with this great burden on her back, the snail shell, Rosa was smiling as the sun looked down upon her. When she shared her *LifeMap* with the class, she explained the severe traumas she had to confront, but also expressed the liberation she felt in recognizing that these challenges were not her fault, and that she could create a vision of herself that was whole and exactly who she wanted to be.

Rosa's character, quiet and confident, and her amazing story, not just surviving trauma, but thriving, was compelling and gave us the chance to envision a language of transformation as she had, showing that this could be possible for each of us.

Obviously, the idea of reflecting on past trauma can be a serious challenge and extremely uncomfortable, but both in MAESTR@S and our classes, our work on the first phase of this process led us to realize that the pain that each of us carry has a profound impact on us, often subconsciously, throughout our daily lives. We learned that our work was to support each other through a process of acknowledging that reality and beginning to understand its impact.[19]

Phase 3: Living Social Justice

The final phase of the process is the most vital simply because of how overwhelming the issues raised in the first two parts of the model can be. One of the greatest challenges of social justice work is the paralysis that can come from analyzing injustice and oppression. It can leave students and teachers alike feeling hopeless. Raza who go through this process need the opportunity, therefore, to envision the ways in which they want to live their lives as whole people. They must do this work in community, where they can begin to connect and align their daily action for social justice to that of others in the community and collectively move toward confronting injustice by walking social justice.

In MAESTR@S, one of the ways we embarked on this task is through a mask-making exercise (Figure 9.2). By making plaster gauze masks as a group, we commit to supporting each other through a visioning of who we want to be, as we struggle with all of our histories and experiences and work for social justice in our own small ways. For me [Pizarro], I entered the

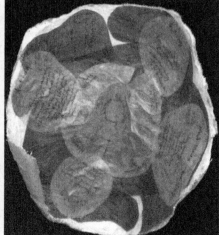

Figure 9.2

exercise apprehensive, but, because of my trust in the group and the support of the community at this gathering, I eventually gave in to the process and let someone slowly cover my face with the plaster. It was the next step that surprised me even more, as I eventually took my written *TraumaMap* and glued it to the inside of the mask, demonstrating the ways in which my multilayered traumas, my complex emotional responses to them, and the fears that I had developed that were limiting me, all represented the challenges I carried with me that no one ever saw. On the outside of the mask, despite my lack of artistic confidence, I painted my *PrayerMap*, my visual representation of who I wanted to be, burning like fire, organic and growing like corn, strong and fluid like water, deeply connected to the land, and fed by the sun. I later shared this work, explaining how it represented my vision of who I want to be and asking the community to help me live that. This walking of social justice is so difficult, but it is the community that makes it possible to take each step as we work together, connect our lives, and constantly see each other as a community in which our stories, our traumas, and our prayers are all connected in a web of support. The process of sharing these visions with a community supports us to live the work, knowing that others have affirmed and committed to walking this path with us, and developing specific plans for manifesting our prayers. This specificity is also solidified in action plans that are broken down, for example, on grids that cover everything from a particular goal we each want to reach to the daily actions that will lead to its achievement and the strategies we will take to confront the challenges we know we will encounter.

The students in our class engaged in this process in a different way. Their final assignment for the class ended with a vision of who they wanted to be and how they would take our work forward with them in their lives. They each did this in their own way and shared it in our final classes with the community as a way of ensuring that the community heard their prayers and could help them live these prayers. Rosa, whose *LifeMap* is discussed in the previous section, wrote a poem/mission statement for herself as part of her final project, integrating pictures of her family, and titled *Sacred Purpose*.[20] She used parts of our model and highlighted a vision of herself on the physical, spiritual, intellectual, and emotional levels of her life. In this work, she explained, "I will make sure I take care of myself before I surround myself with others"; "I will be the living example of what I want to see in my family and community"; and "I will continue living a balanced life of reciprocity." This final vision actually connected back to her *LifeMap* earlier in the semester, in which, on the green body of the snail, despite all of the burdens she carried on her back, she began creating a vision of who she was becoming,

Aside from being a successful Chicana, I want to get married & have kids. I want my husband & I to be loving parents. I want us to celebrate birthdays and holidays together. I want us to live & breathe what it means to be a family by respecting, loving, caring, trusting & being loyal to one another.

Through her work on the *LifeMap* and her final prayer for herself, Rosa was developing not just a vision of who she wanted to be, but *how* she was going to be that person, beginning that day.

The greatest demonstration of the strength of our process was that so many of the students wanted to continue the work after the class was over. In the second version of the class, we provided an opportunity for them to come together the next semester and do an independent study with us as a way of continuing the work, applying the lessons learned in the development of support groups in a local community center. One-third of the students in the class took us up on this offer, not even receiving a grade for the class. As they explained, they wanted this community to help them live the work we had started and to share it with others. They understood that they were learning ways of walking social justice that reflected who they are, where they come from, and where they wanted to go as a community.

Our work in MAESTR@S and in our classes showed us clearly that raza students, teachers, and communities need this work. Even among successful educators, MAESTR@S found that we had succumbed to the normalization of inequality and racism in our communities and that, despite our consciousness, we had also internalized much of this deep in our psyches. Most of all, we learned that we wanted to counter the individualization we had learned and accepted over the course of our lives. As we built a collective understanding, connected that to our individual and communal stories, and developed a vision of who we could be individually and as a group, we recognized that at each step in this process we needed others to help us make sense of ourselves. It is in this process of understanding ourselves through the stories of others that we are able to make sense of who we are, as we fight for who we will be. Related to this, we also recognized how much we needed support throughout this work. Fully engaging in these processes requires a community of support. In both contexts, we saw that we needed that community to help us do the challenging work of confronting the contradictions we face on a daily basis and the obstacles that we simply cannot overcome without ongoing support. The students in our classes affirmed this through their deep, personal commitment to each other that, as they explained, far exceeded anything they had ever done with peers in a classroom setting, which led to ongoing support long after the classes ended.

The Impact of Walking Social Justice on Students

What does this mean for teachers in the classroom? What does it mean for school leaders who strive to build a community of support for their teachers? As this chapter and the previous one have shown, the challenges that Latina/o students in disenfranchised communities must face can be significant. Although credential programs focus on curriculum to a large degree, along with some important work on pedagogy, as this analysis has shown, teachers also need to be prepared to meet their students where their greatest needs are.

Raza students have to fight against the internalization of racism that dominates the racial landscape of life in the United States today. Many simultaneously battle against the realities of living in disenfranchised communities and the personal challenges they face in their daily lives. As explained above, to better understand how we can support these students, we have brought our model into the college classroom in a special topics course: Working for Social Justice in Disenfranchised Communities. Through this course, we wanted to explore both how our model would meet undergraduate student needs and if we could begin the process of training them for this work.[21]

Having explained some of what we did in the class above, we will consider the effect of our process on students. As the students explained at the end of each semester, they greatly appreciated the opportunity to reflect on and understand their own experiences in the context of their family and community histories. Two of the constructs that resonated most deeply each time we taught the course were historical trauma and the internalization of racism. Throughout the semester, students wrestled with these ideas as they looked at their own and their families' lives. In our first version of the class, Carlos Navarrete explained what our work meant for him.

> Upon reflection, I did not know why I was ashamed sometimes of being poor and Mexican. I remember as a kid that I was ashamed that my mother had to work two jobs and still could not buy us nice clothes. I remember crying when my mother would take us to the church to get free meals on the weekends because I was worried that somebody would see me. I remember I did not want to hang out with the kids that had just arrived from Mexico, but I did not know why. I now understand that I had bought into the stereotypes about Mexicans, though I myself was Mexican. The reading[22] really is eye opening to me now. I have seen in my family how my sisters worried about getting dark. Whiteness in my family, as well as in Mexico, is valued as an aesthetic. Dark is ugly. Indigenous is ugly.

Carlos took our process to heart and used it as a chance to reanalyze his and his family's life stories, and he went through each of the steps of the process to arrive at this analysis. This gave him the motivation not only to strive for success, but to re-think his goals, creating an educational and career path that would allow him to share this approach with others. As Carlos told Pizarro in the months that followed, this process also gave him a sense of confidence and affirmation as he learned the ways in which he could give meaning to things he always felt but had never known how to put into words or practice.

Martha Naranjo, another student in our first class, reflected on her experiences in the class after it was over.

> I was confused for so long about who I was and what direction I was going. I was extremely hard on myself for every mistake I ever made in my life. For a long time, I believed that it was my fault for growing up in the dysfunctional environment that I did, surrounding myself with negative influences in my life, and disciplining myself by coping with substances such as drugs and alcohol. I always had low expectations for myself because of all the barriers that I faced throughout my life, from not fitting in at school to not understanding myself and my family. Even though I was attending college and had a stable job, I did not feel complete. I felt something was missing in my life and I found that something in the class, which is understanding who I am.

As Martha explained in our final class sessions, this process allowed her to first understand and forgive herself, which was critical to her ability to work effectively in communities. Her first step toward this goal was with her own family. She told us that by understanding herself in the larger context of our community's experiences over time, she was able to approach her own family members with a new sense of understanding and possibility and, as she described to our class, this realization, along with the strategies that she began to learn, allowed her to create new connections within her family relationships.

What we witnessed both times we taught this class is that the students became deeply committed to the process. For almost all of the students, they stopped approaching our group as a class and became less concerned with their grades and much more focused on what they were doing that was going to help them reach their life goals. They began to make direct connections between historical trauma and the specific ways in which they and their families and communities had internalized racism. They adapted specific tools to develop their understandings and to live their lives as whole people. We found that the students worked extremely hard, often outside of the boundaries of the college class structure, as they continued on this path after the semester, attending community gatherings that were not required or even part of the class, and creating their own communities for applied social justice work in their daily lives. In addition, with regard to academic achievement, the students dedicated themselves deeply to their work in the class and, in the second version of the class we had, completed the most powerful and compelling set of final projects Pizarro had in over 15 years of college teaching.[23] Furthermore, many of them, for the first time in their lives, saw themselves as true students, and several changed their academic paths, realizing that they could be successful as graduate students.

Applications for K–12

Since writing the chapters that appear in this volume, Pizarro brought these models to a local high school. Working with an 11th grade English teacher, we adapted all of the facets of the model in the creation and implementation of a Latina/o literature version of English 5–6. The high school students had the chance to develop a collective and shared understanding of their lives, building on the constructs covered in the previous chapter. They then carefully considered the effects of these experiences and processes on their lives, and even began creating a vision for themselves about how they could take this work forward. This was accomplished through reading autobiography, literature, poetry, and social science research and asking students to create their own versions of these works by relying on their experiences. The curriculum was aligned to the Common Core standards and approved by district officials.

The heart of the work we did with the students was through the process itself, where students were centered and knew that they mattered. This was greatly shaped by the aforementioned ethics that we brought to the classroom: seeing ourselves in others and others seeing themselves in us, deep honesty grounded in familial love, and community accountability to and nurturing of each individual. We exhibited these ethics in everything we did and by the end of the year the students had adopted them as their own because they had experienced their power in building communities of support.

Students ended the school year with increased confidence and engagement, but also with a deep attachment to these new communities, as they expressed their appreciation for each other in emotional end-of-year goodbyes. One student showed the power of this work in her final evaluation of the course:

> [This class] showed me why we have become unmotivated. Factors like internalized racism and subtractive schooling have been affecting me and I had no idea. Now I know how to combat that. . . . It was a class that dealt with real world problems that everyone could relate to. There wasn't a day where I felt bored. It was the kind of class I could go home and talk to my parents for hours about. It was the only class I feel I really learned from and will help me later on after high school.

The lesson for K–12 teachers and school leaders, in our experience, is that by focusing on the deepest needs of our students, those issues that students confront daily, but for which they have no support, teachers can create spaces where students are able to make sense of their lives, as they learn and adapt tools for explaining their experiences. Through this process, students can then also make sense of what it means to be a student, can connect that to who they are and to who they want to be, and can also create realistic blueprints in community for achieving these goals. In short, raza who go through this process learn to be more whole, and that allows them to be much better students.

This work is challenging. It can seem like a daunting task to take a classroom full of students through this process, especially when we have the obligation to cover standards, reach benchmarks, and prepare our students for college and careers. The lesson from this project, however, is that our students need this and they thrive academically when they have it. Teachers can bring aspects of this work into the curriculum in ways that help with community building, link student goals to their specific work on a course, and achieve deep engagement in the learning process. Much of this work can be front-loaded early in the school year and then carefully weaved in throughout the year in synch with the ebbs and flows of school schedules and the student needs that emerge and evolve.[24]

We began this chapter emphasizing the importance of how we learn to walk social justice in our schools. A critical lesson from our observations of the process is that it not only meets students' needs but also teachers' needs. MAESTR@S realized that we could not just talk about and develop approaches for helping students. We needed to understand what we were dealing with as former students who had lived these realities, as teachers who witnessed the tremendous struggles of our students and their families, and as caring people who are hurt by the pain in our communities. As we have shared our work, we have found that teachers in disenfranchised communities need the space and time to confront those facets of their lives in community. Doing so helps them, but it also helps them see and be with their students through an *in lak ech* mindset to how they walk social justice. School leaders need to create these opportunities for their staff. Again, this can seem like one more entry on a long task list for a school leader. Creating spaces for teachers to explore their own challenges and critical issues, like the pain involved in working in a disenfranchised community, shifts the way in which teachers connect with each other and the community and impacts the culture of the school. This work can have dramatic effects on bottom-line issues like teacher effectiveness, student engagement, and student success.

Obviously, there are content lessons from our work with the students, as well as pedagogical insights. More important for school leaders, however, is how we created community and student engagement. This engagement was the product of our ethics in the classroom, which impacted all of our work with the students and, as the students told us at the end of the year, began the process of building their self-confidence and commitment to achieving their goals in the school. School leaders who are committed to addressing racial justice issues in their schools can model these ethics, allow school staff to explore their own ethics, and create a school culture in which community matters more than anything else. In our work, we found that as our community strengthened, student attendance increased, student effort rose, the quality of work increased, and the intellectual energy in the room continually grew.[25]

Recently, Pizarro began working in an EdD program focused on educational justice and equity. The students in this program are all school leaders, many of them working in disenfranchised communities that serve large numbers of families of color. These leaders almost all come to the program with a desire to address issues of educational inequity. The realities of daily life working in schools, however, lay an often unconscious assault on those goals. They feel constrained by the focus on test scores, balanced budgets and attendance, and any number of policies and laws that demand specific practices. These job requirements govern what they do so that explicit plans for addressing equity issues are an afterthought, if that. The work in this chapter is intended to flip the script on these approaches to school leadership. It asks the school leader to focus on what dominates and shapes the culture of the school, to attack the historical forces that determine student identities, often without their recognition, by helping teachers center racial justice work as part of their daily practice. It does not mean that leaders or their teachers should, or can, ignore policy or the daily demands of their jobs, but emphasizes recognition of the fact that if we do not deal with the issues highlighted in these chapters, our effort to address any of those job demands will be severely hindered. In contrast, if we focus on the issues discussed here, gradually, as we shift the nature of the discourse around race and schooling, concerns such as test scores and attendance will be addressed in more substantive and long-lasting ways. Building strong communities and schools through leadership requires that we begin by understanding the deepest needs of our communities, acknowledging the forces that have led to those needs and creating spaces in which we can begin to meet the needs concretely through daily practices. This must be at the heart of our school leaders' job descriptions.

FINAL REFLECTIONS

This chapter and the previous one represent MAESTR@S' journey to walk social justice with raza communities committed to addressing the educational inequities that dominate the landscape of life in the United States today. There are many lessons from the extant research on Latinas/os in school that can help us on this path. There are also many teacher credential programs that work exceptionally hard to train future teachers to dedicate themselves to equity issues in the classroom. Still, the work being done in credential programs and the research being conducted often do not deal with some of the most powerful and complicated forces affecting disenfranchised raza communities today. Through our work as a collective of social justice educators in these communities, we have been able to develop a framework for making sense of these complexities. This has helped us to understand the centrality of historical trauma in the life of these communities and the direct connection between this sociohistorical force and the evolving deficit models that are so central to the story currently being told in the United States to explain racial inequality. This reality serves as the foundation on which we build the normalization of both that inequality and the racism that feeds it. We have seen countless examples of how this set of forces impacts our communities through our learned individualization of school failure, which in turn fuels the internalization of racism, whereby large numbers of Latinas/os growing up in disenfranchised communities learn to blame themselves and their race/ethnicity for their failure, often without even consciously recognizing that this is what they are doing.

As MAESTR@S learned and developed a path of "making sense" of this reality, we knew that we had to move towards ways of confronting it and transforming our own experiences in our work with raza youth. This is the point of all of our work: to develop a model of engaging raza youth and communities in processes of confronting, resisting, and transcending these toxic social forces and their impact on our daily lives. The model laid out in this chapter represents our efforts over several years to engage in this process. The approach is centered on the importance of creating communities where we can begin to understand our own stories individually and collectively. This demands that we confront the biggest challenges we each face, because our experiences have shown us that even the best academic programs mean very little when students still struggle to be able to make sense of all the obstacles and contradictions they confront. As the examples from MAESTR@S and our classes demonstrated, this evolving model for working with raza students showed the power of creating a clear path for youth to recognize the ways in which they were taught and had learned to *normalize* Latina/o school failure and the complex, contemporary manifestations of racism they face. It gave them a space to overcome the *individualization* of their own challenges and failures, through which they had also learned to blame themselves for systemic issues that deeply impacted their lives. They were transformed by the opportunity to recognize these processes as part of a legacy of *historical trauma* connected both to the ever-evolving *deficit approaches* to raza schooling and the *internalization* of racism and, to dissect the ways in which they had gone through these processes. Most importantly, they thrived in a space where they were able to build on the strength gained by going through this process and creating a realistic vision for how they could use these insights to develop a path for themselves to walk social justice and realize their own goals individually and as a community. In the end, although the model covers critical theoretical ground, as the MAESTR@S community and the students both explained repeatedly, this is a model for healing. Both communities understood this healing as most essential to their needs as people, while also demonstrating the dramatic impact it had on their work as students and teachers.

The complexity of this process is significant, and while the examples hopefully help readers begin to "visualize" it, we know that the true power of our model is in the people who come to it and the commitment they bring once given the space to do the work that they want for themselves and their communities. Rosa helps us see this best in one of her final reflections on our work in the class:

> Being able to acknowledge all the struggles one has endured can be therapeutic to one's soul. I grew up bottling up so much pain, not showing emotion but holding back a lot of resentment that was preventing my spirit from having joy. I did not know I was causing it more pain by holding in things that were killing me inside. Once I was able to do that in class, I felt a huge weight get lifted from my shoulders; to be able to say it all without holding back made me feel at peace. That day was the beginning of a new me. I felt light. I walked out feeling relieved and happy. I never knew how much talking about my suffered trauma would help heal my spirit. I felt like I could finally breathe and I want kids to experience what I experienced the day I acknowledged all my baggage to the class.[26]

Looking back at my own time as a classroom teacher, I now understand what I needed but never received; the training that our teachers in MAESTR@S, who are working in disenfranchised communities, also needed but did not get.[27] This approach is simply about addressing the most powerful needs of raza youth in disenfranchised communities and of their teachers, so that they all can heal and, in the process, develop the tools to be successful in the classroom and in life. It is our definition of what school leadership needs to be.

NOTES

1. One of the participants in this project decided to remain anonymous because of the family stories that he shared and his desire to protect his family members.
2. MAESTR@S is a Bay Area-based collective of teachers and educational justice workers dedicated to addressing the needs of Latina/o communities and students. I will describe the group in more detail as the analysis evolves. The previous chapter also provides more background on the group.
3. I use a variety of ethnic labels in this paper. Latina/o is used to refer to all Latin American descent peoples. Chicana/o is commonly used amongst organizers in our communities because it refers to Mexican descent Latinas/os

(the vast majority of Latinas/os in many parts of California) and also because it implies a radical political analysis that many in these communities adopt, including some non-Mexican Latinas/os. I also use raza because it is an umbrella term and it is often used in communities. Chicano and Latino are used specifically to refer to males, and Chicana and Latina for females. I use these ethnic labels interchangeably because that is how they are used in our schools and communities.

4. This approach to method is informed by earlier methodological work I had done to rethink my approach to research (Pizarro, 1998), as well as crucial insights from indigenous researchers (Smith, 1999; Wilson, 2008) who pushed for innovations based on the importance of relationship building, creating research with communities that is informed by their own knowledge systems.

5. As a tenured university professor, I have the luxury to be able to integrate unconventional approaches to classroom work without repercussions from administrators. Even when I bring this work into high school classrooms, my status allows me to engage in innovations that other members of our collective cannot without being critiqued or reprimanded by administrators.

6. As with all research and community work, there are power dynamics involved in the group. Pizarro coordinated both MAESTR@S and the classes discussed. The approach in both contexts, however, is to focus on meeting the needs of all participants and building relationships that extend beyond organizations and classrooms. In both contexts, we worked to create *familia* and *respeto* that transcended whatever originally brought us to the class or group. We also sought to develop a collective understanding of our work that is shared in the chapter. Still, we recognize that this is always fraught and contested.

7. In this chapter, I am providing an overview of the model to help those who are interested in developing a social justice approach to working with disenfranchised raza youth. To implement the model, readers are encouraged to contact the author and participate in a training session to more deeply understand how to apply this approach to specific contexts.

8. Each phase of the model is captured in italics in two different ways. The first is a description and the second is the shorter heading used in the visual model that follows this section.

9. The LifeMap can be done in a number of different ways. Examples follow in the next section and can include an actual visual representation as a map, poetry, lists, spider diagrams, or whatever works for the individual.

10. Since this model focuses on raza in disenfranchised communities, typically those involved do have traumas and pain that they easily tap into. Still, we also create a space for those who are not in touch with deep pain or trauma to share this reality and explore it in the context of the work being done as a community. This can be revelatory for all and requires careful attention.

11. The model includes the Mexica concept of Ollin, which refers to movement, often used to describe how communities work together to move toward collective goals for the betterment of all. The model also references CCW (community cultural wealth). Yosso (2005) provides a powerful analysis of the cultural strengths of Latina/o communities that need to be acknowledged and tapped into in schools.

12. Obviously, the way in which we adapt the model to a K–12 school classroom is different, but the examples from college students seem particularly applicable because much of what the students discussed comes from their experiences as teens in their schools, families and communities.

13. When discussing the examples from class, "we" is used because Pizarro team teaches the course with Mario Ozuna-Sanchez, who does similar work with gang-impacted youth in the community. We do all of our planning together. Mario also uses the *Joven Noble* curriculum (see Tello, 2008) in his work and in our classroom, which overlaps in many ways with the MAESTR@S model but also adds other components. We hope to write more about that in forthcoming work.

14. Although it is very common for those living and working in disenfranchised communities to experience trauma in some way, not everyone does. This is important. Some participants have experienced challenges, but not in the same way as those with severe traumas. In these cases, we have to help those without such experiences feel like they are part of the community, and we can do this by explaining that our goal is to raise a generation without trauma and by reminding everyone of the power of being a mirror to each other despite our differences, as we support each person through this process.

15. This is a pseudonym. Jaime felt that much of what he shared with us was very personal, and although he felt a sense of trust with those in the class that allowed him to share these thoughts, he wanted to keep his family's struggles anonymous in this publication.

16. So many of our young men learn that being a Latino male means never expressing emotions other than anger in public spaces, and Jaime exposed the lessons for all of us from engaging in this kind of work with a supportive community. It allowed others to share personal experiences and their emotional impacts.

17. In the class, we just called this the LifeMap, although the students mainly focused on the challenges they faced, and so this exercise was primarily covering the process discussed in the TraumaMap section above.

18. There is so much emphasis on judgment in schools. Even in artistic assignments, students feel the burden of being judged and often learn that, "I can't draw. I'm not an artist and never will be." In our class, we strive to eliminate the judgments and focus on the process. We also highlight students' unique contributions conceptually, in terms of how they think about the work, rather than simply how it looks.

19. I am not providing examples of the EmotionMap or the FearMap, but these steps can be taken in the same way as the TraumaMap, providing participants with multiple ways of exploring these themes individually and collectively, and focusing on the larger meanings of our shared experiences.

20. In the class, Mario explains that each of us has a sacred purpose and that it is our responsibility to live it.

21. This class was informed by the lessons of the MAESTR@S process. While many community-based, college courses (service-learning and others) focus on immersing students in community work, our approach was based on recognizing that the students needed to understand themselves before they even

considered going out to work with anyone else. For this reason, for most of the semester, the students were never engaged in direct community work, but instead focused on their and their families' experiences and understandings, and how that applied to doing social justice work.

22. Carlos is referring to Tello (2008).

23. The student projects were both complex and sophisticated, extending beyond assignment requirements, as the students were focused on meeting their personal and life goals through their work rather than on just completing an assignment. This led to many engaging in a powerful weaving together of their readings, the concepts we highlighted through our processes as a collective, and their personal experiences both in the class and in their daily lives.

24. In our work, we argue and have found that even in subjects like science and math, where the connections do not always seem obvious, these processes can make a dramatic difference in students' connectedness and commitment to their classes. Obviously, this work requires serious dedication and creativity on the part of the teachers.

25. Toward the end of the year, we had students who could not make it to class texting those who were in class updates on their work and planning for the next day. When we ended the class, students acknowledged specific peers who had helped them learn, often talking about how they were surprised by what they learned about and from peers whom they had previously negatively categorized. The district found that the students in our classes surpassed their peers in terms of attendance, test scores, and grades. More background on the class and its impacts on students can be found in the previous chapter.

26. It is important to note that everyone approaches the work in her own way and at her own pace. Rosa, for example, was removed from her past both in terms of space and time, which allowed her to go deep into this process. The strategies she developed earlier in her life may not have been the most beneficial for her long-term health, but they did allow her to survive at that time. Related to this, when students may not have other safe spaces to explore this work, we have to offer them the opportunity to adapt it to their lives in ways that are affirming and useful, while still allowing them to make it through their daily lives. Again, readers interested in exploring all of the nuances of the model should contact the author about going through training.

27. I am indebted to the MAESTR@S collective for all the lessons I have learned from our work together, and for entrusting me with documenting our evolving model. I learned immensely from each part of this process and from each of our members. I am also grateful to the students in our classes who have trusted us to guide them through this process and allowed us to learn from them and to share these lessons with others. Both the MAESTR@S and the students are true warriors for social justice.

28. The previous chapter (Chapter 8, this volume) includes references that are helpful to understanding the concepts covered in this chapter.

REFERENCES[28]

Boyle, G. (2010). *Tattoos on the heart: The power of boundless compassion.* New York, NY: Free Press.

Gutstein, E. (2010). Critical multicultural approaches to mathematics education in urban, k–12 classrooms. In S. May & C. E. Sleeter (Eds.), *Critical multiculturalism: Theory and praxis* (pp. 127–137). New York, NY: Routledge.

Pizarro, M. (1998). "Chicana/o power!": Epistemology and methodology for social justice and empowerment in Chicana/o communities. *International Journal of Qualitative Studies in Education, 11,* 57–80.

Smith, L. T. (1999). *Decolonizing methodologies: Research and indigenous peoples.* New York, NY: Zed Books Ltd.

Tello, J. (2008). El hombre noble buscando balance: The noble man searching for balance. In R. Carrillo & J. Tello (Eds.), *Family violence and men of color: Healing the wounded male spirit* (pp. 37–59). New York, NY: Spring Publishing Company.

Wilson, S. (2008). *Research is ceremony: Indigenous research methods.* Halifax, NS: Fernwood Publishing.

Yosso, T. (2005). *Critical race counterstories along the Chicana/Chicano educational pipeline.* New York, NY: Routledge.

ABOUT THE CONTRIBUTORS

René Antrop-González is Dean and Professor of Urban Education in the School of Urban Education at Metropolitan State University in Saint Paul, Minnesota. He has taught bilingual education/ESL courses at the elementary, secondary, and postsecondary levels in Puerto Rico and the United States. His research interests include African American and Latin@ sociology of education, urban school reform, African American and Latin@ high achievers, and Latin@ youth in the New Latin@ Diaspora. Antrop-González received his AA from Valencia Community College, a BA in Spanish from the University of Central Florida, a MEd in the teaching of English as a second language at the Pontifical Catholic University of Puerto Rico and his PhD in curriculum and instruction with an emphasis in bilingual education from the Pennsylvania State University. Prior to his current position at Metropolitan State University, Antrop-González was the Goizueta Foundation Chair in Education at Dalton State College (Dalton, Georgia) and Professor of Second Language Education in the Department of Curriculum and Instruction at the University of Wisconsin-Milwaukee.

Antonette Aragon is an associate professor at Colorado State University's School of Education and the Center for Educator Preparation. Her scholarship is grounded primarily in the intersections of social justice systemic change, equity, technology, and educational opportunity utilizing culturally responsive teaching. A Latina activist scholar of color, her research focuses on bringing theory into practice. Predominantly teaching preservice teachers, educational leaders, counselors, and adult educators, her pedagogy centers critical multicultural education, critical feminist theory, critical race

Envisioning Critical Race Praxis in K–12 Leadership Through Counter-Storytelling, pages 211–215
Copyright © 2016 by Information Age Publishing
211

theory, and social justice emphasizing understandings of self, systemic inequities and cultural awareness. She has presented at major conferences such as American Education Research Association (AERA), National Association for Multicultural Education (NAME), and the National Network for Educational Renewal (NNER). Her publications include a co-edited book, several chapters, and journal articles in such journals as *Urban Education, Multicultural Education & Technology, Teaching Education, Multicultural Teaching and Learning,* and *Journal of Hispanic Higher Education.*

Aza Baylor is an education and research professional with over 20 years of experience in the field of education specializing in the interrelationships between schools and society, education and culture. She is a proven effective instructor (K–12 & college level), Teacher coach, Teacher performance evaluator and instructional leader. She has leadership expertise in professional development training and cultivating a school culture of high academic achievement. Her research Interest include: Black Feminist Pedagogy, Critical Race Theory in Education, Diversifying the teacher/school leadership population, Culturally Relevant Pedagogy and Educational Leadership.

David Fernandez* is currently a high school sophomore. He was born in Los Angeles, CA to immigrant parents from El Salvador. As the middle child of the family, his life has largely been shaped by having to look out for his sisters. David is interested in literature, poetry, science, history and English. He is an excellent poet and spends his free time writing poems and spoken word pieces. He plans on going to college and getting a degree in literature and writing. Daniel plans on pursuing a career in creative writing after college.

Nicholas D. Hartlep is an assistant professor of Educational Foundations at Illinois State University. Prior to that, he was an Advanced Opportunity Program Fellow at the University of Wisconsin–Milwaukee, an "Urban 13" University, where he earned a PhD in the Social Foundations of Urban Education and was named an "Outstanding Doctoral Student." Dr. Hartlep also has a Master of Science Degree in K–12 Education and a Bachelor of Science Degree in Teaching, both conferred from Winona State University. As a former public school teacher he has taught in Rochester, Minnesota and Milwaukee, Wisconsin, as well as abroad in Quito, Ecuador. Dr. Hartlep's research interests include urban in-service teachers' dispositions, the impact neoliberalism is having on schools and society, the model minority stereotype of Asians, and transracial adoption. He received the University Research Initiative (URI) Award in 2015 from Illinois State University. His

---

* Pseudonyms were used to protect the identities of these students as they are still enrolled in the school district at the time of publication.

scholarly books include *Going Public: Critical Race Theory & Issues of Social Justice* (2010), *The Model Minority Stereotype: Demystifying Asian American Success* (2013), *Unhooking From Whiteness: The Key to Dismantling Racism in the United States* (2013), and *The Model Minority Stereotype Reader: Critical and Challenging Readings for the 21st Century* (2014), *Killing the Model Minority Stereotype: Asian American Counterstories and Complicity* (2015), and *Modern Societal Impacts of the Model Minority Stereotype* (2015). He is currently working on a book entitled *The Neoliberal Agenda and the Student Debt Crisis in U.S. Higher Education: Voices of Students and Faculty* to be published in the book series: Routledge Studies in Education and Neoliberalism. You can follow his work on Twitter @nhartlep or at the Model Minority Stereotype Project (www.nicholashartlep.com)

Christopher B. Knaus is a race scholar, critical race theory practitioner, educator, and community advocate dedicated to the overthrow of the standardization of schools, cultures, and public space. He is a Professor of Education at the University of Washington Tacoma, with practitioner-based research and hands-on projects that examine the global impact of colonial school systems and related policies on communities of color. At the core of community and systems transformation, Dr. Knaus centers critically conscious urban youth voice as a way to help educators create inclusive, challenging classrooms and schools that arm children to transform the immediate world they live into a world where addressing social inequalities becomes the purpose of education. Dr. Knaus served as a Fulbright Scholar to South Africa, which led to his most recent book (co-authored with M. Christopher Brown II): *Whiteness is the New South Africa: Qualitative Research on Post-Apartheid Racism.* Dr. Knaus was the founding director of the Doctorate (EdD) in Educational Leadership Program at the University of Washington Tacoma, and previously served as a Professor of Educational Leadership at California State University, East Bay, and in the African American Studies Department at the University of California, Berkeley. In addition to numerous articles and books about racism in education, Dr. Knaus has taught classes in high schools in Seattle, Oakland, and Berkeley, CA.

Daniel D. Liou is as an assistant professor of Educational Leadership and Innovation in Mary Lou Fulton Teachers College at Arizona State University. Daniel's research focuses on the social and institutional analysis of educational pathways and inequities across race, class, gender, and immigration status. Daniel's research centers on the institutional dynamics of academic expectations from the perspectives of the students, teachers, school leaders, and the P-20 educational pipeline. Daniel is committed to understand how these dynamics influence students' classroom experiences, equity, and college readiness. In addition to his expertise in education, Daniel brings perspectives from ethnic studies, sociology, and critical race studies to his work. For the past 21 years, Daniel has worked and researched in schools in Boston, Des Moines, Los Angeles, Phoenix, and the San Francisco Bay Area. Daniel is the first in his family to graduate from high school and to attend college, and seeks to work on research and engage in teaching topics central to this experience. Daniel is the 2015 recipient of the AERA Leadership in Social Justice Teaching Award (LSJ SIG).

Eligio Martinez Jr. is a postdoctoral research fellow at the University of California, San Diego. He received his PhD and MEd from the University of Washington in Educational Leadership and Policy Studies. Eligio's research interests focus on the intersection of race, class and gender in the educational experiences of men of color and their pursuit for higher education. As a practitioner, Eligio has created several mentoring programs for middle school and high school students. Eligio also coordinated the Men of Color Mentoring Program in Fort Worth, Texas, a community college mentoring program geared at improving educational outcomes for African American and Latino Males. Eligio grew up in Santa Ana, CA and graduate from UCLA.

Guadalupe Montes[*] is a high school sophomore. Born in Southern Mexico, his parents brought him to the United States at a young age. He is the third child in his family and spends a lot of time baby sitting his little sister. Guadalupe looks up to his older brother and wants to follow his footsteps and go to college. Guadalupe is grateful that his parents have given him great advice about friends and got him involved in sports, which have allowed him to stay focused academically and out of trouble. He is a member of his high school's football, soccer and basketball teams. In his spare time, he enjoys hanging out with his brother and his friends. Guadalupe plans to attend college after high school and major in sports management.

Isaac Perez[*] is a high school sophomore who grew up in the Pacific Northwest. Isaac has a close relationship with his parents and spends a lot of time hanging out with his younger brother. Isaac is a member of his high school's football team where he tries to set an example to his teammates by showing them the importance of being a good student athlete and putting school first. In his spare time, Isaac enjoys working out and hanging out with friends. He plans to attend college after high school and pursue a career in the health sciences.

Marcos Pizarro teaches in Mexican American Studies at San José State University. A former school teacher, Pizarro works with Chicana/o students at various stages in their schooling and tries to understand how interventions can help these students develop strategies that might aid them in their efforts to succeed in school and pursue social and racial justice in their communities. Currently, he coordinates MAESTR@S, a social justice organization developing and implementing a transformative education model with Latina/o communities. He also works with schools on the development and implementation of Latina/o Studies curricula to enhance Latina/o student engagement, having completed a year-long project that involved teaching in a local high school. Recently, he has been co-coordinating a campus-wide effort to improve the ways in which SJSU supports the retention and success of Latina/o students. Finally, he is the co-coordinator of the Institute for Teachers of Color Committed to Racial Justice.

Rachelle Rogers-Ard is an educator and administrator with over 23 years' experience modeling Culturally Responsive instruction and Leadership Development. Her work around recruiting, retaining and growing diverse educators is a main focus; Dr. Ard also demonstrates expertise in providing training around Project-Based/Linked Learning curricula aligned to common core standards. Her main goal is helping educational organizations create systems designed to retain and grow educators across disciplines and divisive subcultures. For the past six years, Rachelle managed Teach Tomorrow in Oakland, a federally funded program within the Oakland Unified School District focused on building systems to support the recruitment and retention of teachers of color. Currently, Rachelle is the Director of Leadership Development and Employee Engagement within OUSD's Office of the Superintendent. Dr. Rogers-Ard is also the Regional Director for the National Association of Multicultural Education, a visiting professor in the Urban Education program at CSU East Bay, and is the author of several publications. In her "spare time," Rachelle is a wife and mother of four, ages 25, 23, 16, and 10, and the founder, composer, and director of the East Bay Anointed Voices, a contemporary gospel ensemble.

Dr. Stephanie Masta Zywicki is an Assistant Professor at Purdue University and a member of the Sault Ste. Marie Tribe of Chippewa Indians. Her work focuses on the use of critical qualitative methodologies in educational research. Stephanie's current projects focus on the application of Indigenous methodologies to study the experiences of Indigenous youth in P–20 mainstream schools.

CPSIA information can be obtained at www.ICGtesting.com
Printed in the USA
BVOW06s0053090916

461562BV00004B/10/P

9 781681 234083